ENDORSEMENTS

"More and more resources are being provided to those who are questioning their beliefs and deconstructing their faith. Here, Heather offers her unique contribution with her own story by reimagining, reshaping, and reinterpreting some of Christianity's major components into food that will benefit many on their own spiritual journeys."

— **David Hayward** (@nakedpastor), Artist, Cartoonist, Author of
*Questions are The Answer: nakedpastor and the search
for understanding* and *Flip It Like This!*

"If you're ready to move through faith deconstruction and into whole-life transformation, Heather Hamilton is your guide. At turns disarming and incisive, Heather shares vulnerably from her journey through Bible-belt fundamentalism to a truly mythic understanding of Jesus the Christ. No matter where you're at in your spiritual journey, *Returning to Eden* invites you to move beyond spectator religion into the fullness of participatory living, reflecting full Divinity precisely by embracing our full humanity."

— **Mike Morrell**, founding organizer, Wild Goose Festival; founder,
Wisdom Camp; co-host, Mystics Summit (The Shift Network);
collaborating author with Richard Rohr, *The Divine Dance:
The Trinity and Your Transformation*

"For anyone who has found themselves increasingly incompatible with the husk of the Christian institution and hungering for a more mystical and inclusive version of that faith, Heather Hamilton serves as a compassionate mytho-poetic midwife...gently guiding readers into the unknown germinating potential within."

— **Brie Stoner**, Artist, Musician, Host of *Unknowing* Podcast, and Co-Host of *Another Name for Every Thing with Richard Rohr* Podcast

"For me personally, never have the words "sacred," "inspired," and "infallible" felt more appropriate for describing the Bible than they did as I was reading this book. All of the arguments about literalness and historicity notwithstanding, Heather Hamilton transcends the fray, inviting us to take the Bible more seriously than most of us have ever imagined possible. Through page after page in this well-crafted book, Heather removes any doubt: the Biblical story is my story, your story, our story. In reading the Bible, we are not simply revisiting ancient characters and narratives. No. We are reading our own biographies, our own spiritual travel diaries. So, regardless of your relationship with the world's long-time best-selling book—whether that relationship is warm, strained, or estranged—this book will be a gift in your life. I mean it when I say: get ready to have your mind stretched and your heart healed."

— **Stan Mitchell**, Founding Pastor, GracePointe Church, Nashville, TN; Teaching Pastor, The Village Church, Atlanta, GA

"The images we paint and stories we tell about our faith, church, God, the Bible, and Jesus often influence us for years or decades or even generations. As we mature in our faith, these stories and traditions can either produce strong foundations for our growth, or create gaps that need to be filled with new answers. In *Returning To Eden*, my friend Heather Hamilton encourages us to ask questions about ourselves, the text, our traditions and, ultimately, what we believe...not as an exercise simply in deconstruction, but as an exercise in art restoration. She encourages us to strip away the dirt and dust and gunk and religion that can distort and cover over the truth and beauty of Jesus. Reading Heather's insights may not provide you with the answers you are looking for, but they will lead you to questions you need to ask."

— **Dave Adamson**, Social Media and Online Pastor (@aussiedave), Bestselling Author of *MetaChurch: How to Use Digital Ministry to Reach People and Make Disciples*

"This is a health-giving and refreshing book, proclaiming the Christ who comes to restore our deepest selves to wholeness. Heather Hamilton opens up the scriptures of both Testaments in such a way that they work therapeutically on our psyches. She employs biblical stories, parables, and symbols brilliantly, drawing also on saints and spiritual writers in her application. While I have always been hesitant to use the terms "False Self" and "True Self," she defines these concepts so well and so vividly that all my reservations vanished as I read. And it was good to see her make use of invaluable insights from the writings of such important seminal thinkers as Carl Jung, Marie-Louise von Franz, and Joseph Campbell, who are too often misunderstood and misapplied. The book is also beautifully illustrated. All in all, a marvelous work."

— **Addison Hodges Hart**, author of *Strangers and Pilgrims Once More: Being Disciples of Jesus in a Post-Christendom World* and *Silent Rosary: A Contemplative, Exegetical, and Iconographic Tour Through the Mysteries*

"Our ways of understanding God, ourselves, and the world need more than tweaking. They need an overhaul! In this accessible book, Heather Hamilton rethinks a host of key issues and beliefs. I felt both relieved and buoyant after reading it!"

— **Thomas Jay Oord**, Theologian, Bestselling Author of *God Can't* and many other books

"Heather has bravely and compassionately captured her journey and shared the wisdom she's gained to serve as a lantern in the misty darkness. For anyone wanting to embrace Christian faith traditions but feels disconnected, disappointed, or disillusioned in the examination of their beliefs, this book feels like finding a decoder ring in a favorite box of cereal. *Returning to Eden* brings new life to familiar texts and invites us all to the important work of dying and being born anew."

— **Candi Shelton**, Writer, Producer, Creative Consultant

"In *Returning To Eden*, Heather offers us a thoughtful and thorough turning of the gem. Her words help us see from a deep and different perspective what has long been covered up by convenient theology, comfortable traditions, and a careless form of "christianity." It is evident through this beautiful book that Heather has not only done her homework but has also done her *own* work. This book is the overflow of that work, and I believe it will unlock something both fresh and freeing in you."

— **Jarrett Stevens**, Co-Lead Pastor of Soul City Church, Author of *Praying Through*, *Four Small Words* and *The Deity Formerly Known as God*

Addison—
Thank you so very much
for all your support and
encouragement. I am so honored
by your endorsement. I will forever
be grateful for your
enthusiasm, and I'm happy
to have connected with a
like-minded thinker.

Heather Hamilton

RETURNING
to
EDEN

A Field Guide for the Spiritual Journey

HEATHER HAMILTON

All photos included in this work are public domain.
Illustrations included herein created by the author.
Permission granted to the author by Malcolm Guite to use the excerpt from his poem *The Stations of the Cross, Poem X: Jesus is Stripped of His Garments.*
Permission granted to the author by Brian Zahnd to use his quote in chapter 2.
Permission granted by the Joseph Campbell Foundation to use quotes in chapters 4, 19, and 43.
Permission granted by Stan Mitchell to use his quote in the epilogue.

Cover design by Rafael Polendo (polendo.net)
Interior Layout by Matthew J. Distefano

ISBN 978-1-957007-43-4

This volume is printed on acid free paper and meets ANSI Z39.48 standards. Printed in the United States of America

Published by Quoir
Chico, California
www.quoir.com

I dedicate this book to my three precious children, Norah, Jacob, and Florence. You give me the courage to love, to be myself, and to tell the truth. Thank you for choosing me to be your mother. I love you.

CONTENTS

ACKNOWLEDGMENTS   XV

FOREWORD   XVII

INTRODUCTION   XXI

PART I   1
FILLING IN THE GAPS

1. THE CHRISTIAN OF THE FUTURE   3

2. FINDING CHRIST IN THE BIBLE   7

3. THE ANATOMY OF A SEED   13

4. THE FUNCTION OF MYTH   21

PART II   27
DISCOVERING THE TRUE SELF

5. RETHINKING ADAM & EVE   29

6. THE TOWER OF BABEL   35

7. THE TWO BECOME ONE FLESH   39

8. JONAH & THE WHALE   43

9. THE VIRGIN BIRTH   49

10. BECOMING A VIRGIN   53

11. JACOB'S LADDER   55

12. NOAH'S ARK: A BAPTISM IN TEARS   59

13. THE CROSS SYMBOLIZES INCARNATION IN   65
EVERY HUMAN

14. GO TO HELL   69

15. GOD SEES THE WORLD THROUGH YOU   79

16. GOD HIDES HIS FACE?   85

17. DEMONS & DEVILS   91

18. PARTING THE RED SEA   97

19. WORK OUT YOUR OWN SALVATION   101

20. GO INTO YOUR CLOSET & CLOSE THE DOORS   109

21. IN THE WORLD, NOT OF IT   115

22. HATE YOUR MOTHER & FATHER   121

23. ORIGINAL SIN   127

24. THE EYE OF THE NEEDLE   131

25. JESUS STRIPPED OF HIS GARMENTS   137

26. PAUL (THE TRUE SELF) WAS HIDDEN WITHIN   141
SAUL (THE FALSE SELF)

27. THE WELLSPRING OF LIFE IS WITHIN   145

28. PARABLE OF THE HIDDEN TREASURE & THE   149
PEARL OF GREAT PRICE

29. PARABLE OF THE WEEDS   153

30. THE PASCHAL MYSTERY (THE CHRIST MYSTERY)   159

31. EAT MY BODY; DRINK MY BLOOD   165

32. FATHER, SON, & MOTHER SPIRIT   171

33. THE KINGDOM OF HEAVEN IS WITHIN YOU   175

PART III   181
CREATING HEAVEN ON EARTH

34. CARRY YOUR CROSS   183

35. FORGIVENESS IS TRANSMUTING ENERGY   191

36. THE WORD MADE FLESH   199

37. JESUS IN DISGUISE   203

38. THE TRINITY   209

39. THE SECOND COMING OF CHRIST   213

40. THE KINGDOM BELONGS TO CHILDREN   221

41. THE PRODIGAL SON   227

42. I AM THE WAY, THE TRUTH, & THE LIFE   231

43. A NEW EARTH   235

EPILOGUE   239

END NOTES   253

BIBLIOGRAPHY   267

ABOUT THE AUTHOR   277

ACKNOWLEDGMENTS

I would like to acknowledge those who helped me bring this book into the world.

To my husband, Jared, thank you for being such an incredible partner. Your unconditional love has given me the environment I needed to grow and evolve. Your support, encouragement, and understanding gave me the confidence, time, and security I needed to dig deep into the depths of my soul and bring this book back with me. Thank you for that and for the hours of reading and feedback. I'm grateful for a partner who can critique my work with clarity, precision, and graciousness.

To my dear friend, Jessica Condrey, thank you for your unending, non-judgmental friendship. You'll never know the love I felt that night on the Burger Bus, bearing my soul to you. You gave me hope that all would not be lost. You are a gift to me. Thank you for the hours and hours of reading and critiquing. Your questions and pushback were invaluable to this work.

To my writing coach and editor, Jim Palmer, thank you for having confidence in me from the beginning of this endeavor. It's probably safe to say that this book would not have existed had you not been sure of my ability to write it before I was. You have been the wind in my sails on many occasions and helped me rise to the task. I cannot think of someone better to have written the Foreword to this book. I feel truly grateful to have you in my corner.

Thank you to Keith Giles, Matthew Distefano, Rafael Polendo, and the team at Quoir Publishing for all the efforts to bring this project to fruition.

From design, to formatting, to marketing, your contributions have been immense. I'm grateful for your investment in me and my work.

To those who endorsed this book, I have great admiration for each of you. Your work, contributions, and personal character inspire me. I am so humbled and honored that you felt this book was worthy of your time and endorsement. From the bottom of my heart, thank you.

Thank you to Candi Shelton. You planted the seed for this book a few years ago. I knew I wasn't yet ready to write it, but you named it that night at dinner and sparked a new possibility in my heart.

Thank you to Joe and Charleen Seidel for your love and mentorship in my family's life. Your home is a haven for us.

Thank you to my therapist, Jennifer, for helping me "fix the pipes" so that this book could flow through me.

Thank you to everyone on my launch team for helping me get this book into the world. Thank you for believing in me, cheering me on, and giving this book a signal boost. I'm so grateful for each of you.

To my family, friends, "my people," who have been a source of endless encouragement and unconditional love over the years: thanks to each of you who have shared your heart and received mine over coffee, or food, or work, or kids' play dates, or hang-outs, or trips, or porch chats, or walks, or...*life*. Thank you to the steadfast friends who have shown up for me and my family during difficult times when we needed help. You are the salt of the earth. Thank you to my friends and fellow creators who encouraged me in this endeavor and helped me navigate the vulnerable quest of bringing this book into the world. You are each a well of love I have drawn from many times over as we've journeyed through life together. Thank you.

FOREWORD

Let me begin this Foreword by stating clearly the reason why I view Heather Hamilton's book, *Returning to Eden: A Field Guide for the Spiritual Journey*, as a groundbreaking and profound contribution to the journeys of countless people who have left religion. Given how the Bible has been weaponized by large swaths of Christendom to induce and indoctrinate fear, shame, and control among the faithful, the deconstruction process requires church leavers to disentangle themselves from toxic theology. However, this does not necessarily mean one must give up any notion of God, reject the historicity of Jesus, or write-off the Bible entirely.

In a time when people quickly switch sides from fundamentalist Christian to fundamentalist atheist, Heather's book, *Returning to Eden*, offers a middle way.

For the past twenty years I have counseled people through the process of recovering from spiritual abuse, religious trauma, and toxic indoctrination. The journey involves rethinking one's approach to life's greatest existential questions about ultimate reality, the meaning and purpose of human existence, and what it means to live life fully.

There are many different paths people take after leaving religion. Many ex-Christians cease believing in God altogether and become atheists. It's not uncommon for them to view the Bible as ridiculous, pointless, and worthless. It's understandable. If a person was traumatized by oppressive and abusive biblical teachings that produced shame, fear, depression, and anxiety, it may be a lot to ask for them to re-think a more positive approach to the Bible.

To write the Bible off entirely, even for those who were once victimized by it, may be unfortunate. Unfortunate, because once you detach the Bible from a fundamentalist and literalist framework, you discover it's a treasure trove of universally applicable themes and motifs for the lived human experience and a profound spirituality.

There is a long history of non-religious thinkers who found deep meaning in the Bible. The philosophy of religion and psychology are two fields of endeavor that have found significant value in the narratives, stories, and figures in the Old and New Testaments. In her book, Heather weaves in these viewpoints from notable individuals in these fields.

In order to unpack the treasures of the Bible, you must understand myth and mythology. For most Christians who have left their faith, not only do they not understand it, they were likely taught that viewing the Bible as myth or mythology is perilous, evil, demonic, and good reason to be condemned to eternal hell in the afterlife. Here are some of the obstacles a deconstructing or ex-Christian would have to overcome in order to give the Bible another chance:

1. Vilification of the Bible as a tool of oppression and abuse
2. Lack of knowledge and experience with myth and mythology
3. Residual fears of condemnation for profaning the Holy Book

One can and perhaps should take the Bible as a literary anthology—a collection of varied literary genres written by multiple authors over the span of many centuries. In its details, too, the Bible is a literary book. Most of it is embodied in the genres of narrative, poetry, letters, myth, law, and visionary writing. The Bible is an Epic, telling the saga of humankind. It speaks to the central themes of our existence, including life and death, good and evil, the nature of reality, meaning and purpose, the non-material or transcendent dimension, suffering and flourishing, love and hate, politics and religion. Personally, I think the originality of the story the Bible tells makes it a fascinating and profound piece of literature.

Many ex-Christians view the Bible as absurd because they assume that the biblical writers intended us to take sections like the creation story, Adam and Eve, the Fall, Noah's Ark, Jonah and the whale, and others, literally. No, there is not a Gandalf-God in the sky who asked Abraham to kill his son, commanded holy troops into battles and wars, or struck down people dead for disobedience.

In my view, attacking the Bible because you think it's a joke that the biblical writers invented the creation story, Adam and Eve, Noah's Ark, and the virgin birth of Jesus as literal events, are missing the point of the stories. Just because fundamentalist Christians shoehorned their toxic theology and interpretations into the Bible isn't the Bible's fault.

But even given all of that, because of how the Bible was abused to damage people spiritually and psychologically, it may never be a piece of literature that some people will be able to embrace meaningfully. That's okay too. There are many spiritual, sacred, and literary works that you may find worthwhile such as the Tao Te Ching, Buddhist Sutras, The Vedas and The Upanishads, Bhagavad Gita and others.

The ultimate authority of one's life is not in any book. It is not something written by men and frozen in time. It is not from a source outside oneself. One's ultimate authority is the voice of truth within one's own soul. What Heather points out in her book is that the Bible, taken as myth or mythology, awakens that voice of truth within us and guides us toward a more authentic, profound, transcendent, human, transformative, and liberating spirituality.

You don't need a PhD in the Philosophy of Religion or be an expert in mythology to benefit from understanding the Bible on radically different terms. To get started, all you need to do is read the book you are holding in your hands. Consider *Returning to Eden* as your introduction into what every true spiritual seeker ultimately discovers—that the highest truths that set us free are hidden in places most people are not looking. The mystery of life and transcendent reality cannot be captured directly in words or images.

Symbols and mythic metaphors, on the other hand, point outside themselves and into that reality.

Heather's book is not dry and pedantic, elaborate or esoteric, or woo-woo and gobbledygook. Her writing and ideas are sound but pioneering, practical but liberating, profound but down-to-earth. *Returning to Eden* is not a content dump about the history and mechanics of mythology. Heather invites us into her journey of leaving religion and deconstruction, and how discovering the Bible as myth was a pathway of personal liberation and transformation. I never thought I'd ever say that a book about biblical mythology was a book I could not put down from reading. Heather's book is both enlightening and entertaining.

Many people who leave religion may never pick up and read a Bible again for the rest of their lives. I get that. Each of us must follow our own way that we find meaningful. But for those who feel that their religious system, among other things, cheated them out of gaining the true meanings and messages of the Bible, you must read Heather Hamilton's book. She's been there. She understands. And she offers a path forward.

Sometimes you have to leave religion to find God, become a heretic to uncover the deepest truth, and be a bit profane to discover what is truly sacred. The proper field guide for this is *Returning to Eden: A Field Guide for the Spiritual Journey*.

— **Jim Palmer**, Author of *Notes from (Over) the Edge*, and *Inner Anarchy;*
Founder of *The Center for Non-Religious Spirituality*

INTRODUCTION

There's a comedic irony when salvation is found in your religion falling apart.

Growing up as an evangelical Christian, there was a notable emphasis in the church on sharing your personal testimony. This is the story of someone's conversion to Christianity. I used to bemoan my personal testimony because I found it rather boring. Though I still cringe a little to admit it, my vices in life are rooted in wanting to be special. Not ordinary. *Not boring.* I always felt a tinge of envy when someone would share a compelling story about how they became a Christian. Not having a very unique story, I unconsciously endeavored to be a special kind of Christian. I did this in the only way I knew how—*sincerity*. I was what the church called a "sold-out-for-Jesus" kind of Christian.

When I was seven years old, I attended a summer Vacation Bible School (VBS) at a Baptist church in Georgia. VBS is common in the American South. Churches offer week-long summer camps where kids play games, eat snacks, and learn about the Bible, while the parents get a break. At that young age, a pastor told me that there was a heaven and a hell. I was going to one of those places when I died. He explained that because I had sinned, God couldn't look at me or be with me anymore, because He hated sin so much. I was destined for hell where I would burn forever in agony. The worst part wasn't that my skin would be melting off, nor that I would never see my family again, but that I would be separated from God.

But there was good news! Because God is just and needs a payment of death for sin, Jesus came to die on a cross as a substitute payment. He rose from the dead to prove He was God's Son. I could trust that this pastor's message I was hearing about this cosmic arrangement was The Truth. Period. Hard stop.

If I just believed that this was all true and said aloud that I was a sinner who needed forgiveness, Jesus would come into my heart and save me from hell, and I would go to heaven when I died. When God looked up my name in the Book of Life, he wouldn't see me. He would see Jesus's name and blood covering my name. *(Somehow, I was simultaneously precious to God and also so abhorrent that He couldn't look at me.)*

Like any frightened seven-year-old hearing this would do, I prayed. I asked Jesus to come into my heart and decided to be baptized later that week. I remember being too small for any of the gowns the church had. So, I stood alone in the hall waiting my turn, swallowed up in a huge adult robe dragging the ground. I was baptized in front of hundreds of VBS kids, many of them peering over the glass into the pool. I was a small, earnest, sensitive child. The experience felt very noisy and chaotic. But I just wanted to be in God's family. To be with *my* family. To be loved and accepted. I didn't want to be unworthy of acceptance and love because I had lied to my mom that one time. Even that small sin committed in fear was enough for me to burn. I longed to be a good girl. But obviously, I was a bad girl. God created me and loved me. Yet, I didn't deserve God's love. I didn't deserve to be in His family.

When you are seven, you accept as true whatever grown-ups tell you. This specific paradigm of God—heaven and hell, plan of salvation, and eternity—was the foundation upon which I oriented the next twenty-five years of my life.

After I was "saved" through this initiation, my life's purpose became telling other people the "good news." On the elementary school playground, I told my schoolmates about heaven and hell and Jesus. At the ripe old age of twelve, I decided my calling was to be an overseas missionary. I slid tracts into the lockers at my high school. These little "gospel" pamphlets, usually illustrated with cartoons and Bible verses plucked out of context, offered a simple and persuasive formula for salvation. Some literally had "The ABCs of Salvation." I was too shy to just walk up to my peers and ask them if they had accepted Jesus into their heart. This lack of boldness bothered me, but I reasoned that a colorful gospel tract from an anonymous person would do the trick.

I went on mission trips in high school. For weeks I wore the same princess dress in Peru, performing a drama and "sharing the gospel" through a translator to hundreds of people on the street. Our group would roll up to a corner on a busy street—flash mob style—plug in the PA, and start our performance. I'm still not entirely sure what the drama actually communicated, but I got to do a backflip at one point in it, which hopefully wowed a few spectators to salvation. As silly as it sounds, this was a special time in my life. On these trips I particularly noticed how much genuine joy some of the poorest people seemed to have. It was a joy noticeably missing in the Christianity back home. Later, in my adult years, I worked shooting baptism testimony videos of kids. Curiously, I noticed that the majority of children telling their stories had a similar story as mine. Adults told them "the truth." Children believed it. Children grew up to become adults that tell more children "the truth." And the wheels on the bus go round and round.

I occasionally would muse over the good fortune I had to be born in America at the time that I was. After all, this "gospel" was bequeathed to me as a child. I also wondered about being born in a different part of the world at a time when this "truth" wasn't prevalent or easily accessible. In so many different scenarios, figuring out the formula to get to heaven would have required a great deal of effort, sacrifice, and suffering. "Thank God I didn't have to go through all that," I would think to myself at times. I just happened to live in a time and place in history where the truth was readily accessible. And yet, the stakes were so high. Eternal life was on the line. It didn't quite compute why God would make it so easy and obvious for myself and the people I loved and so difficult for others, but I was grateful.

My conversion to Christianity didn't feel special or unique. I couldn't control that. But I could control the sincerity and effort I put into being a devoted Christian. I wanted to lead people to Jesus. I didn't earn my salvation, but I could earn a "well done, good and faithful one" from God when I died.

I strived to earn my stamp of divine approval. I wanted God to know that I took the mission seriously and gave it my all.

Not surprisingly, my zeal was rewarded by the evangelical church. I was continuously invited into circles of leadership. This trajectory continued, and by the time I was thirty, I had firmly established myself as a leader at a very large megachurch. My husband is a musician and had found our church to be a place where he could spread his wings musically and play with the best musicians in the city. Eventually, he became the music director leading a service for tens of thousands of people each week. We had written a good story that we were proud of, and it seemed God had blessed our efforts.

What happened next is what finally produced my not-so-ordinary story. A few weeks after I'd given birth to our third child and just before my thirty-third birthday, I experienced what could be conventionally labeled as a nervous breakdown. As unresolved traumas began surfacing, that led to terrifying episodes of PTSD, although I did not have the language to understand what was happening at the time. I began suffering waves of debilitating panic attacks and was overcome with hopelessness and despair. These episodes became increasingly severe and frequent. Over the course of a few days, they became constant to the point where I had lost control of my body. Nearly overnight, my life went from being the model of a well-behaved, successful, Christian, American woman, to someone whose underground anxiety had erupted like a volcano of spewing molten lava. Looking back, I realized I had suffered from anxiety since childhood. *But I couldn't even label the feeling because it was such a normal internal state. You can't know something is wrong if you've never known anything different.*

As I continued spiraling into more and more intense panic, I also had the inner knowing that what was happening to me was deeply spiritual. It felt as if I was dying. I was spiritually dying. I felt my soul descending deeper and deeper into an abyss of despair. As I wailed and begged God for help, for the first time in my life, I felt nothing. My soul felt absolute abandonment and alienation. The image of God I had carried with me was vaporized. In my most desperate hour, as I was crying out for God, *there was nothing.* No comfort. No presence. No nothing.

A few years earlier, my uncle had died by suicide. He had two children (my cousins) who loved him very much. It had been difficult for me to understand why someone would take their own life, especially when they leave behind people that love them. I have three children of my own, and any parent must know that their children will suffer when a parent takes their own life.

Perhaps one of the most frightening parts of my breakdown was a distinct moment when I realized: "I get it. I cannot live like this." I understood, for a moment, what my uncle might have felt. I was not imminently suicidal, but a sobering realization told me if I continued on like this much longer, it would get to that point very quickly. The complete absence of God in my desperation and despair was crushing to my soul. All light and hope had been eclipsed by this absence. Whoever I was calling out to was not there. *I was in hell.*

I knew at this point that my life was in danger. I mustered all the courage I had and whispered three words to my husband: "I need help." My husband called 911. A few minutes later, I opened the door to my house to find a transgender woman standing on my porch who had arrived to help me. She was part of the emergency response team. My first reaction to this was *fear.* Growing up as a Christian, I viewed myself as the rescuer. My fear came from years of a church background which perpetuated the idea that I was different from those in the LGBTQ+ population. That, in some way, they needed my rescuing. In my ignorance, I thought this was a loving, compassionate view. I was the one who was supposed to be helping "people like her." Not the other way around.

But suddenly, a palpable love began to emanate from this woman. There was something inside of me that immediately recognized this presence as Christ. It was an ineffable essence that was at once new and immediately familiar, like a feeling I'd suddenly remembered from another life. It was the most *real* moment I had ever experienced. The irony was not lost on me that I was a leader at this influential megachurch, but Jesus was standing on my porch in a body I would least expect to find him in.

In that sacred moment, Jesus flipped the table of my life.

Over the next several months, I had similar experiences as this one. Moments where I would suddenly feel an ineffable presence, as if my reality was suddenly saturated with a thick, benevolent texture. It reminded me a little of the liminal state between dreaming and waking—except I was completely alert, and my body was fully absorbing the energy of whatever or whomever was in my presence. I began to experience premonitions in my dreams where I'd foresee an interaction with someone and then later experience the interaction in real time. All of these moments had similar qualities to them, and my senses began to become familiar with the nature of these experiences.

Reflecting upon my life before this, I can identify a similar experience occurring the moment I gave birth to my first child, Norah. It felt as though the perceivable intensity of heaven was emanating from inside of both me and my daughter, but also pressing out from us and pushing in on us at the same time. Like gravity pulling and grace lifting, such that I felt suspended in a capsule outside the boundaries of time. It felt like *eternity*.

After Norah was born, the window of that feeling slowly closed, and I associated that experience exclusively with childbirth. My mistake was attributing this experience of heaven with an external event (the birth of my daughter). In actuality, what had occurred was that my mind had become still long enough for my heart and body to *be here now* and sense my own soul. In reality, the experience came from within.

Following my encounter with the transgender woman who was channeling Christ on my front porch, this experience of the *eternal* was occurring often in very ordinary situations and had longevity and fluidity to it. It felt like a state of awareness that opened up and became fully available to me with greater frequency.

During this season of my life, I was becoming increasingly aware that many of the tenets of my evangelical faith no longer made sense. I was experiencing more and more cognitive dissonance between what I had been taught in church my whole life and what I was experiencing in real time along the everyday paths of life. Ironically, many Bible stories that had become rote over the years suddenly became fairly accurate and relevant metaphors to describe my experiences, which I later came to define as *mystical* experiences.

My personal encounters and spiritual revelations began to contradict much of what I was taught from an early age about God and the nature of reality. My evangelical theology required me to force pieces of the puzzle together that I knew no longer fit. My goal in this book is to offer a new paradigm through which to consider objective spiritual (and by extension, *natural*) laws. In my search to understand the nature of God, the universe, and humanity, I stumbled upon the study of biblical mythology and was struck by its accuracy in illuminating the lived human experience. It offered a precise diagnosis of the plight of the human soul and charted a map for spiritual growth and transformation. If the term "myth" throws you, hang tight—I'll dive into it in Chapter Four, *The Function of Myth*. It doesn't mean what you're afraid it does. If you'll stick with me, my hope is to lead you to a well of undiscovered potency hiding in the biblical stories that has the power to both revitalize your life and encourage your sharpest reasoning skills. The time has come for the heart, mind, and body to come fully alive. The world is yearning for a breakthrough beyond our well-worn religious tropes.

Maybe the hell I've always feared
Was burning inside of me?
And the only way to heaven
Was to walk right through the fire
Falling forward I ignite
My mind and body engulfed in heat
I've made a mistake
Let me drift back to sleep
Give me the inferno I thought was heaven
The combustion I called love
This pain is suffocating
My self is melting off
My life bursting into flames
I'm writhing in the violent death
Of everything I knew burning down

But as the smoke begins to clear
And ash settles on the ground
I dust off a brilliant diamond
At last, I am found
The Garden I'd been longing for
Was waiting on the other side of hell
The blaze of truth spread like wildfire
Until finally I was free
Now I inspect Eden to ensure all embers are extinguished
A match and gasoline ready in each hand
I'll light a controlled burn next time
But I'm not going back to sleep
Except to rest peacefully under the Tree of Life

— **Heather Hamilton,** Burning in the Garden, Feb. 22, 2019

PART I

FILLING IN THE GAPS

ONE

THE CHRISTIAN OF THE FUTURE

The Christian of the future will be a mystic, one who has experienced God for real, or he or she will not exist at all.[1]

— **Fr. Karl Rahner** (1904–1984)[2]

THERE IS A PROFOUND story in part of the testimony of St. Francis of Assisi. Like many religious people, Francis experienced his religious group tribally and had an abhorrent fear of certain "outside" groups of people. For many Christians in the world today, that fear and disdain might be directed at LGBTQ+ persons, different religious groups such as Muslims or Hindus, or non-religious groups such as atheists and humanists. For Francis, his disdain was directed towards lepers, and he avoided them at all costs.

One day while riding his horse, Francis encountered a leper with his hands out, asking for charity. His initial instinct was to turn away to avoid this man whose skin had been eaten away by leprosy. But to Francis's surprise, he was suddenly filled with compassion and turned towards the man. He dismounted his horse, gave the man money, embraced him warmly, and kissed him tenderly on the lips. He literally put his lips on that which disgusted him most. This was the watershed moment in Francis's spiritual life. When he got back on his horse and looked around, he no longer saw the man. He eventually came to understand that it was Jesus Christ himself whom he had kissed.

St. Francis later wrote, "This is how God inspired me, Brother Francis, to embark upon a life of penance. When I was in sin, the sight of lepers nauseated me beyond measure; but then God himself led me into their company, and I had pity on them. When I had once become acquainted with them, what had previously nauseated me became a source of physical consolation for me. After that I did not wait long before leaving the world." It was soon after this encounter that Francis left his life of wealth and power, began spending time with lepers, and started his ministry.[3]

The Greek word for sin, *hamartia*, means "to miss the mark." It is quite a different understanding than the conventional modern notion of sin as a violation of a written law or, more simply, "bad behavior"—however that behavior may be defined in any given cultural context. Francis's behavior when he was "in sin" was the result of a misperception of who and where God was. In his embrace of the leper, Francis's sight was corrected. He now recognized Christ not just as a man who lived for thirty-three years, but as the indwelling Spirit of every human being, including the leper. For Francis, this Spirit extended to all creation. He came to see all people as a manifestation of the Spirit of God, or *Christ*. Although the characters were different, my encounter with the transgender woman on my porch led me to the same conclusion as Francis. The leper, the transgender woman, and everyone else was a vessel for the indwelling Spirit of Christ. There were no exceptions; therefore, there was no longer anyone to disdain or avoid. Only different manifestations of Christ to love. The Apostle John calls the indwelling Spirit of Christ "the Word":

> *In the beginning was the Word, and the Word was with God, and the Word was God. He was in the beginning with God. All things came into being through Him, and apart from Him not*

even one thing came into being that has come into being. In Him
was life, and the life was the Light of mankind. And the Light
shines in the darkness, and the darkness did not grasp it.

— **John 1:1–5** (NASB)

The Word, or *Christ*, is the Spirit that flows out from God and manifests all things in physical form. This is the spiritual reality, which the mystic sees. To be "in sin" is to be in *darkness* or blind to this reality. The result of this blindness is the *perception* of separateness from God and others. Sin is not a state that one consciously chooses to enter into by willful decision. It is an inevitable state of human development. The condition is not *original*; rather, it is *inevitable*. Like Francis, there must be an encounter in each person's life where this perception of separateness is corrected and sight is restored—revealing the indwelling Spirit of God in every human and all creation.

The person of Jesus incarnates this formless, expansive Spirit of God pulsing through all of creation (Christ) and distills it through one person, expressing in human form the very essence of God and ultimate reality. The life and teachings of Jesus as portrayed and mythologized in the New Testament took on a powerful symbolic spiritual meaning, which has endured for two millennia and has profoundly shaped the course of Western civilization and the world.

The following verses express the nature of Christ, revealed through Jesus:

For He rescued us from the domain of darkness, and transferred
us to the kingdom of His beloved Son, in whom we have redemp-
tion, the forgiveness of sins. He is the image of the invisible God,
the firstborn of all creation: for by Him all things were created,

both in the heavens and on earth, visible and invisible, whether thrones, or dominions, or rulers, or authorities—all things have been created through Him and for Him. He is before all things, and in Him all things hold together.

— **Colossians 1:13–17** (NASB)

Once one is aware of the truth of this reality, mainly that Christ is the imminent Spirit of God animating all of creation, a love that was once reserved only for Jesus suddenly extends boundlessly to everything: *because the fundamental essence of Christ is hidden in everything.* The person of Jesus is then the gateway, or portal, out of the darkness—the darkness of seeing divinity exclusively in Jesus and nothing else. Through the gateway of Jesus, we transfer into the *kingdom*—where we recognize Christ as the indwelling essence of everything that exists.

The Christian mystic is one who has made the leap from loving Jesus to loving everything because they see Jesus in everyone and everything else. This is the reality from which they see.

> Only the Divine matters.
> And because the Divine matters,
> Everything matters.

— **Thomas Keating, O.C.S.O.** (1923–2018)[4]

Two

FINDING CHRIST IN THE BIBLE

With that foundation laid, let me describe how I now read the Bible, which is important for understanding the rest of this book. My hermeneutic is based on the theory that the character of God has never changed, but that the human understanding of God's character has. This evolution of human consciousness concerning God is summed up succinctly by Brian Zahnd:

> God is like Jesus. God has always been like Jesus. There has never been a time when God was not like Jesus. We haven't always known this, but now we do.

— **Brian Zahnd**[1]

Zahnd is emphasizing here that we should understand the Bible as a narrative of human consciousness struggling to understand God—and often misunderstanding. The human understanding of God matures throughout the text until the invisible nature of God is finally revealed through Jesus. Jesus "upgrades" our understanding of what God is like, so that we can correct our mistaken perceptions about God.

To put it plainly, I look for Jesus in every Bible story—even if the story says nothing about Jesus. As I said in the previous chapter, Christ is the imminent Spirit of God animating all of creation. Christ has been present since the beginning, breathing creation into life and sustaining it. Christ was the Spirit that animated Jesus's life. We can understand Christ with nuance, in that, although Christ has always been present, the exact nature of Christ was not fully revealed until the incarnation of Jesus. Jesus's temporal incarnation on earth gives concrete definition to the nature of Christ. Jesus makes visible the Christ which is invisible. Jesus and Christ are paradoxically distinct and also one. An imperfect metaphor for this is thinking of air in a balloon. The air (representing Christ) is constantly present, but by filling a balloon (representing Jesus), we can better understand the properties and characteristics of the air (Christ). The balloon (Jesus) temporarily embodies the air (Christ), and through that embodiment, we realize that the air (Christ) has always been here and will continue to be. Forgive the unsanctimonious metaphor, but I hope it helps illustrate the distinction.

The purpose of Jesus is to reveal the true character of God. So, in every Bible story, including Old Testament stories, I look for the character who most closely resembles the Spirit of Christ as revealed by Jesus. *Sometimes the character who most resembles Christ is not the "God" character.* I know what God is like through my personal encounter with Christ on my front porch. I know what God is like through the life of Jesus in the New Testament. *So, if the "God" character in a Bible story does not reflect the character of Jesus, then I know that the "God" character is not God.* Sometimes the "God" character in a Bible story is not Christlike and the Spirit of Christ must be found elsewhere in the story. You might be thinking, "Huh? How can the God character in the story not actually be God?" Good question. Reading the "God" character as God is indeed one way of reading Scripture. There are many other ways to read it though. Jesus's repeated formula for people devoted to their particular reading of scripture is: "You have heard it said . . . but I say . . ."

There is a big difference between what God is actually like (Jesus) and what humans *think* God is like. *When the Bible presents a depiction of God that is contrary to the exact nature of God as revealed in Jesus, I know that the depiction I'm reading is not actually God.* Rather, it is a depiction of what humans *think* God is like. Is God a vengeful tyrant who demands firstborn sons be sacrificed? *Or is God like Jesus?* Is God violent and egotistical? *Or is God like Jesus?* Does God commit genocide with floods? *Or is God like Jesus?* Does God punish people? *Or is God like Jesus?*

An example would be the story of Abraham and Isaac. When you look at the three main characters in this story—God, Abraham, and Isaac—which character looks most like Jesus? Is it the "God" character who demands a brutal child sacrifice? Or is it Isaac who is non-violent and loving towards the person who is about to murder him? I insist that Christ is revealed here in Isaac.

The human perception was, *and largely still is*, that God requires an innocent human sacrifice for the atonement of sins. In his book *What is the Bible?* Rob Bell points out that before Abraham takes Isaac up the mountain to sacrifice him to God, he says to his servants, "Stay here with the donkey while I and the boy go over there. We will worship and *then we will come back to you*" (Genesis 22:5).[2] Before even taking Isaac up the mountain, Abraham assures his servants that *both of them will return*. Abraham knows God does not require sacrificial killing! But he still has to act out the whole ritual up until the point of the violent ending everyone is expecting. The human mind usually needs to be shocked into the truth about God. "You have heard it said... but I say..." From the very first book of the Bible, humans with a clear knowledge of what God is really like have been saying, "You think God requires a sacrifice for the atonement of sins...but I say God is non-violent and all-merciful."

> *For I desire mercy, not sacrifice, an acknowledgment of God rather than burnt offerings.*
>
> **— Hosea 6:6** (NIV)

Little by little, Scripture seems to nudge the human perception of God—as wrathful, violent, and punitive—towards a more loving and merciful understanding of God, as finally and fully revealed in Jesus. *It is not God who changes throughout the text; it is the human understanding of God that is shifted.* This shift is often shocking, awe-inspiring, and humiliating—especially for Christians! How else would we learn humility without realizing we had God all wrong?

Before becoming doctors, medical students must take the Hippocratic Oath in which they pledge to *"first, do no harm."* This is an act of humility which demands that doctors do not overestimate their ability to heal, or underestimate their capacity to harm. The aim is for doctors to be vigilant about the power that they hold—to strive to remain sober-minded before jumping into action. We should adopt this principle with the Bible. Can you imagine if Christians were required to take an oath to "first, do no harm" with the Bible?

I have a good friend named Jessica who, during her own questioning of the character of God in light of Jesus, found herself teaching Bible stories to children in a private Christian school. The curriculum was given to her to teach, and as she began reading old familiar Bible stories to prepare for the school lesson, she began to feel conflicted about presenting God in the unflattering light in which the character was portrayed in the stories. She would often reach out to me saying, *"This version of God doesn't reflect who Jesus is."* We would then search the story to find *someone* in the text reflecting love that appeared Christ-like. It often was not the "God" character. Jessica decided to operate using the "do no harm" principle. If she couldn't find a reflection of Jesus in the story, she'd skip that part. She realized that she held the power to turn God into an angry tyrant to be feared by the children she was responsible for teaching. She was humble enough to do nothing rather than risk harming children's hearts and minds by carelessly reading the text at face value. Reading the Bible literally, like a news report, robs us of understanding its intrinsic depth of wisdom and saddles us with a rigid, fearful, and lifeless understanding of God.

> *If anyone causes one of these little ones—those who believe in me—to stumble, it would be better for them to have a large millstone hung around their neck and to be drowned in the depths of the sea.*

> **— Matthew 18:6** (NIV)

The Bible deals with life's greatest mysteries and humanity's struggle to understand, flourish, and live in harmony with mystery. The key to unlocking the depths of the Bible is in awakening to the essence of Christ as revealed in Jesus. Only then can one recognize Christ in the Bible where Jesus is not explicitly named. An accurate recognition of Christ corrects our distorted perception of God. That distorted perception is reflected over and over again by characters written about in the Bible (including the "God" character), and we risk falling into distortion with a strictly literal interpretation of the text. It is essential that a person reads the Bible through the lens of Christ, which requires an unwavering certitude in the qualities of the character of Jesus and the Spirit that animated his life. Apart from that, one will take the words of the text as impetus for violent behavior towards themselves, other humans, and creation.

> *Leave them; they are blind guides. If the blind lead the blind,*
> *both will fall into a pit.*
>
> — **Matthew 15:14** (NIV)

THREE

THE ANATOMY OF A SEED

IT'S IMPORTANT BEFORE WE get farther into the book that I establish some terminology that I will use moving forward. Although it is impossible to speak of spirituality and mystery with exact precision, metaphors can provide the mind a handle by which to grasp spiritual concepts so that they can be discussed.

A major principle that eventually surfaces on the path of spiritual seeking, including within the tradition of Christianity (in contemplative and mystical paths), is the concept of the True Self and False Self. Unfortunately, this teaching is usually not found within contemporary Christianity. My personal feeling is that this is not a willful omission. Rather, many mainstream religious teachers and adherents are unaware of it or do not understand it. The Bible alludes to this spiritual reality in many of its metaphors, but I feel it is necessary now to describe this principle of spirituality explicitly in order for humanity to move forward together. Spiritual ignorance continues to foster unnecessary personal and global division, which is unsustainable. Through advancements in psychology, we can now assert that the principle of the True Self and False Self is not simply an ambiguous spiritual theory. Rather, it has increasingly become essential in the science of understanding human development, trauma, neurosis, and psychological healing.

In the field of psychology, the human psyche is defined as containing all elements of a person's mind and soul, conscious and unconscious. The different parts of the psyche are not physically concrete like anatomical parts of the brain, but it is necessary to label them in order to work with them. There are various labels that refer to the True Self: *soul, essence, essential nature, inner child, etc.* Likewise, the False Self might also be called: *ego, flesh, dualistic mind, egoic personality, persona, mask, etc.* For simplicity, I will use the terms True Self and False Self in this book.

Following my mystical encounter with the transgender woman on my porch, I began voraciously seeking literature that would help me make sense of my shifting perceptions about religion and spirituality. I stumbled upon an obscure commentary written by Maurice Nicoll. It opens with an entry entitled *Letter to Mr. Bush.*[1] In his letter, Nicoll describes the psychological and spiritual stages of human development corresponding to the life cycle of an acorn. From then on, I could not get that metaphor out of my head, as a reflection of what I knew to be true of my experience. That inspiration planted a seed in me that grew into what was eventually this book.

> *He presented another parable to them, saying, "The kingdom of heaven is like a mustard seed, which a man took and sowed in his field; and this is smaller than all other seeds, but when it is fully grown, it is larger than the garden plants and becomes a tree, so that the birds of the air come and nest in its branches."*

> **— Matthew 13:31–32** (NASB)

In this metaphor, Jesus is describing the concept of the True Self and False Self. In order to understand the metaphor, it's essential to understand the anatomy of a seed. If you were asked the question, "What does a seed look like?", most likely you would picture the round, smooth, intact object that you can hold between your index finger and thumb. The outside of the seed is, in fact, only one part of the seed. But it is the part that our brains identify as the *whole* seed. In reality, there are more parts below the surface. The anatomy of a seed is a useful way of envisioning the True Self and False Self.

When opened, the seed actually contains an embryo within the shell. In order for the seed to grow into a tree, the outside shell—the part of the seed that we identify as the whole seed—actually has to break open and die. It is the embryo inside of the shell that then takes root and, once the roots are firmly established, grows into a tree. This is illustrated in the diagram below. The seed coat, or outer shell, represents the False Self, and the embryonic seed leaf and root represents the True Self.

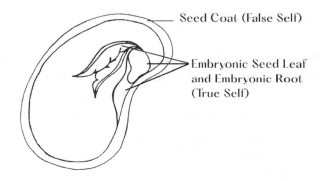

Seed Coat (False Self)

Embryonic Seed Leaf and Embryonic Root (True Self)

The seed's process of germination mirrors what must happen in order for a person to access their True Self—which Jesus calls *"the kingdom of heaven"* in the parable of the mustard seed. The tree on which a seed originates is like a *first womb* from which the seed grows, and it symbolizes God who gives *birth* to all creation. The seed experiences itself as one with the tree, a part of the whole. This is a child's state of consciousness, experiencing itself as one with its mother. The seed, or fruit, must then *fall* from the tree. This is a good and necessary process for life to continue and for each seed to fulfill its potential destiny of becoming a tree all its own. Like the seed falling from the tree, a child's consciousness eventually shifts from experiencing reality as connected to the source of its existence (God, represented by the tree), to experiencing itself as *separate from God* (the seed fallen from the tree). The human mind now identifies itself with the outer shell, experiencing itself as separate and fallen from its source. The conscious mind is unaware that what it is, the seed, is a self-contained tree. The source of its life and potential growth is inside the outer shell. *The True Self (embryo) is hidden inside the False Self (outer shell).* The human being (represented by the seed) senses deep down that their purpose is to become a tree. But they don't know how to accomplish this. They only see the outside of themselves. They identify completely with their outer shell, their False Self, and lack awareness of the True Self hidden within. Consequently, the False Self becomes a personality which strives to imitate the potential of the True Self. But because it is an imitation of the True Self and not the real thing, the False Self, or egoic personality, becomes inflated and self-loathing.

This state of consciousness is what the Bible refers to as *sin*. In Chapter One, *The Christian of the Future*, I mentioned that the Greek word for sin, *hamartia*, means "to miss the mark." The state of sin arises when the False Self is aiming to realize itself as a potential "tree" through an inflated, egoic personality. The result of this striving leads to addictive, compulsive, and narcissistic behaviors in an effort to emulate the True Self. Until a human becomes conscious of the fact that they are, in fact, *not* the False Self, *not* the outer shell, they will continue to suffer in this state of sin, or missing the mark, because they will attempt to become a tree while circumventing the process required to grow into a tree. The False Self is like a little seed gazing up at the majestic trees around it, either pretending it is already a tree when it is not, or self-loathing over the apparent impossibility of becoming one. The False Self is ignorant that it contains within itself the keys for transformation.

Like a seed, the False Self (outer shell) must be buried in the ground, which is like a *second womb*. It is from this second womb that one can be spiritually *born again*. Once buried, the False Self can begin to break open and subsequently die, allowing the True Self (embryo) to first take root in the ground and secondly sprout back up to the surface and continue its growth into a tree.

It is important to back up and note that the embryo, or True Self, cannot survive without the outer shell, or False Self. The treacherous journey from the fruiting on the original tree—to the fall to the ground—through the brutal elements of nature—and finally burial in the ground—would not be possible without the outer shell. The embryo would never be able to complete its necessary journey without the protection of the outer shell. Likewise, the flourishing of the True Self would not be possible without the development and subsequent protection of the False Self. It is only once the True Self is ready for *rebirth in the second womb* that the False Self no longer serves a purpose and must die and be buried. This is the process of *dying to (False) Self.* Indeed, the state of sin, represented by the False Self (outer shell), is actually a natural and necessary state of development, without which we would not survive to realize our full potential and experience grace in God. What an antidote to guilt and shame! We can surrender the False Self at the proper time, understanding its purpose which frees us from self-loathing. The English mystic, Julian of Norwich, calls sin necessary:

> It was necessary that there should be sin; but all shall be well, and all shall be well, and all manner of things shall be well.

— **Julian of Norwich**[2] (c. 1342–c. 1416)[3]

This process of dying to the (False) Self is the *Way* described by Jesus and visually represented in his crucifixion, burial, and resurrection. Through this cruciform process, the human's consciousness is restored to wholeness, identified as the True Self grounded and sustained by God and in harmony with all of nature. The consciousness now identifies itself as a *child of God* or offspring of the Tree, growing in the likeness of the source from which it fell. It recognizes that this was always its identity, and that it was simply unaware of this truth before. This misplaced identity—this identification with the False Self, this unawareness of the True Self, this "missing the mark"—is *sin*. It is not an *original* state of consciousness as most of Christianity has come to believe through the doctrine of original sin. The term "original sin" is not found in the Bible. The idea was proposed by St. Augustine hundreds of years after Jesus. The Bible actually begins with a declaration in Genesis 1 and 2 that we are "good . . . good . . . good . . . good . . . good . . . *very good.*" I will delve into original sin further in Chapter Twenty-Three, *Original Sin*.

Fr. Richard Rohr, OFM is a Franciscan priest whose work and teaching have been extremely illuminating for me. He names the pattern of spiritual transformation, which begins with our individual and collective goodness.

He emphasizes humanity's Original Goodness as inherent and asserts the potential humans have to realize our true nature and let it flourish:

> From the very beginning, faith, hope, and love are planted deep within our nature [the embryo]—indeed they are our very nature. Christian life is simply a matter of becoming who we already are.

— Fr. Richard Rohr[4]

Identification with the False Self, or the state of sin, is a necessary and unavoidable level of consciousness that serves as a vehicle for the survival and development of life. However, once the shell of the False Self has served its purpose, resisting the call to die becomes detrimental to the birth of the True Self. If the False Self (outer shell) is not crucified, or *sacrificed*, the True Self (embryo) cannot resurrect and become a tree. Apart from this process, a human soul is *lost*—like a seed blown by the wind, unaware of its true identity and purpose, and unable to fulfill its destiny.

Having now understood the concept of the True Self and False Self, read the words of St. Paul in 1 Corinthians 15 (The Message). Imagine the False Self when he talks about the seed and the True Self when he discusses the plant:

> *Some skeptic is sure to ask, "Show me how resurrection works. Give me a diagram; draw me a picture. What does this 'resurrection body' look like?" If you look at this question closely, you realize how absurd it is. There are no diagrams for this kind of thing. We do have a parallel experience in gardening. You plant a "dead" seed; soon there is a flourishing plant. There is no visual likeness between seed and plant. You could never guess what a tomato would look like by looking at a tomato seed. What we plant in the soil and what grows out of it don't look anything alike. The dead body that we bury in the ground*

*and the resurrection body that comes from it will be dramatically di
fferent.*

*You will notice that the variety of bodies is stunning. Just as
there are different kinds of seeds, there are different kinds
of bodies—humans, animals, birds, fish—each unprecedented
in its form. You get a hint at the diversity of resurrection
glory by looking at the diversity of bodies not only on earth
but in the skies—sun, moon, stars—all these varieties of beauty and brightness. And we're only looking at pre-resurrection
"seeds"—who can imagine what the resurrection "plants" will
be like!*

*This image of planting a dead seed and raising a live plant is a
mere sketch at best, but perhaps it will help in approaching the
mystery of the resurrection body—but only if you keep in mind
that when we're raised, we're raised for good, alive forever! The
corpse that's planted is no beauty, but when it's raised, it's glorious. Put in the ground weak, it comes up powerful. The seed sown
is natural; the seed grown is supernatural—same seed, same
body, but what a difference from when it goes down in physical
mortality to when it is raised up in spiritual immortality!*

*We follow this sequence in Scripture: The First Adam received
life; the Last Adam is a life-giving Spirit. Physical life comes
first, then spiritual—a firm base shaped from the earth, a final
completion coming out of heaven. The First Man was made out
of earth, and people since then are earthy; the Second Man was
made out of heaven, and people now can be heavenly. In the same
way that we've worked from our earthy origins, let's embrace our
heavenly ends.*

I need to emphasize, friends, that our natural, earthy lives don't in themselves lead us by their very nature into the kingdom of God. Their very "nature" is to die, so how could they "naturally" end up in the Life kingdom?

But let me tell you something wonderful, a mystery I'll probably never fully understand. We're not all going to die—but we are all going to be changed. You hear a blast to end all blasts from a trumpet, and in the time that you look up and blink your eyes—it's over. On signal from that trumpet from heaven, the dead will be up and out of their graves, beyond the reach of death, never to die again. At the same moment and in the same way, we'll all be changed. In the resurrection scheme of things, this has to happen: everything perishable taken off the shelves and replaced by the imperishable, this mortal replaced by the immortal. Then the saying will come true.

Death swallowed by triumphant Life!
Who got the last word, oh, Death?
Oh, Death, who's afraid of you now?

It was sin that made death so frightening and law-code guilt that gave sin its leverage, its destructive power. But now in a single victorious stroke of Life, all three—sin, guilt, death—are gone, the gift of our Master, Jesus Christ. Thank God!

— 1 Corinthians 15:35–57 (MSG)

FOUR

THE FUNCTION OF MYTH

Half the people in the world think that the metaphors of their religious traditions, for example, are facts. And the other half contends that they are not facts at all. As a result, we have people who consider themselves believers because they accept metaphors as facts, and we have others who classify themselves as atheists because they think religious metaphors are lies.

— **Joseph Campbell** (1904–1987)[1]

I MENTIONED IN THE Introduction that after my own spontaneous mystical experiences, I stumbled upon the study of mythology. Joseph Campbell, who was a professor who taught about comparative mythology and religion, received notoriety for bringing the themes of mythology into popular culture through his lectures and writings. His work illuminated the common themes and universal wisdom threading through the myths and religions across the world. As an evangelical, however, I was discouraged from exploring this fascinating field of study.

Through my upbringing in the evangelical church, I had come to understand that faith was an unwavering belief that all biblical stories were literal, historical events. However, I was beginning to have mystical experiences that were too great and intense to be described in words. The best way I could seem to describe them was through biblical metaphors. "I felt like I was in the belly of the whale...I felt like my whole world was flooding...I felt like I was dying and resurrecting…" I began to wonder if there was, in fact, a deeper meaning to the biblical stories that otherwise seemed rationally unbelievable. Perhaps I was missing something valuable by viewing the Bible through the false dichotomy of a "literal or lie" lens.

I discovered an important function of myth that had been absent from my biblical education in church: for a human life to actually experience revitalization from a myth, one must step out of the mindset of historicity and enter into the work of excavating the deeper spiritual truths hidden underneath the trappings of the story.

In fact, many religious stories are so outlandish on the surface, it's almost as if the authors were seeking to make it obvious that the story shouldn't be taken literally.

> If myth is translated into literal fact, then myth is a lie. But if
> you read it as a reflection of the world inside you, then it's true.
> Myth is the penultimate truth.
>
> — **Joseph Campbell**[2]

The word *myth* has several definitions, but in many fundamentalist churches it has a distinctly negative and misleading connotation. The popular usage of the word *myth* is synonymous with "fiction" or "a lie;" it implies a made-up story that has no basis in fact or reality. For people who feel deep meaning or emotional connection to their religious belief, the notion that their beliefs are myth is reprehensible. When they perceive a flippant dismissal of deeply held beliefs, their response is often a tighter grip. The emotional charge elicited by someone making light of a genuine belief can often lead to a concretization of not only the belief, but the specific interpretation of that belief. This is understandable and even predictable. There *is* power and energy in biblical stories that connect to people on a deep level. It is arrogant to deny that or minimize the human need that the stories are speaking to. In fact, that deep resonance humans feel with the stories is evidence for the power of myth as a doorway to deeper truth. Myth points to a reality beyond the historical facts of an event. Once understood correctly, the argument of historicity largely becomes irrelevant, and the stories become valuable for both the religious-minded and atheists alike.

Rather than providing historical accuracy, the most powerful function of myths is as windows into the underlying spiritual energies and experiences at work inside humans.[3] The purpose of mythological stories is to unlock our own deep meaning, understanding, and experience of life. To ancient civilizations, it was the meaning that was contained in the story that was sacred and most important, not the literal truth of the details surrounding the particular story. An important fact to note is that in the study of comparative mythologies across world cultures, similar religious symbols emerge roughly around the same time period in different geographical locations and cultural contexts. One example would be similar immaculate conception stories, which appear in Christian, Greek, Hindu, Buddhist and other mythologies. Mythological symbols emerge from the human psyche and speak to the human psyche. They pull us into a place deep within ourselves and illuminate universal truths that render the question of historicity irrelevant.[4] Simply put, biblical mythology should not be read like a news headline from the Associated Press.

This brings me to address those who have pivoted completely towards the view that biblical stories are "mere folklore." The stories are dismissed as completely obsolete and without value because, taken literally, they seem irrational. This position, while perhaps functional for a time of deprogramming from religious fundamentalism, is also incomplete. Reducing biblical mythology to "once upon a time" ignores the undeniable evidence that has arisen from the science of analytical psychology that symbolism originates *out* of the human psyche. These stories are not just made up out of thin air; they are maps for the human soul.

Carl Jung, a prominent 20th century psychiatrist and psychotherapist, founded analytical psychology, which explores the relationship between the conscious and unconscious. He noted the prolific occurrence of symbols and images in the dreams and unconscious projections of his patients. He observed that by working with these images, patients could achieve relief from their neurosis and suffering.

> But beyond that [the intellect] there is a thinking in primordial images, in symbols which are older than the historical man, which are inborn in him from the earliest times, eternally living, outlasting all generations, still make up the groundwork of the human psyche. It is only possible to live the fullest life when we are in harmony with these symbols; wisdom is a return to them.
>
> — **Carl Jung** (1875–1961)[5]

I began to notice that experts in different fields, such as Fr. Richard Rohr, Joseph Campbell, and Carl Jung, were observing similar phenomena. Although they were expressing their observations in different "languages"—such as religion, mythology, or psychology—they were all pointing to the same invisible truths and patterns.

Mythological stories and symbols are not ends in themselves. They point towards something deeper; something *beyond* the image or story. They provide clues by which we might navigate the inner workings of our psyches—yielding insights into our behaviors, addictions, neurosis, longings, and meanings of our particular and collective life. They provide a "road map" to navigate our deep inner landscape below the surface of our False Self. Of course, the map is not *the* adventure. But maps provide guidance to an otherwise dark journey through the wilderness. Just like on a road trip, the chances of a successful journey increase with some guidance. The possibility of reaching my highest potential pulls me towards my destiny, and myths chart a map to get there.

My husband and I recently took our children to visit Ruby Falls in Tennessee. Ruby Falls is an underground waterfall deep within a cave under Lookout Mountain in Chattanooga. In the 1920s, a chemist and cave enthusiast named Leo Lambert dreamed of opening the cave to the public. At the time, he was unaware that there was an undiscovered waterfall deep within the heart of the cave he wanted to explore. Drilling and eventually opening the cave to the public seemed like an impossible task, but Leo could not let go of the idea. He followed the longing of his heart. In 1928, jackhammers plunged through a void that opened up to the magnificent Ruby Falls, a breathtaking 145-foot underground waterfall.[6]

Ruby Falls inside Lookout Mountain in Chattanooga, Tennessee

As we made our way farther below ground and deeper into the cave, I couldn't help but notice how the journey into the heart of the cave felt like a living myth. By staying on the surface, no human could know the treasures underneath the ground they walked on. Leo's longing seemed to mirror the longing of the human heart to discover the mysteries hidden in life that elude us if we fail to dig deep into ourselves.

That is the purpose and power of myths: to awaken us to our deepest selves; to give us clues on our journey of self-discovery; to pull us into deeper truths we didn't know existed, so that we might discover the Living Water cascading deep inside the caves of our own hearts. Myths are the portal through which humans answer the highest calling in life. Through this portal lies the actual *experience* of being alive—the rapture of existing.

With a basic foundation of mythology laid, let's go back to the beginning of the Bible with Adam and Eve. I believe that by using mythology as a map, we can dig beneath this well-traveled surface into the realm of undiscovered personal knowledge and universal wisdom deep within us. Perhaps you'll experience a rapture all your own.

Know thyself, and thou shalt know the universe and God.

— **Temple of Apollo at Delphi**

PART II

DISCOVERING THE TRUE SELF

FIVE

RETHINKING ADAM & EVE

EVANGELICALISM TEACHES THAT FAITH is a white-knuckled belief in certain stories as literal events. The faithful must force themselves to believe stories literally that are often impossible to reconcile logically. The plausibility of the stories in our modern context becomes so remote that awareness of the story is pushed out of our daily consciousness and relegated to the Sunday School room for an hour of pondering and then moving on: "Wow . . . Noah built this huge boat all by himself while everyone thought he was crazy. What a brave guy. I hope I'd be so brave. Anyway, where are we going for lunch after the service?"

Those who actually do insist that events of biblical proportion are imminent are sometimes swept away by delusion. I once knew a lovely mother who whole-heartedly believed the end of the world was approaching. She ended up in a mental hospital, unable to care for her young children. In less extreme cases, these beliefs simply create an emotionally destabilized life. I'm reminded of my friend who, as a teenager, spent New Year's Eve in the year 2000 (Y2K) hiding in a closet in his church's youth room awaiting Armageddon.

My aim is to give you permission to suspend this way of thinking, just for a bit, and allow yourself to ponder these stories through a different lens. What clues do biblical stories give us for our own emotional and psychological healing? Through the paradigm of the True Self and False Self, the allegory of Adam and Eve begins to make more sense and becomes immediately relevant for every person. Approached through a psychological lens, the characters and settings in the story take on a different significance, with perhaps greater relevance for our personal understanding of ourselves.

The Garden of Eden reminds me of an infant's environment inside its mother's womb. Perhaps it symbolizes the womb of God, which itself represents the holding environment every embryo needs before birth. The Tree of Life portrays human consciousness in the state of wholeness, harmony, and interconnectedness with nature. This is how infants experience themselves and the world. Although they are separate people, they do not experience themselves as such. At this stage of development, infants perceive themselves to be one with their mother, their source. There is no conscious perception of separation from her. This is the state described in the Garden of Eden. The conscious state of unitive and symbiotic relationship experienced by Adam and Eve with their source is the exact experience of our earliest developmental stage. Developmentally and psychologically, all humans begin life in the Garden.

Going back to the anatomy of a seed: in order for the True Self to set off on the journey of life, it is necessary for the embryo to be hidden in the outer shell of the False Self, or personality, and *fall* from the tree. The seed of a tree is its *fruit*. This developmental transition is represented by Eve eating the fruit of the Tree of Knowledge of Good and Evil. Traditionally, this act has been portrayed as a moral failure. But from a psychological perspective, eating the fruit or "pushing off" from the parent is necessary for a healthy life to develop. Eve, or the feminine life force in each human, is responsible for this yearning towards realizing life and gaining wisdom.[1] However, once the knowledge of good and evil is acquired, the mind is no longer in a state of wholeness or unity with its source. The mind now splits into dividing things as "good" or "evil", among other categories. In Genesis 3:7, Adam and Eve become conscious of and identify only with the False Self, repressing their awareness of the True Self, or embryo, inside. They each perceive their outer shells to be separate and incomplete from one another, thus feeling naked, afraid, and ashamed.

It's necessary to pause and clarify here that, mythologically, this story is operating on two different levels. On one level, Adam and Eve each represent this human condition of alienation from the True Self that occurs in every individual. So, they are seen interacting as separate individuals in relation to one another. But on a deeper level, within each human Adam represents the masculine mind and Eve represents the feminine soul. I will be further analyzing the myth from the latter level to show how both Adam and Eve represent parts within each individual human. Both Adam and Eve represent parts of *you*.

It's important to emphasize explicitly that in this context, Adam and Eve, masculine and feminine, do not refer to gender. They refer to energies inside each human being that must be differentiated and parsed out in order to understand their relationship to one another and their functions inside of each of us.

Genesis 2:21–22 says that Eve was "taken out of man."[2] Psychologically speaking, Adam's consciousness could be considered originally androgynous, containing both the masculine and feminine within the one, whole psyche (before Eve was "taken out of man"). Now that the psyche has been divided, the masculine and feminine forces are in opposition to one another. Another way to put it: while it was once whole, the awareness of the feminine soul was taken out of man's conscious mind. Eve, who now personifies the feminine drive to create life, is repressed, as it is this feminine force that said "yes" to the life process and ate the fruit from the tree. In reality, Eve—this feminine, generative life force—is loving, courageous, and brave. She thrusts life forward.

> *Adam named his wife Eve, because she would become the mother of all the living.*

> — **Genesis 3:20** (NIV)

We perceive Eve to be dangerous because she has disrupted the psyche's comfort in the womb, the Garden of Eden, and has propelled life forward. The psychological womb of the Garden creates the perception of comfort and safety; however, staying in this stage limits our growth and potential for self-realization. Our desire to live and to realize our potential in our life requires the "push off" from the psychological womb of the Garden, and this process is personified by Eve. Any mother knows that a child cannot stay in the womb indefinitely, or both mother and child will die. It is Eve who recognizes the wisdom to be gained by eating the fruit.[3] It is through the process of trial, error, and learning from mistakes that we eventually acquire our own wisdom, and Eve initiates this process. During the formation of the False Self, our conscious memory of the Garden is buried deep within us, becoming unconscious, and we experience this as a great loss. It is this loss that creates suffering for the False Self and pushes it to seek to resolve its suffering.

> *So, He drove the man [the mind of False Self] out; and at the east of the Garden of Eden He stationed the cherubim and the flaming sword which turned every direction to guard the way to the tree of life.*

— **Genesis 3:24** (NASB)

Notice that the text says that only Adam was driven out of the Garden; not Eve. Eve, the soul of the True Self, represents the wisdom to eat the fruit, which was necessary for the next stage of life. The True Self within each person carries the memory of unitive consciousness experienced in the Garden. It is Adam, the False Self created by the mind, who is cast out of this state of consciousness.

The seed that has fallen longs for the comfort of the unitive consciousness represented by the Tree of Life, when it experienced oneness with its source. Of course, the seed cannot go backwards. It must set forth on its journey to *become* its own Tree of Life that it longs to be and is destined to be, and this process is propelled by Eve, the inner wisdom.

The True Self and False Self are now unconsciously in conflict with one another. The False Self resists the journey forward and utilizes the personality to create a sense of safety. This is personified by the masculine Adam, who is unaware of his inner feminine soul, the True Self, personified by Eve. The False Self, Adam, longs for reunification with the True Self, Eve. But Adam is unaware that Eve is within, and so he seeks to satisfy that longing externally. Another important development in human consciousness to mention here is the symbolism of the Tree of Knowledge of Good and Evil. "Eating the fruit" from this tree initiates the stage of development in the human mind that begins to label and divide. As soon as the False Self perceives itself to be separate, it begs the question, "separate from what?" It is at this stage in human development that we begin to think *dualistically.*

In order to solidify our shell of separation and fortify the defenses of the False Self, the human mind begins to label and judge. Good versus evil, right versus wrong, black versus white. This way of thinking confirms the False Self's belief that it is indeed separate and reinforces a sense of separate identity. Eating from the Tree of Knowledge of Good and Evil represents the False Self nourishing and strengthening itself with dualistic thinking. Once again, this is a *necessary* stage of human development. For survival, a child must establish that they are independent from their parents and others. They must learn boundaries and gain a sense of confidence in their individual abilities. A period of healthy narcissism is essential for a human to develop a sense of self and to progress on the journey of life.

But this dualistic labeling, or eating from the Tree of Knowledge of Good and Evil, only gets us so far. Dualistic thinking eventually becomes malignantly narcissistic and destructive to ourselves and others. *I'm better than. I'm smarter than. My family is the best. My country is the winner. My religion is the only truth.* This state of sin—our identification with the False Self—eventually leads to destructive addictions rooted in anger, pride, vanity, envy, greed, fear, gluttony, lust, and sloth. The behaviors that arise out of these addictions serve to numb the pain of separation from the True Self. In short, we have lost contact with our soul, which remains in the Garden. It is hidden deep with us in embryonic form. The soul, Eve, is always accompanying the False Self, Adam, hidden deep below his conscious awareness. But the False Self is unaware of this because it has been banished from the Garden.

The dualistic mind cannot exist in the realm of unitive consciousness. The germination of the seed would destroy the outer shell.

SIX

THE TOWER OF BABEL

ONCE THE FALSE SELF has been firmly established, the mind knows no other language than that of dividing and labeling. The dualistic mind divides up every part of reality, both internally and externally. Conscious communication with the True Self is eventually lost, which leaves us in the state of sin. This state of sin is much more an inevitable, unconscious psychological dilemma than a conscious moral choice. The development of the False Self is essential for healthy psychological development, but it leaves us alienated from our True Self, our soul.

Having lost awareness of itself in the context of the whole seed, the False Self looks upward in search of itself. It desires to become a great tree, but is unaware that the source of its life and destiny is hidden within. Attempting to fulfill its destiny, the False Self tries to construct this tree externally. The impulse is correct, but the method is futile. This state of striving in vain is depicted in the Tower of Babel.

Now the whole world had one language and a common speech. As people moved eastward, they found a plain in Shinar and settled there.

They said to each other, "Come, let's make bricks and bake them thoroughly." They used brick instead of stone, and tar for mortar. Then they said, "Come, let us build ourselves a city, with a tower that reaches to the heavens, so that we may make a name for ourselves; otherwise we will be scattered over the face of the whole earth."

But the Lord came down to see the city and the tower the people were building. The Lord said, "If as one people speaking the same language they have begun to do this, then nothing they plan to do will be impossible for them. Come, let us go down and confuse their language so they will not understand each other."

So the Lord scattered them from there over all the earth, and they stopped building the city. That is why it was called Babel—because there the Lord confused the language of the whole world. From there the Lord scattered them over the face of the whole earth.

— **Genesis 11:1–9** (NIV)

The myth of the Tower of Babel personifies the impulse of the True Self to fulfill its destiny. The True Self seeks to realize itself as the "city on a hill" (just like the seed strives to become a tree). That unconscious impulse to fulfill destiny is what drives the behavior of the False Self. Since the False Self is a temporary structure, it seeks to "make a name for itself" in order to outlast itself. It is a temporary form that desires eternity. The problem is that we identify exclusively with the temporal form of the False Self. Therefore, we fear annihilation of the temporary form. The temporary form serves a necessary and good purpose, but in our spiritual amnesia, we forget that our true identity lies in the formless and infinite True Self. The False Self is only a temporary vehicle carrying the True Self within. We wrongly identify ourselves as the vehicle.

Since we have now identified with the transient external form, we try to construct forms outside of ourselves that will represent us and outlast us. However, these efforts are in vain, because all forms are temporary. The more the False Self identifies with external roles and attaches its worth to temporary forms, the more confused and frustrated it becomes. The conscious and the unconscious become more and more confused and at war with one another. They are *scattered* (Genesis 11:9).

This state of confusion between the True Self and False Self first manifests inwardly, but extends outwardly. We try to work out this internal confusion in our external lives—individually, societally, and globally. Soon, it is the unconscious passions of Adam, the False Self, that govern our lives and the life of the planet. Anger, pride, vanity, envy, greed, fear, gluttony, lust and sloth. *These unconscious passions are the underlying "languages" confusing us and the world around us*, rendering us incapable of realizing the city we long for. They keep us looking up at the external towers outside of ourselves searching for eternity, rather than building the tower within where the eternal foundation lies.

It is Eve, the True Self deep within, that beckons us to make contact with her. This causes great anxiety for Adam, the False Self, as he knows that heeding Eve's call will lead to his death. The False Self compulsively engages in addictive behaviors in a futile effort to fulfill its purpose. It knows that, when it gives this up, it will "return to dust":

> *To Adam [the False Self] he said, "Because you listened to your wife and ate fruit from the tree about which I commanded you, 'You must not eat from it,' [the mind fell into dualistic thinking]*
>
> *"Cursed is the ground because of you; through painful toil you will eat food from it all the days of your life. It will produce thorns and thistles for you, and you will eat the plants of the field.*

By the sweat of your brow you will eat your food until you return to the ground, since from it you were taken; for dust you are and to dust you will return."

— **Genesis 3:17–19** (NIV)

Our addictions quell the anxiety of the False Self temporarily. It often takes a great deal of suffering and acceptance of the futility of our efforts before the False Self will begin the process of surrendering and sacrificing itself, so that the True Self can emerge from the depths within. Until then, Adam and Eve, the False Self and True Self, the conscious and unconscious, remain in opposition to each other. The False Self is trapped in a perpetual state of suffering, or sin, alienated from the True Self, toiling in vain to build itself up. From this point, the relevant question becomes: where do we go from here? How do Adam and Eve unite once again in Eden?

SEVEN

THE TWO BECOME ONE FLESH

Every man carries within himself the eternal image of woman,
not the image of this or that particular woman, but a definite
feminine image. This image is fundamentally unconscious, a
hereditary factor of primordial origin . . .

— Carl Jung[1]

THE MARRIAGE THAT THE Bible is primarily concerned with is not between
two separate people. It's a personification that is concerned with the separation of the masculine and feminine forces, symbolized by Adam and Eve, that
exist within your own body. Each human contains both masculine and feminine energies. Through the process of normal psychological development,
the masculine and feminine split from one another to form the conscious
and unconscious, as we saw in the story of Adam and Eve.

The feminine energy is creative, emotive, nurturing, and concerned with
matters of the Heart, such as love, compassion, wisdom, empathy, and transformation. Carl Jung associated the feminine with the maternal Eros.[2] It
pulls you in and captivates you. It's the untamed essence of Nature itself. It is
receptive and goes with the flow, if you will. The feminine Spirit also creates a
holding environment for pain and suffering and sustains us in our weakness
and vulnerability. This is God as Mother, represented by the Holy Spirit. In
the languages Jesus used (Hebrew and Aramaic), *Rúach* (spirit) and *Rúach
Hakodesh* (spirit-the-holy) are feminine nouns.

The masculine energy is decisive, discerning, structured, knowledgeable, and provides order. It is logical, skillful, and concerned with the Mind and meaning. Jung associated the masculine with paternal Logos.[3] It provides the container that holds the feminine Spirit. Masculine energy initiates action. It brings form and grounding to the flow of its feminine counterpart. This is God as Father. The feminine can be imagined like a rushing river and the masculine like the river bank, giving containment and direction to the untamed water.

The task of good religion is to wed the masculine and feminine into a balanced, sacred relationship. It is to bring the two seemingly opposing forces at work within each person back together into alignment and harmony. *The two become one flesh.* When this marriage is achieved, opposites are reconciled and a person's inner and outer nature come into harmony with each other. Internal suffering subsides as the conscious and the unconscious are no longer in opposition. The masculine mind no longer tries to repress the feminine Spirit, but instead gives form and direction and allows her to flow. The two becoming one flesh is the consecration of your spirit and your body; the life of your spirit animating your life on the physical plane.

This process consecrates the person to Nature, and they suddenly come to feel at home in their body and in the universe. Instead of fearing the destructive power of the feminine Spirit, the masculine mind allows her to flow, yet provides structure, so that direction and focus is given to the spiritual energy. This harmonious and generative relationship between the masculine (Father) and feminine (Mother) is symbolized as Christ. This is God as Son, the Christ child. We see this sacred marriage of masculine and feminine in the body of Jesus. The Son is the perfect fusion of Father and Mother, birthed from the union between the two. Jesus represents a masculine body containing a feminine soul; a perfect union of the two in one flesh.

Jesus saw some babies nursing. He said to his disciples, "These nursing babies are like those who enter the (Father's) domain."

They said to him, "Then shall we enter the (Father's) kingdom as babies?"

Jesus said to them, "When you make the two into one, and when you make the inner like the outer and the outer like the inner, and the upper like the lower, and when you make male and female into a single one, so that the male will not be male nor the female be female...then you will enter [the kingdom]."

— **Gospel of Thomas**, Saying 22[4]

Consider this spiritual principle reflected in the most basic, ordinary exchanges. A male and female have sex and the two become one in the form of a child. When a woman becomes pregnant, the outside (her body) becomes like the inside (with child). The one becomes two again when the child is born. The two become one again when the infant nurses from the mother's breast and the milk flows into the infant's body. The mother's milk inside the infant's body digests to become a growing human. The inside has become like the outside once again as the mother's milk becomes the baby's body. *There is no moral or ethical commandment here.* The picture of the two becoming one flesh is a meditation on a deeper spiritual principle about integrating the True Self with the False Self. The innate self with the learned personality. The feminine with the masculine. The inner with the outer. *The two become one flesh.*

This is an important matter to clarify in our culture now. The picture of marriage in the Bible is not a moral command to choose a spouse of the opposite gender. The story of Adam and Eve is not a mandate for heterosexual relationships. It's a personification of an internal process involving the reunification of masculine and feminine, Adam and Eve, False Self and True Self. The text is not meant to be taken literally, but symbolically. It is potent imagery referring to the internal psychological and spiritual processes for each individual human being to achieve wholeness within themselves.

So, how is this union achieved? The story of Jonah and the Whale gives us clues into the mechanics of achieving this union.

EIGHT

JONAH & THE WHALE

HAVE YOU EVER OBSERVED your own cognitive dissonance when the story of Jonah comes to mind? Noting the implausibility of surviving in a whale's belly for three days, but then chalking it up to "with God, nothing is impossible"? Holding tight to literalism deprives us of the mythical treasure offered in this story.

The story of Jonah and the Whale provides an excellent mythological map for the process of transformation. In it, we see that when Jonah is in his state of sin, he becomes increasingly distressed by the conflicts of his True Self and False Self. Like a seed remaining on the surface of the earth, avoiding descent into the unconscious below, Jonah is tossed around by the wind. His exterior shell fails to control the storm brewing inside of him.

> The belly is the dark place where digestion takes place and new energy is created. The story of Jonah in the whale is an example of a mythic theme that is practically universal, of the hero going into a fish's belly and ultimately coming out again, transformed . . . It's a descent into the dark. Psychologically, the whale represents the power of life locked in the unconscious. Metaphorically, water is the unconscious, and the creature in the water is the life or energy of the unconscious, which has overwhelmed the conscious personality and must be disempowered, overcome and controlled.

— **Joseph Campbell**[1]

Think of this story as a personification of the psychological process you have been coming to understand in this book. Great suffering of some kind often drives a person to surrender their False Self to the depths. When one comes to the threshold between the conscious and unconscious mind, represented by the water, it is natural to resist as Jonah does. It is dark, dangerous, unfamiliar, uncharted territory. It is only when the suffering of resisting the call becomes too painful that one surrenders to the process of dying to the False Self. Internal resistance not only creates internal chaos and suffering, but it also creates the same for the world around us.

Like Jonah, it is sometimes out of concern for others that people heed the call. In my own life, it was not until I truly saw how my own addictive and narcissistic behaviors were harming my family that I consented to examining my unconscious mind and getting to the root of what was driving my behaviors. Sometimes our addictions and behaviors do not seem overtly harmful. We don't recognize them as unhealthy. But they are covertly manipulative. We fail to act when we should. We say "yes" when we want to say "no." We repress our emotions in order to appear easygoing. We fawn over others and people-please to gain affection. We serve and perform for admiration and future favors. We betray ourselves to maintain a false sense of peace in our environment. It wasn't Jonah's overt harm to others, but his negligence, that was causing chaos. Many people feel that they can quietly go through life without creating any waves, even though internally they are not truly at peace. Sometimes it is those we love that remind us that bringing peace to our world requires reconciling the True Self and False Self within ourselves. There's no escape but surrender to this psychological and spiritual process.

Then the men became extremely afraid, and they said to him, "How could you do this?" For the men knew that he was fleeing from the presence of the Lord, because he had told them. So they said to him, "What should we do to you so that the sea will become calm for us?"—for the sea was becoming increasingly stormy. And he said to them, "Pick me up and hurl me into the sea. Then the sea will become calm for you, because I know that on account of me this great storm has come upon you."

— **Jonah 1:10–12** (NASB)

The unconscious is represented as water in myths all throughout history. Once a person surrenders to the psychological process, the sea monster then swallows them. Jonah 2:2 says, *"out of the belly of hell cried I."* The Belly, or *hell*, is the place where the old man is digested and transformed into new energy—a new creation. We will explore the nature of hell further in Chapter Fourteen, *Go to Hell*.

At this point, it's important to understand that passage *through hell* is an essential part of becoming a new creation. It is not a state to be avoided on the journey. In the human digestive process, the stomach produces heat because energy is required to break down and transform the food product. As a general rule, the hotter the temperature inside of the Belly, the faster the transformation. In other words, *the hotter the hell, the more dramatic the new creation.* From that point of view, we could conclude that, out of all the biblical stories of transformation, Jesus was transfigured by the hottest hell.

> *For as Jona[h] was three days and three nights in the whale's belly; so shall the Son of man be three days and three nights in the heart of the earth.*

— **Matthew 12:40** (KJV)

At the end of Jonah's journey, he says *"Salvation is of the Lord."* The Belly, the second spiritual womb, or *hell*, delivers Jonah back onto dry land (the ordinary, conscious world)—except that he brings back the wisdom that was attained in his journey through his unconscious underworld. He is *"reborn"* out of the Belly. Like a seed, the True Self, the embryo, has been born out of the Belly of Mother Earth. Jesus again describes *The Way* to Nicodemus in John saying:

"Very truly I tell you, no one can see the kingdom of God unless they are born again."

"How can someone be born when they are old?" Nicodemus asked. "Surely they cannot enter a second time into their mother's womb to be born!"

Jesus answered, "Very truly I tell you, no one can enter the kingdom of God unless they are born of water and the Spirit. Flesh gives birth to flesh, but the Spirit gives birth to spirit. You should not be surprised at my saying, 'You must be born again.'"

— **John 3:3–7** (NIV)

Jesus makes it abundantly clear that no one can realize heaven without being "born of water and Spirit," psychologically and spiritually, in that order. As we have seen, the water represents a descent into the unconscious mind, where one is swallowed by the Belly, or *hell*. The False Self, outer shell, first Adam, or old man is digested within the Belly—or "cooked" by the fires of hell. Then the True Self, embryo, second Adam, or new man emerges from the depths of the Belly. The new creation is resurrected as a new form integrating the masculine form of the Father and the feminine energy of the Mother. The new creation is *Christ*, a child of God.

I should note that after Jonah's journey through the Belly of hell, he has completed the task before him, but he is not yet fully realized. The shell of the False Self breaks open and the embryo germinates in the Belly, and Jonah integrates the experience. However, at the end of the book of Jonah, he feels judgment and indignation towards the people of Nineveh.[2] Although Jonah feels enlightened by his experience, his resentment reveals another layer of the False Self that will later have to be surrendered and digested for transformation. The death and rebirth process may happen many times over as we continually surrender pieces of our False Self, digest, and utilize the new energy for growth. After the first major transformation however, we are awake and more conscious of how the process works. Once the germination process has begun, the True Self takes root and begins to grow. It does not return to the completely unconscious state of the False Self inside the shell. It simply takes time to mature as with anything in nature that is newly born.

True faith isn't an unwavering belief in the historical plausibility of a folktale such as Jonah and the Whale. It's the trust that the journey into hell creates heaven on earth. *The two (heaven and earth) become one flesh in the body of the person who has surrendered to this sacred process of death and rebirth, over and over again.* Your physical body (earth) manifests spiritual reality (heaven) through the process of psychological healing (hell). Faith is the courage to actively show up for and surrender to the process of transformation in all its stages and iterations.

NINE

THE VIRGIN BIRTH

I ONCE HEARD A story about a little evangelical boy who had accepted Jesus into his heart. He later developed a heart condition and had to have heart surgery to repair it. He became greatly distressed, because he worried that the surgery would hurt Jesus, who lived inside his heart.

While this story might elicit an "aw" from an adult, the fact is that many people are taught to think this way in Western Christianity. We mistake symbolic realities for historical fact, thus closing ourselves off to participation in spiritual processes. We are asked to believe that a girl named Mary was miraculously impregnated by the Holy Spirit (who, ironically, we've now established is feminine). Mary never physically had sex but became pregnant and gave birth to a son named Jesus. We then pray and ask this Jesus to come live in our hearts, and that's how he arrives there. You can understand the little boy's fear of harming Jesus with a scalpel.

The True Self, represented by the embryo inside of the seed, is the Imago Dei (image of God) inherent in every human being. This objective reality is revealed to the mystic when they discover through their own germination process that *the birth of Christ occurs from within. It was not something received from outside of themselves.* Once this fact is realized, the mystic then obtains *the mind of Christ*, which is the mind that perceives the real and present Imago Dei in other humans. The Imago Dei, which the mystic perceives, is the potential in every human being to be transformed into the *likeness of Christ*, because the ingredients for transformation are already present within them in a latent state *from the beginning.*

As we have established already, the marriage of masculine and feminine is a spiritual union that happens within, specifically in the spiritual heart. The *virgin birth* symbolically represents this divine union that happens in the womb of the spiritual heart where the Christ child is conceived. The Christ child is the birth of the True Self from within, which grows into the likeness of Christ. Through a psychological and spiritual lens, the virgin birth is the generation of the spiritual life within a person, not a biological anomaly occurring once two thousand years ago. The seed waiting to be fertilized is within your heart, and it's always been there.

It is the first womb of the Garden where the False Self, the animal man, the *First Adam* is born, and sets out on the journey to discover the True Self, or authentic human within. In the Garden, the whole is split into separate parts, masculine and feminine. It is the second womb of the spiritual heart where the split is reconciled and virginity is restored, or the two become one again. In the heart, the psychic opposites—masculine and feminine—are held in pregnant tension, until finally the *Second Adam, or Christ,* is then born of a "virgin."

The motivations of the False Self, animal man, or First Adam concern security, reproductive, and competitive impulses, which serve to sustain the false identity it's formed. Examples of this could include obsessive worry over money, having children or reproducing yourself in some way (business, charity, art) in order to preserve your legacy, and compulsively feeling the need to win at all costs to perpetuate a feeling of superiority. Concerns for security, reproduction, and competition are not inherently moral or immoral. It's more about the motivation and energy with which they are approached, and to what end they serve. The motivations of the False Self always come from a place of scarcity and fear, so there is never enough security, reproduction, or winning to satisfy long-term.

Once conception of the Christ child has happened within the womb of the heart, the former False Self with all its animalistic concerns begins passing away, and those old energies are metabolized to fuel the germination process of the second birth. In other words, the outer shell of the False Self is broken down and integrated into the True Self. We do not cut off our parts. As we know from the Law of Conservation of Energy, energy can neither be created nor destroyed, only converted from one form of energy to another.[1]

Once the energy of the False Self is broken down, it is then converted and utilized by the True Self. The True Self—authentic human, or Second Adam—is concerned with matters of compassion and love, becoming a human temple through which Christ sees and experiences the world. It is the eye of the heart that is opened. It is the birth of truly humanitarian love that identifies with the sufferings of others, including so-called "enemies," and is grounded in complete solidarity with humanity. It is a state of internal freedom that no longer clings to others for personal benefit, while, at the same time, feeling a deep sense of oneness with others. It is in this newly-opened heart that the bridge between heaven and earth is tethered. As the heart continues to transmute more energy from the old self into new life, the realm of heaven and earth eventually collapse into one another. There is now the delicate balance of seeing Christ as Jesus and Christ in *All*. The love that at first was densely concentrated on the fixed point of Jesus now extends out from that point in a boundless sphere while maintaining its density in all directions and dimensions. The "center point" of Christ is now everywhere. The experience is described by Mother Teresa:

> I see Jesus in every human being. I say to myself, this is hungry Jesus, I must feed him. This is sick Jesus. This one has leprosy or gangrene; I must wash him and tend to him. I serve because I love Jesus.

> — **St. Mother Teresa** (1910–1997)

This mystical vision extends to the physical eyes as well. Mystics often experience seeing objects with a greater vitality. Colors appear more vivid. They perceive a palpable energy which seems to make objects vibrate subtly. The spiritual dimension known as heaven permeates the material dimension known as earth. This is experienced as both an intuitive knowing and sometimes a physical phenomenon.

. . . having the eyes of your hearts enlightened, that you may know what is the hope to which he has called you, what are the riches of his glorious inheritance in the saints . . .

— **Ephesians 1:18** (ESV)

TEN

BECOMING A VIRGIN

MORE RIVETING THAN A physical anomaly, the virgin birth is about *your own spiritual immaculate conception*. I remember very vividly when I experienced this virgin birth within myself. This miraculous conception inside of the womb of my spiritual heart wasn't anything I went looking for. It was something that happened to me. I had a clear awareness that something was indeed happening inside of me that was *real*. There was a palpable entity inside of me that felt both completely new, yet somehow familiar and recognizable. It was akin to waking up from amnesia and slowly recovering awareness that had been lost.

It was like realizing there was a small child—*me*—buried alive inside of me. I had unconsciously been searching for this lost child my entire life and finally heard a faint cry from deep within. Once I heard that cry, I could not unhear it.

I felt like Mary. *Alone*. I could feel this child moving inside of me. I was to nurture and love it. I was to be its *Mother*. But I was also afraid. I knew that this whole experience would sound not only unbelievable, but insane. I knew it was real, but I also knew how crazy it would sound to others, because it would have sounded crazy to me before my own experience. It contradicted everything I understood about my faith and religion. My entire identity—my False Self—had been constructed around being an evangelical Christian. Everything about my life—my work, relationships, decisions, and sense of self—was rooted in that identity. And suddenly I realized that this False Self was not the real me. This inner child, my True Self, was the real me. The shell of the False Self was cracking open and dying quickly. I was overcome with despair, but pulled forward by the new life inside of me, which I sensed was sacred.

It felt both exhilarating and terrifying. I knew that I could lose everything in my life that I'd gained up to that point. With the conception of Christ in the sacred womb of my heart, I was both the mother and the child. I was also a threat to the old world. *Would my husband believe me? Would my family believe me? Would my friends? Would I lose my church? Would we lose our jobs?*

The answers to those questions would turn out to be mixed. My husband, like Joseph, believed me and stayed. He too had dreams that gave him peace about what I was experiencing, and he was steadfast in his love for me. There were certain environments that we had to flee because we were no longer welcome. We were actually perceived as a threat to the power structures. I did lose some friends. I did lose some income.

But then there were other moments, like when I sat across from my friend Jessica and told her what had happened to me. And like Mary visiting Elizabeth, the inner child in Jessica leaped from the womb of her heart with joy. And I knew that I was not completely alone.

> *When Elizabeth heard Mary's greeting, the baby leaped in her womb, and Elizabeth was filled with the Holy Spirit. And she cried out with a loud voice and said, "Blessed are you among women, and blessed is the fruit of your womb! And how has it happened to me that the mother of my Lord would come to me? For behold, when the sound of your greeting reached my ears, the baby leaped in my womb for joy. And blessed is she who believed that there would be a fulfillment of what had been spoken to her by the Lord."*

— **Luke 1:41–45** (NIV)

ELEVEN

JACOB'S LADDER

Later in the Renaissance in the seventeenth century, Jacob's
Ladder was interpreted symbolically as being the sounds and
vowels of human speech, or the different qualities of the world,
or the different numbers of the world. The basic idea of different systems of thought was projected onto the ladder. But
in all cases the ladder symbolized a continuous, constant connection with the divine powers of the unconscious. We could
say the dream itself was such a ladder. It connects us with the
unknown depth of our psyche. Every dream is a rung on a
ladder, so to speak.

— **Marie-Louise von Franz**[1] (1915–1998)[2]

THIS BRIDGE BETWEEN HEAVEN and earth, between True and False Self, is
reflected symbolically in the story of Jacob's ladder. The stone under Jacob's
head is symbolic of his False Self upon which he is sleeping. He is not yet
awake to the order of the universe which links the physical and spiritual
world. The top of the ladder, where we find angels, represents the True
Self, which unifies these two worlds in the union of the sacred marriage of
masculine and feminine. The virgin birth then gives way to Christ when
Jacob awakens to his True Self exclaiming:

"The LORD is certainly in this place, and I did not know it." He was afraid and said, "How awesome is this place! This is none other than the house of God, and this is the gate of heaven."

— **Genesis 28:16–17** (NASB)

Jesus refers to himself as the gate of heaven when he declares, "I am the way, the truth and the life" (John 14:6). However, we see Jacob declaring the same thing here, hundreds of years before Jesus, and anointing the rock on which he slept to symbolize "the gate." It makes no sense at all to take these verses literally. How can both Jesus and this rock be "the gate"? But we can now see that when "the gate" is a symbol for this sacred process of the birth of Christ within your heart, calling it "the Way" makes perfect sense. Jacob is anointing the rock as Christ to mark the center point through which heaven and earth were bridged for him. Jesus later symbolizes this rock and exposes the revelation of this center point within the human body. He declares it rather obviously in Luke 17:21 when he says, *"The kingdom of God is within you."*

The ladder that Jacob saw is reflected in frescoes in cathedrals around the world. At first glance, we might be tempted to think that heaven is to be found in the sky. But what if the frescoes in cathedral ceilings are actually a *reflection* of what's below them? Their intention is not to keep us looking up and outside of ourselves, but below—inside of ourselves—into our unconscious mind and the depths of our hearts. The dream world is like our own personal fresco, projecting a picture of our unconscious world up into our conscious mind. As Marie-Louise von Franz says in the quote at the beginning of this chapter, dreams are the ladder, bridging the unconscious spiritual world with our conscious material world.

Jacob's Ladder by Raphael. Fresco on the ceiling of the Vatican (Sanzio da Urbino, Raffaello. Jacob's Ladder. 1513–14. Stanza di Eliodoro, Palazzi Pontifici, Vatican.)

And he dreamed that there was a ladder set up on the earth, and the top of it reached to heaven; and behold, the angels of God were ascending and descending on it!

— **Genesis 28:12** (RSV)

Everything you see in the fresco, Jacob saw in the rock. The pattern is usually to recognize "the gate" first in something or someone else, such as Jesus. Then, it is reflected back to us, and we realize that heaven emanates outward from our inmost center. Finally, heaven extends out from our own center until we see everything else simultaneously included in our sphere and also as its own center point of origin.

To paraphrase an idea from Fr. Richard Rohr, heaven is not a location that you see. Rather, it is a state *from which* you view everything else.[4] It is recognizing the invisible divinity in everything visible, such that heaven and earth are consummated as one. Earth (meaning the material world) becomes the hiding place for heaven. There is nowhere to go to "get to" heaven. It's wherever you are, whether you have the vision to see it or not. Like seeing through glasses for the first time, what was always there is suddenly crisp, vivid, and breathtaking. Nothing actually changes except your perception.

Ordinary matter is the hiding place for Spirit and thus the very Body of God. Honestly, what else could it be, if we believe—as orthodox Jews, Christians, and Muslims do—that "one God created all things?" Since the very beginning of time, God's Spirit has been revealing its glory and goodness through the physical creation. So many of the Psalms assert this, speaking of "rivers clapping their hands" and "mountains singing for joy." When Paul wrote, "There is only Christ. He is everything and he is in everything" (Colossians 3:11), was he a naïve pantheist or did he really understand the full implication of the Gospel of Incarnation?

— **Fr. Richard Rohr**[5]

TWELVE

NOAH'S ARK: A BAPTISM IN TEARS

MANY OF US FIRST learned the Noah's Ark story in Sunday School. There might have been cute animals on a felt board. We may have colored pictures of a rainbow. The story, taken literally, is a tragedy for nearly the entire human race. There is a lot of cognitive dissonance that must be sustained in order to take this story literally as an adult. Surely, there's a better perspective on what this story means.

Noah's Ark is a symbolic picture of Christ and takes us back to our metaphor of the seed. The wooden Ark is like the outer shell of the seed, the False Self. It must be constructed to ensure the embryo, the True Self, can withstand the treacherous storms and elements of the first half of life. The Ark, or outer shell, represents a will to live, to stay intact though the attacks from the outside environment. If the Ark, like the outer shell, is not built solidly enough, it will eventually be washed out, along with everything precious inside of it. This is a psychological model. The outer shell is a testament to the will to live. It is essential to form this layer of protection around the embryo of the True Self, or it simply will not survive. Also, the False Self cannot safely give up its defensive functions until the environment is safe enough for that process to happen. In Genesis 8:9, we see the dove signaling to Noah that it is not yet time to crack open the Ark.[1] If opened too soon, the waters of the unconscious will overcome the vessel and the inner contents will drown.

Practically speaking, this is why it is important that a healthy False Self be established. The use of mind-altering substances at a young age can interfere with the process of building the False Self, allowing the unconscious to leak inside the shell prematurely. Trauma, abuse, and neglect can also interfere with the process of constructing a sturdy Ark, leaving too many holes between the conscious and unconscious. Generally, a person needs to be able to function adequately in society with their outer shell before they can embark on the task of metabolizing it and integrating it into the True Self. We must build ourselves a container strong enough to carry us through the process. That is step one. If that first step is not adequately accomplished in childhood, the first task of a therapist would be to help build a healthy and solid sense of self, or ego structure. Without a functioning False Self, a person remains in a childlike state, unable to mature, because they are still grasping for a solid sense of self. Construction must come before deconstruction.

The False Self looks outside itself with a dualistic mind, seeing only pairs of opposites, as represented by the male and female animals. In order to label something "good," something else must be "evil." The False Self uses this function of the dualistic mind to bolster itself as *separate, good, and better.* The False Self creates necessary boundaries, but it can always find someone or something else to which it is superior or inferior. *My religion will prevail. My country is exceptional. My children are the best.*

Once the illusion of the False Self is revealed, there comes a period of grief and remorse for the harm the False Self has perpetuated on others. The masculine and feminine, *the opposites,* must now be reconciled within the heart of the Ark.

> *For you are all sons and daughters of God through faith in Christ Jesus. For all of you who were baptized into Christ have clothed yourselves with Christ. There is neither Jew nor Greek, there is*

*neither slave nor free, there is neither male nor female; for you
are all one in Christ Jesus.*

— Galatians 3:26–28 (NASB)

Noah is the person who has taken every disappointment, failure, loss,
hatred, sorrow, and contradiction in life into the Ark of his heart and flooded
his entire world with tears of sorrow and remorse. Remorse is necessary and
productive for self-reflection, making amends, and taking right action. This
is an intense internal process. A sturdy Ark is needed to contain and bear it.

The more common word for this process is *forgiveness*. In her book *Rising
Strong*, Brené Brown recalls a time she was listening to an Episcopal priest
named Joe Reynolds speak about forgiveness. He said, "In order for forgiveness to happen, something has to die. If you make a choice to forgive,
you have to face the pain. You simply have to hurt."[2] Reflecting later on the
epiphany she had during this sermon, Brown said in an interview:

> *Love is not easy. Love is not hearts and bows. Love is very con-
> troversial, really . . . In order for forgiveness to really happen,
> something has to die . . . Whether it's your expectations of a
> person, there has to be a death for forgiveness to happen. In all
> these faith communities, where forgiveness is easy and love is
> easy, there is not enough blood on the floor to make sense of that.
> And so I thought about why forgiveness is so hard in our culture.
> Because there are two affects (or emotions) that people fear the
> most, and it's shame and grief.*
>
> *If something has to die in order for forgiveness to happen, and
> people are deathly afraid to feel grief, then we just won't forgive
> anybody. Because I don't want to feel grief. I thought faith would
> say, I'll take away the pain and discomfort. But what it ended
> up saying is that I'll sit with you in it.*[3]

This radical forgiveness is not only extended to others, but also to your False Self for the sins it committed in ignorance. Fr. Richard Rohr describes this forgiveness as reaching to include *reality itself*:

> Forgiveness becomes central to Jesus' teaching, because to receive reality is always to "bear it," to bear with reality for not meeting all of our needs. To accept reality is to forgive reality for being what it is, almost day by day and sometimes even hour by hour. Such a practice creates patient and humble people.

— Fr. Richard Rohr[4]

> Forgiveness remains the only path that leads out of hell. Whether we're forgiving our parents, someone else, or ourselves, the laws of mind remain the same: As we love, we shall be released from pain, and as we deny love, we shall remain in pain. Every moment, we're either extending love or projecting fear, and every thought takes us nearer to Heaven or hell. What will it take to make us remember that 'the ark is entered two by two,' that there is no getting into Heaven without taking someone with you?

— Marianne Williamson[5]

Once the tears recede, a new heaven and a new earth will emerge inside you, and everything that was once opposite will be reconciled. The paradoxes of life, those things which seemed to be in opposition to one another inside the Ark, will be put into balance. What was once seen as black-and-white and irreconcilable has been taken within and integrated into a rainbow. The True Self is freed to *be fruitful and multiply* as the tree that can now spread its branches and bear fruit.

If God, in His mercy, had not granted to men this second baptism, then few indeed would be saved.

— **St. John Climacus** (c. 579–649)[6]

These tears of repentance (represented by the flood) are the baptism of the Holy Spirit (represented by the dove). A water baptism in a church foreshadows the baptism in the Spirit to come. You agree to begin building the Ark within your heart and summoning the opposites: life and death, saint and sinner, good and evil, joy and sorrow.

The soul can have no rainbow if the eyes have no tears...Tears of sorrow are tears that glisten with hope for a better tomorrow. Such tears are, in fact, like a rainbow, a God-given sign of hope. This spiritual rainbow is caused by the rays of the Son of God striking the tears of penitence and transforming them into sparkling droplets of joy and hope.

— **Philokalia: The Bible of Orthodox Spirituality**[7]

The American journalist and activist Dorothy Day once wrote, *"I really only love God as much as the person I love the least."* To love God is to love the whole of reality, which includes everything and everyone. Instead of trying to escape certain people and keep them out of my personal "Ark" (e.g., life, country, church, work, organization, business, etc.), this picture of Christ as the whole opens me to a radical inclusiveness. The moment I exclude anyone from my sphere of compassion is the moment I have placed Christ in exile. I have thrown Jesus off of the Ark.

Thirteen

THE CROSS SYMBOLIZES INCARNATION IN EVERY HUMAN

It is the role of religious symbols to give a meaning to the life
of man.

— **Carl Jung**[1]

HUMANS NEED SYMBOLS. RELIGIOUS symbols draw us into and through
them. They point to a reality deeper than and beyond the symbol itself. A
symbol is a metaphorical door that you walk through. The purpose of a door
is to go through it, not stop at it.

The cross is a symbol of objective reality. A statement of *the way things
are*. It articulates our relationship to nature. It is not something that changes
fundamental reality; rather, it changes our perception of reality and our
relationship to it. Rather than changing ultimate reality, the cross offers a lens
through which we can view reality so that we can be brought into harmony
with it.

The cross gives humans a singular point through which to enter into the
fullness of life as it actually is—that is to say, the present moment. *Now. Real*

Time. This is impossible to do, unless we perceive reality as it actually is, and not as we *think it to be, or think it should be.* When we perceive reality incorrectly or wish it to be different, we suffer. It is only when our perception of reality is corrected that our internal state comes into harmony with the external reality. It is not that we no longer feel pain. It is that we do not resist pain, and so we no longer create suffering for ourselves. We *yield* to what *is.*

The picture of Jesus hanging on the cross unlocks the mysterious divinity hidden in everyone and everything. The theological term for this *natural divinity* is "Incarnation." The cross symbolizes the intersection of humanity and divinity realized in the spiritual heart of human beings.

Western Christianity neutered this message when it limited the Incarnation to only Jesus and nothing else. It put him on a pedestal, higher than and removed from our world.

But Jesus never rids himself of his humanity. He includes it. He carries his story and his scars. "Touch me,"[2] he says to Thomas, to remind us that our bodies and souls—in whatever form—keep a record of our human history, both individually and collectively. His scars represent the paradox of suffering as a part of reality. Our wounds somehow belong and are the keys to unlocking our gifts that we give to ourselves and the world. Redemption is not an erasure of the wounds, but the mysterious invitation by which we lean in closer to what we're afraid to touch. In doing so, we experience the miracle of inner peace, *shalom,* an ultimate surrender to the beautiful mystery of life. We fear our sufferings will be unbearable. Yet, we somehow can and do bear them, and they transform us—if we allow it. Jesus calls himself the Son of Man as if to reinforce his message: "I am one of you. I come from you. I am with you. There's no separation, distance, or difference between us." Jesus shows us how to truly live by yielding to the whole of life, the pain and the pleasure. By allowing the mystery to unfold in our lives, we become the peace we're searching for.

Jesus doesn't symbolize a transcendence of humanity. He symbolizes a saturation of humanity with divinity. A soaking of nature with divinity. On the cross, we see Jesus's blood penetrate the ground, such that what grows from the earth will be rooted in and nourished by his blood. The food that we eat from the ground will thus be grown from his body. And that food will become our body. The earth is saturated with Jesus's blood and our bodies are physically made from the blood-saturated earth. We are all physically one body *in Christ*.

It is this *physical reality* that the Eucharist or Communion is meant to make us conscious of. We are literally eating the body of Christ, thus becoming Christ. In Catholic theology, transubstantiation is the name of the ritual wherein practitioners believe that the bread and wine are converted into the physical body of Christ. In reality, all physical matter is already the body of Christ. The ritual simply makes us aware of this reality. No magic happens other than the miracle of us becoming aware that physical reality is soaked in divinity. It is all sacred. It is all Christ. Little by little, our consciousness is becoming aware of the fullness of this reality.

Here is the mystery of this incarnation summed up in the cross:

Everything we sense on the Horizontal (physical, earthly) plane (—) intersects with the Vertical (spiritual, heavenly) plane (|).

*Byzantine Cross, 9th–12th century, Metropolitan
Museum of Art*

Every rock *is* the gate of heaven. Every bush *is* burning. The wine *is* the blood. The bread *is* the body. Everything physical *is* spiritual. Everything natural *is* supernatural.

Christ is all, and is in all.[3]

Jesus saves humanity by giving humanity the symbolic truth to save itself. Thank you, Jesus, for the cross.

FOURTEEN

GO TO HELL

The doors of hell are locked from the inside!

— **C.S. Lewis** (1898–1963)[1]

FROM THE INSIDE? *FROM the inside?* If the doors of hell are locked from the inside, doesn't that give us the power to free ourselves? This flips the popular understanding of hell on its head.

Perhaps one of the most critical concepts to parse out is the teaching that there is a literal, geographical place called *hell* where people burn forever after they die. In conventional, modern-day evangelical teaching, this belief is a given—a foundational premise that usually isn't even questioned. This fear is often the ultimate motivation for conversion. The only way to avoid this fate is to "accept Jesus into your heart." Usually this is done by praying "The Sinner's Prayer" *sincerely*.

I prayed this prayer at a summer Vacation Bible School at church when I was seven. I remember my parents were a bit surprised when, a year or so later, I prayed the prayer at another church event and got saved again. The church congratulated me with a snow cone, and my parents looked confused when I told them the good news again, but they were reluctant to spoil my snow cone party by pointing out the obvious: that I had just done this and had been baptized not long ago. Apparently at this church, they didn't keep track of how many times you got saved.

In the following years, I would lay in bed countless nights asking Jesus into my heart again, just to be sure my final fate in heaven was sealed. When I got older, I started calling it "rededicating my life to Christ." The youth pastors at church would frequently give teens a chance to do this at youth events.

In theory, the solution to avoiding eternal conscious torment was so simple. *Believe in your heart that Jesus is Lord, confess it with your mouth, and be saved!* I would hear this formula repeated ad nauseum at church.

In practice, the church created a trap of obsession. I, and millions of others, have spent countless hours analyzing and scrutinizing the sincerity of our hearts. This was often prompted by pastors saying things like "Are you sure?" and "99% saved is 100% lost." The anxiety from the possibility of seeing the devil when I passed away always justified just one more prayer. *How could I be sure I was sincere enough?*

In some ways, I seemed to take this matter much more seriously than most people around me. A lot of my fellow Christians didn't seem to spend much time thinking about it. They seemed able to go about their lives fairly normally. On the other hand, there were others who seemed to over-spiritualize everything. A normal consequence in life was viewed as an "attack from Satan." On the extreme end of the spectrum, I knew Christians who spiraled into severely neurotic behavior and suffered from religious hallucinations and delusions.

It surprises me how shocked many Christians are when I say that I took hell that seriously—that *graphically*. As a child, I would imagine myself screaming in terror while my flesh melted off. There are children who are actually sensitive and trusting enough to believe adults when they tell them terrifying things about God and the afterlife. I would think this would be obvious, but apparently it is not. *Curiously, for me, no adult ever tempered the certitude of this narrative with the fact that they'd never personally experienced the afterlife to know for themselves what it was like.*

After my own psychological descent into "hell," when, like Jonah, I had been swallowed by the waters of my unconscious mind, I struggled to integrate the experience into my learned knowledge of what hell was supposed to be. Everyone I had heard teach with authority on the subject had never actually had a personal experience with hell, yet they seemed certain of the truth of their teaching. Yet, here I was. I had undoubtedly experienced it *and come out of it.*

The more I reflected on the impact of my experience, the more that hell felt like a *transitional* state. Less a final destination and more a natural, alchemical process necessary for growth and regeneration. A death of the False Self and birth of a new phase of being. I had an inner knowing that hell was not a place, but rather a metaphorical purifying fire that every soul must endure on its journey of transformation. A caterpillar's metamorphosis into a butterfly comes to mind. The disintegration of form in the cocoon undoubtedly could be experienced as hell from the limited perspective of the pre-cocoon caterpillar. The caterpillar's body "melts" almost completely in the womb of the cocoon before morphing into a butterfly. As violent as it seems, we know that the beautiful butterfly cannot emerge apart from this process. *Hell belongs.*

> Hell is a state of mind—ye never said a truer word. And every state of mind, left to itself, every shutting up of the creature within the dungeon of its own mind—is, in the end, Hell. But Heaven is not a state of mind. Heaven is reality itself. All that is fully real is Heavenly.

> **— C.S. Lewis**[2]

Upon realizing this, I began to see this journey *through* hell reflected as *good and necessary* in the Bible. This view was also affirmed by saints and mystics who had undergone their own metamorphoses. St. John of the Cross called it "the dark night of the soul." I simply had never been introduced to this interpretation of hell as a sacred step in the process of transformation. "Hell" as a geographical location of terror and agony was too powerful a manipulation tool for fundamentalist religion to let go of. Fear is an extremely effective recruitment tactic.

The word "hell" did not find its way into the scriptures until Jerome translated the Greek scriptures into the Latin Vulgate in the fourth century. By this time, Christianity had become the dominant religion in the Roman Empire, where doctrines were beginning to be interpreted and enforced by the most powerful in society. To put a finer point on it: *those introducing the punitive concept of "hell" into church doctrine were the most powerful in the Roman Empire, in the same positions as those who crucified Jesus.* Powerful people threatening the masses with harsh punishments should be held suspect. And even beyond that, our idea of hell being a place of eternal fire and conscious torment was more of a reflection of Dante's *The Divine Comedy* written in the 14th century. *The Divine Comedy* is a world-renowned Italian poem describing an imaginative vision of the afterlife.[3] Our modern-day concepts of hell are much more influenced by a medieval worldview than a biblical one. At the risk of insulting my reader, I emphasize that poetry is not to be taken literally. A poem is a form of literature that often uses symbolism to describe and evoke emotion about ineffable human experiences. Dante's poetry of hell should be treated like any metaphor. For instance, if I said, "my heart broke into a thousand pieces," that picture would draw you into my pain. I hope it wouldn't lead you to picture my physical heart ripped into tiny pieces of flesh. It goes without saying that the latter completely misses the point of the metaphor. The same holds true for biblical metaphor and religious poetry and art.

In *Inventing Hell*, Jon Sweeney dissects the evolution of our modern concept of hell, explaining that it mostly comes from misunderstood metaphors in the book of Matthew.[4] Hell is not found in the Jewish Torah, the Gospel of John, nor Paul's letters. The words Sheol and Gehenna are used in Matthew, but *Sheol*, in Jewish understanding, was simply a holding place for the dead, where *all* humans await judgment and God finally wins.[5] Gehenna, or the Valley of Hinnom, was an actual valley outside of Jerusalem. It was believed that children were burned in sacrifice there, but it may have simply been a crematorium.[6] You can still visit the location today. It's quite nice.

*Gehenna, or the Valley of Hinnom, Jerusalem, c.
1964*

Likewise, what we now call the Dead Sea was often referred to as the Lake of Fire or Fiery Lake in Jesus's time.[7] It sits on a fault line, and in ancient times, it used to erupt tar, pitch, bitumen, asphaltites, smoke, sulfur, and flame. The Greeks named it "Lake Asphaltites." These are examples of the way that local imagery is used in mythology to communicate deeper, universal truths. They should not be taken as geographical or historical fact. There are, for sure, real psychological and spiritual realities to contend with when it comes to the function of what we call hell. But burning forever in eternal conscious torment is not one of them. Many times, this one realization is enough to catalyze the germination process of a person who has spent their life under the thumb of this toxic dogma.

The modern, conventional idea of hell as an eternal fiery furnace is a non-existent concept in the Bible. The terms *Sheol* and *Gehenna* were the metaphors used, but these myths had a specific *function* for spiritual growth. In fact, after the introduction of the term "hell" in the Latin Vulgate, the Scriptures still indicate this "hell" to be a place God resides.

Whither shall I go from thy spirit? Or whither shall I flee from thy presence? If I ascend up into heaven, thou art there; if I make my bed in hell, behold, thou art there.

— **Psalm 139:7–8** (KJV)

The biblical assertion revealed in Jesus is that hell is an initiation into heaven.

Jesus never asks you to accept him as your personal savior to avoid hell. He says, pick up your cross and follow him straight into the belly of the whale (hell).

"Out of the belly of hell I cried, and thou heard my voice."

— **Jonah 2:2b** (KJV)

Jesus says in Matthew 12:39 that he would descend into the belly, or hell, just like Jonah. The phrase *"the sign of Jonah"* was used by Jesus as a typological metaphor for His future crucifixion, burial, and resurrection.

The reality for all of us is that we are going to experience hell before heaven. The question for each of us is: *are you going to go to hell kicking and screaming like Jonah? Or are you going to seek out the inevitable path through hell and surrender to it like Jesus?*

What difference does it make? Well, resisting the inevitable causes you and others a lot more prolonged suffering. You don't have to drag the process out for so long if you surrender. Some people resist their whole lives. They end up facing death with angst and fear, because they have not *died before dying* ahead of their physical death. They have not died to the False Self and are confronted with it in the end. By following Jesus willingly in this life, you can actually bring some heaven to earth before you go. Hopefully, you can *go to hell willingly with God.*

Christ descended into hell (Ephesians 4:9) and revealed the path of salvation to the dead (1 Peter 4:6). Then, the tombs of many people broke open and they were raised from the dead (Matthew 27:52). Jesus is not the only dead man walking!

Early Orthodox Christian art depicts Christ's resurrection as a universal, communal event. Below is a painting of the Anastasis (also called the Harrowing of Hell—Jesus's descent into hell to resurrect the dead). It flies in the face of the West's view of what it means to be "saved." We often forget that, after his death, Jesus "descended into hell," as the Apostle's Creed asserts. The early church art depicts Jesus standing on open gates and pulling people *out of* hell. *Not* saving them from entering. The Spirit of God always resides in Jesus, even in his descent into hell. Through Jesus we *realize* that we are in hell until we see that the gate is open and we are free to walk out. He saves us from the prison we are already in.

> *He was put to death in the flesh [the False Self], but made alive in the spirit [the True Self], in which also he went and made a proclamation to the spirits in prison [hell].*

— **1 Peter 3:18b–19** (CSB)

Descent into Hell by Dionisius and workshop, 15th century, Russia (Dionisius and workshop (Ferapontov Monastery).

Christ in Limbo (The Harrowing of Hell) by Albrecht Dürer, 1510 (Cooper Hewitt, Smithsonian Design Museum, New York).

The Risen Christ is not a one-time miracle but the revelation of a universal pattern that is hard to see in the short run...Jesus's first incarnate life, his passing over into death, and his resurrection into the ongoing Christ life is the archetypal model for the entire pattern of creation. He is the microcosm of the whole cosmos, or the map of the whole journey, in case you need or want one.

— **Fr. Richard Rohr**[8]

Like the seed being buried in the ground, the caterpillar entering the cocoon, and Jesus descending into hell, *"the sign of Jonah"* reveals that hell is a necessary stop along the path of transformation. On one hand, this realization is such a relief after the crushing fear of hell. On the other hand, it reveals that the path of salvation in life is much more demanding of us than we had imagined it to be.

> *Therefore, my dear friends, as you have always obeyed—not only in my presence, but now much more in my absence—continue to work out your salvation with fear and trembling, for it is God who works in you to will and to act in order to fulfill his good purpose.*

— **Philippians 2:12–13** (NIV)

FIFTEEN

GOD SEES THE WORLD THROUGH YOU

The cry, Tetelestai, "it is finished," was not the gasp of a
worn-out life, but the deliberate utterance of a clear consciousness that His work was finished, and all God's purpose
accomplished (Acts 17:4), that all had now been done that
could be done to make God known to men, and to identify
Him with men.

— **Marcus Dods** (1834–1909)[1]

THE POP NARRATIVE IN evangelicalism is that God can't look at evil. The
only way he can look at humans is if they are covered by Jesus's blood. Not to
be crass, but when we really consider the story that's presented, God appears
to be so anal-retentive that the only way he can relax is if everything he sees
is covered by a bloody mess from Jesus. This begs the question: what's so
relaxing about seeing everything soaked with blood? In any other circumstance, we would avoid someone with this kind of morbid fixation. But we
fold it into our understanding of God, creating a distorted relationship with
love. We're forced into a push-pull dilemma where we yearn for someone who
simultaneously terrifies us on some level. We resolve this with a cognitive dissonance of justifying the otherwise disturbing behavior (we can't understand

God, so why bother trying?). Or, we deny the terror; but nonetheless, it is still there on a deep, possibly unconscious level.

Referring back to Chapter Two, *Finding Christ in the Bible*, the function of the confusing Bible stories—where the "god" character appears to be a blood-thirsty tyrant, wiping out groups of people—is to challenge our human understanding of what God is really like. We *think* God wants to destroy all evil humans in a massive flood. But then Noah comes along and builds a safe place where we can imagine ourselves taking refuge in a storm. The real God is more like the character of Noah.

This ultimate explosion of our whole concept of God is finally and fully revealed in the story of Jesus. We thought God couldn't look at evil, but then Jesus does. He walks around looking at sinners his whole life. We thought God condemns evil people, but then Jesus seems to think evil is really just ignorance, and he understands why people do the crazy things they do. He does not condemn; rather, for those willing, he removes the speck in their eye so they can see clearly, which often leads to remorse. We think God defeats the enemy, but then Jesus loves all the enemies. He calls Peter "Satan"[2] and then tells Peter/Satan that they're still good. Apparently, good and evil aren't as black-and-white as we'd like to think.

> *Jesus turned and said to Peter, "Get behind me, Satan! You are a stumbling block to me; you do not have in mind the concerns of God, but merely human concerns."*

> **— Matthew 16:23** (NIV)

Jesus is deconstructing the myth of "Satan" here. By calling Peter "Satan", Jesus is naming Peter's False Self as the enemy or stumbling block. "Satan" is a part of Peter's psyche, but not the whole of him. However, at this point in the biblical narrative, Peter is still primarily identifying with his False Self and only able to worry about "human concerns" such as safety, security, longevity, victory, etc. None of these "human concerns" of the False Self matter to the

True Self—the deepest part of Peter through which he *lives and moves and has his being.*

> *The God who made the world and everything in it is the Lord of heaven and earth and does not live in temples built by human hands. And he is not served by human hands, as if he needed anything. Rather, he himself gives everyone life and breath and everything else. From one man he made all the nations, that they should inhabit the whole earth; and he marked out their appointed times in history and the boundaries of their lands. God did this so that they would seek him and perhaps reach out for him and find him, though he is not far from any one of us. "For in him we live and move and have our being." As some of your own poets have said, 'We are his offspring.' Therefore since we are God's offspring, we should not think that the divine being is like gold or silver or stone—an image made by human design and skill. In the past God overlooked such ignorance, but now he commands all people everywhere to repent [change their minds].*

> **— Acts 17:24–30a** (NIV)

God is repeatedly revealed *through humans*. The character of God is often demonstrated *by humans*, not necessarily by the "god" character in the story. In order to discern the character of God in a story, it is essential to first know Jesus as non-violent and non-punitive. Satan is the personification of the False Self, which must be *"defeated"* to reveal God hidden within the person. Again, as we have seen, the outer shell must die so that the divine embryo within can rise.

Every body is a *temple of God* (meaning a place where God resides). Caryll Houselander puts it this way in her book *A Rocking-Horse Catholic*:

> . . . Reverence must be paid even to those sinners whose souls
> seem to be dead, because it is Christ, who is the life of the soul,

who is dead in them; they are His tombs, and Christ in the tomb is potentially the risen Christ.

— **Caryll Houselander** (1901–1954)[3]

The moment Jesus dies, a Roman centurion, who has just killed Jesus, realizes he's made a big "oops." He knew the "god" of the biblical scriptures just like many Christians. Yet, in his zeal to defend God and country, he kills God! He's so attached to his *idea* of God that he can't recognize God right in front of him. In many ways, we face the same predicament. We're so attached to the "God" figure described in Old Testament Bible stories, that we can't see the true character of God revealed in Jesus. Yet Jesus is constantly saying, "You have heard it said, but I say…" God is not "out there", but a living presence that looks out from the human who has clear eyes.

The eye is the lamp of the body. You draw light into your body through your eyes, and light shines out to the world through your eyes. So if your eye is well and shows you what is true, then your whole body will be filled with light.

— **Matthew 6:22** (VOICE)

The defeat of evil on the cross is described as a veil tearing. A veil simply obscures what is already there. Nothing changes except perception—from obscured to clear. Defeating evil is less a victory and more of an illumination. A divine "oops." It's the realization that we forgot that God was inside of our enemies. That all these humans are temples (houses) of God. That the Promised Land (heaven) is within you and belongs to everyone. As Jesus shows us with Peter/Satan, the land of exile (hell) is within you as well. And it all belongs, because you belong. We simply couldn't see it that way before.

For I desire mercy, not sacrifice, and the knowledge of God rather than burnt offerings.

— **Hosea 6:6** (BSB)

Jesus wasn't a sacrifice to a god who needed to see innocent human blood. He sacrificed himself for humanity so that we could see where God resides. Not off in the sky above, but *in Jesus on the cross.*[4] Jesus is a revelation that God is in him. *Suffering with him. Suffering through him. Suffering as him.*

Jesus is a revelation that God is *in us. Suffering with us. Through us. As us.*

But you can't know this without getting up on your cross and seeing for yourself. To see as God sees is to get up from the foot of the cross, turn around, and look out *from the cross.* From the cross, God sees the world through human eyes. From Jesus's cross, God sees the world through Jesus's eyes. From your cross, God sees the world through your eyes.

SIXTEEN

GOD HIDES HIS FACE?

MOST OF US CAN probably recall the moment in the crucifixion narrative when God turns his face away from Jesus on the cross. Many of us sang hymns and worship songs, like "How Deep the Father's Love For Us,"[1] that included this dark moment. However, the Bible never says that God turned his face away. A pastor perhaps repeated that addition to the story when telling it to you, but it is not biblical.

In evangelical churches, the idea that God can't look at evil is bolstered by the narrative that the Father turned his face from Jesus on the cross. As explained in the previous chapter, the emphasis is that God cannot look at us because of our sin. Again, the life of Jesus contradicts this. Since we know that God is not separate from Jesus, but instead inside of him, God *must* look at sin and evil, because Jesus did. Mark Lowry, who anyone in a Baptist church during the 90s would recognize (*Mary, Did You Know?*, Gaither Vocal Band), illuminated this for me in a podcast with Jonathan Martin in 2019.[2] In the interview, Mark laments over his mistaken conception of God, and the inaccurate teaching of the church regarding God's role in Jesus's crucifixion. I related to his sentiment of truly thinking I understood the Gospel, only to be horrified that I had gotten it so wrong. The humility and sincerity with which Mark spoke deeply touched me:

[God] He was in Christ, reconciling the world to himself. The Father was hanging on that cross, too. He was there. He didn't turn his back . . . if God can't look on sin, then Jesus was not God.

— **Mark Lowry**, Gaither Vocal Band

The idea that God cannot look at sin comes from a verse in Habakkuk:

Your eyes are too pure to behold evil, and you cannot look on wrongdoing;

— **Habakkuk 1:13a** (NRSV)

The prophet here is lamenting that God's eyes are too pure to look upon sin. This is where we usually stop reading. But we stop too soon. There's more:

Your eyes are too pure to behold evil, and you cannot look on wrongdoing; why do you look on the treacherous, and are silent when the wicked swallow those more righteous than they?

— **Habakkuk 1:13** (NRSV)

God supposedly is too holy to empathize with sinners, *but he does it anyway!* Indeed, if Jesus was God, and the Father was in him, then God looked at a lot of sinners while Jesus walked the earth. The idea that the Father looked away from Jesus on the cross is false. The Father was *in Jesus,* on the cross, looking out at sin.

On that day you will realize that I am in my Father, and you are in me, and I am in you.

— **John 14:20** (NIV)

In his sermon titled "The Gospel in Chairs", Brad Jersak points out that when Jesus cries out *"Why have you forsaken me?"* from the cross, he is directly referencing Psalm 22. "My God, my God, why have you forsaken me?" is the first line of that Psalm. On the cross, Jesus is calling attention to the fact that the entirety of Psalm 22 is about him. Psalm 22 is a prophetic description of Jesus's crucifixion. It references pierced hands and feet, a parched mouth, and his bones on display.[3] Psalm 22 also references God:

For he [God] has not despised or scorned the suffering of the afflicted one [Jesus]; He [God] has not hidden His face from him [Jesus].

— **Psalm 22:24** (NIV)

God never turned his face from Jesus. God has never and *will never* turn his face from you. Like Jesus, you have *never* been separated from God. But as humans, sometimes it feels that way for all of us.

So where was God the Father on Good Friday while Jesus suffered? Suffering with him. God was in Christ Jesus on the cross reconciling the world to Himself (2 Corinthians 5:19). There's not a moment in which you've suffered that God has not suffered with you and within you. It is on the cross that our graven image, the idea of a god who lives outside of us, dies. In this image of the crucifixion, God makes a sacrifice to Himself, killing Himself for the regeneration of life. The projection in our minds of a god that was beyond us, above us, and separate from us dies, and *a recognition of God in us is born*. God comes down from heaven and Man rises up from earth to become one flesh.

So from now on we regard no one from a worldly point of view.
Though we once regarded Christ in this way, we do so no longer.
Therefore, if anyone is in Christ, the new creation has come:
The old has gone, the new is here! All this is from God, who
reconciled us to himself through Christ and gave us the ministry
of reconciliation: that God was reconciling the world to himself
in Christ, not counting people's sins against them. And he has
committed to us the message of reconciliation.

— 2 Corinthians 5:16–19 (NIV)

Jesus reveals the way to reconciliation. His sacrifice for us doesn't magically save us in some transaction with a god in the sky. He reveals the way of reconciliation that we each must take to *save ourselves*. We allow our False Selves to die, so that our True Selves may be resurrected as a new creation. We no longer regard others as people apart from God (just like the people did with Jesus when they crucified him for blasphemy). We view people as temples encasing God, *even if Christ still lay dead in the tomb inside that temple.*[4] We know there is a True Self hidden inside their shell.

This Way is demonstrated in the story of Zacchaeus. God, through Jesus, looks at Zacchaeus with compassion. Zacchaeus's True Self then resurrects, and he releases his False Self—which was sustained by compulsively cheating people out of their money. Jesus then says to Zacchaeus, "Today salvation has come to this house..."[5] The salvation Jesus is referring to here is not from some eternal punishment when Zacchaeus dies. It is salvation from himself—his False Self.

Never confuse the person, formed in the image of God, with the evil that is in him: because evil is but a chance misfortune, an illness, a devilish reverie. But the very essence of the person is the image of God, and this remains in him despite every disfigurement.

— **St. John of Kronstadt** (1829–1909)[6]

SEVENTEEN

DEMONS & DEVILS

THE DEVIL. SATAN. LUCIFER. The enemy. A snake.

My conception of Satan, which I held for most of my life, began in childhood. It was open-ended, yet strangely specific. In my mind, Satan was definitely a man who was a singular being. He always seemed to be lurking *somewhere*. He was definitely to blame when something horrible happened. He was always plotting an attack. He lived in hell, which was somewhere "down there", but also wandered around earth. I guess he must have gone back and forth? He was probably red and had horns.

I spoke briefly about Jesus referring to Peter as "Satan", yet still embracing him as a friend. In Western society, most people perceive Satan and demons to be entities outside of themselves and are deeply fearful of any perceived contact. However, Jesus doesn't seem fearful at all. He continues to lean into Peter/Satan and treats the satanic element in him like a minor annoyance impeding what he's trying to do. Jesus then turns the rebuke into a teachable moment for the whole group.[1] There seems to be a wide gap between Jesus's perception of Satan and our western visceral reaction. Again, I think that coming at this concept from a different angle can be helpful. I'm going to explore what we could call "demonic" energies mythologically through the 2016 Disney movie, *Moana*.[2]

In *Moana*, Te Fiti is a goddess with life-creating power. She was the first entity to appear in the world when only the ocean existed. She uses her life-giving heart to create life across the planet, including islands full of vegetation and humans. After her work of creation, Te Fiti lays to rest and forms her body into an island. Her life-giving heart becomes a treasure sought after by humans. Eventually, a demigod named Maui steals Te Fiti's heart, transforming her into a demonic shell of her former self: Te Kā. As a result, the island falls into darkness that begins to spread across all the world.

While Te Fiti is a pure, loving, and life-giving entity, it is the removal of her heart that turns her into a demonic force. These two energies are but two sides of one creature. The dark energy is a response to the loss of her heart. Te Kā voraciously guards the shores of the island from further harm and violently pursues whoever crosses her.

Despite this, Te Fiti's true identity still lies deep within her, and once Moana recovers her stolen heart, she calls out to the deepest part of Te Fiti. Once Moana is sure of the truth, she stands at the ocean separating her and Te Kā and asks the ocean to let Te Kā come to her. The sea then parts (conjuring up an image of the Red Sea), and Moana approaches the demonic Te Kā, compassionately telling her that she knows her name. Her *true* name. She knows what happened to her and sees her true identity.

With this, Te Kā allows Moana to touch her and place her stolen heart back in the center or her being. Te Kā's heart of stone then crumbles to expose Te Fiti underneath the stone, revealing that Te Fiti was the True Self under the outer shell all along. Green, vibrant life is then restored to all the land; the "body" of Te Fiti flourishes. Everything Te Fiti touches is restored to life.

This mythology in *Moana* has strong parallels to the True Self and False Self. The outer shell, Te Kā, becomes demonic *in response to* her stolen heart. It is a great violation and loss of contact with the True Self that creates the pain. The outer shell, Te Kā, becomes a means of protection for the lost identity underneath, Te Fiti. The dark and violent energy is a natural response to the loss of Te Fiti's pure heart. While the True Self (Te Fiti) yearns to give life from within, that energy is blocked by the outer shell (Te Kā). The blockage builds up more and more pressure, turning violent. Te Kā represents what we would call "Satan" and her violent energy represents what we would call "demons."

> My definition of a devil is a god who has not been recognized. That is to say, it is a power in you to which you have not given

expression, and you push it back. And then, like all repressed energy, it builds up and becomes completely dangerous to the position you're trying to hold.

— **Joseph Campbell**[3]

To put it plainly, a demon is the energy of our True Self trying to come forth, while our outer shell is pushing it down. Demons, when pushed down, become devils and become violent—either to self, others, or both.[4] Florence + The Machine, the band, convey this in their 2011 song "Shake It Out," in which they describe the process of excavating the heart and discovering the devil within.[5] We must actually go below the surface of our conscious awareness to retrieve our *true life.* The problem in Christianity is that we've scapegoated the demons, projected them outside of ourselves, and tried to get rid of them, which only worsens our dilemma.

The demons we face are actually the expressions, desires, and energy of our True Selves that we learned were unacceptable to society. Growing up, there was most likely some part (if not all) of yourself that you had to repress in order to function safely in your environment. Occasionally, we are aware of this repression and do it consciously for survival. An example might be a child who has to repress their homosexuality to survive a fundamentalist church environment. Or a young girl who must cover up to try to avoid the advances of predatory men. Both later run the risk of punishing themselves for their innate sexuality because of the persecution it brought them.

Most of the time, however, this is an unconscious process. The function of the False Self is to keep the powerful life in us from germinating before we are psychologically ready and to contain us in that environment until it is safe to grow out of our protective shells. The False Self denies and represses beliefs, thoughts, and information that would contradict our perceived reality and security. Any person or idea that contradicts our worldview is then shunned and scapegoated so as to remove the threat to our False Self. We project our unwanted desires externally and then persecute them in other people to avoid dealing with our own internal demons. Or, we persecute ourselves because we are unable to rid ourselves of unwanted desires or behaviors. The more we repress and deny our True Self, the stronger and more violent the energy becomes, demanding to be recognized, becoming a "devil."

One way to picture the life-giving spirit of your True Self is as water flowing through pipes. The pipes represent your psychology. When it is too painful to be yourself, your brain does not allow the flow of your spirit. There is a "block" in the pipe, if you will. Now, we know that if a water pipe is blocked, twisted, bent, or broken, then eventually water will begin dripping from places it's not supposed to, or explode out of the pipes altogether. The natural consequence of the faulty pipes is water damage. There's nothing inherently evil about the water or the pipes. The problem is that the water is not able to flow through the pipes. Your spirit is not able to flow through your mind and thus your body. The repression of the spirit, unable to flow naturally, becomes violent when it can't travel through the pipes and has nowhere else to go. The violence is the spirit of the True Self within, demanding recognition. This causes all sorts of psychological conditions such as depression, anxiety, addiction, and psychosis. Sometimes the repression manifests as physical *dis-ease* (lack of ease) in the body.

The consequence of this phenomena is what we call "the devil." A devil is a dynamic energy of your life that is not permitted by your psyche to express itself and so becomes violent. The Christian personification of this natural phenomenon is Satan.

The solution is to *love your enemies*—the ones within yourself—the parts of yourself that you've discarded and banished to hell. By traveling into your unconscious mind and facing your demons, the psychological block can be identified and removed, allowing these demons to be reconciled to God—or reconciled within yourself—allowing the flow of your spirit within you and out from you.

It is only by identifying or naming the psychological wound and removing the block that the demon can be "exorcized." The spirit within can be permitted to flow out. As we heard in Moana's song, she names Te Fiti's wound, the loss of her heart that created Te Kā. The naming of the demon is simultaneously an acknowledgment of Te Fiti's true identity. Likewise, in

Mark 5:9, Jesus asks a demon inside of a man, "What is your name?" Before a demon can be healed, it must be named specifically. We cannot heal and free from bondage what is unacknowledged, or unnamed, within us. Often, it requires a conscious person such as Moana (who represents Jesus in the myth) to mirror us and our wound accurately, so that we can see correctly.

Once the repressed desire is acknowledged and the psychological "pipes" are fixed, that unconscious energy can then be integrated into the conscious, outward life. The person is healed and the spirit of the True Self can flow freely again.

> *But we all, with unveiled faces, looking as in a mirror at the glory of the Lord, are being transformed into the same image from glory to glory, just as from the Lord, the Spirit.*

— **2 Corinthians 3:18** (NASB)

EIGHTEEN

PARTING THE RED SEA

The Red Sea is the baptism reddened by the blood of Christ,
in which our enemies, namely our sins, are drowned.

— **Honorius of Autun** (c. 1080–1140)[1]

WHILE THE SPLITTING OF a sea makes for a dramatic cinematic scene (I loved the 1956 movie, *The Ten Commandments*), we've previously established that water symbolizes the unconscious mind. The parting of the Red Sea, so that Moses could lead the Israelites out of slavery, is an illustration of the crossing of this threshold. As Honorius of Autun points out to us, it should be read as allegory, with Egypt symbolizing our sin—the grip of our False Self ensnaring us as slaves to our addictions unwilling to relinquish us to freedom without a fight.

We have to approach the threshold of the unconscious knowing very well that it could swallow us up. We could drown. We could sink into the unconscious and not come back up. But, for the willing and pure in heart, you come to the point where you cannot turn back. Behind you is the slavery of your addictions closing in, threatening to ensnare you again. You've lived that already and are certain that it will lead to a lifeless life and a slow death. *The False Self now knows it is dying, but baits us to look backward, promising that the death will be slower and less painful than the potentially imminent death of drowning should we cross the threshold.* It is at this point that the temptation to turn around is the most intense. It is the False Self's last stand.

In the 2019 film, *Harriet*, there's a powerful scene where Harriet Tubman is cornered on a bridge by slave catchers as she attempts to flee her life of slavery. They would have captured her by force if they were able. But she outran them, and now they risk losing her as she's on the brink of jumping over the bridge. Her master attempts to coax her back to the plantation, reminding her of certain comforts and loved ones she'd be leaving behind. Harriet takes a moment of pause, as if to consider the entirety of her life up until that moment. And then, she looks into her master's eyes and says, "I'm going to be free or die."[2] She then leaps off the bridge into the rapids below, putting her faith in the water to deliver her to her destiny, whatever that is. The only certainty she has is that her destiny is not a return to slavery.

The point when one turns towards the Red Sea and proceeds forward into the unknown is *the* great act of faith. "I don't know what will happen, but I can't go back" is the catalyst for the seed's germination process to begin. It is the *will* to live, even if physical death is a possible outcome. You don't know for sure if you'll survive going forward. But you *do* know for certain your spirit will eventually die staying where you are. It is this *life-or-death* energy to which life responds and opens itself up, as the Red Sea symbolizes. For the pure in heart with the will to live, the baptismal waters open up a passage to salvation, as we saw with Moana—washing away the sin of the unconscious False Self, which bound us to the slavery of death and destruction, by way of our addictions rooted in anger, pride, vanity, envy, greed, fear, gluttony, lust, and sloth.

> The Red Sea is a water of death for those that are "unconscious," but for those that are "conscious" it is a baptismal water of rebirth and transcendence. By "unconscious" are meant those who have no gnosis, i.e., are not enlightened as to the nature and destiny of man in the cosmos. In modern language

it would be those who have no knowledge of the contents of the personal and collective unconscious. The personal unconscious is the shadow and the inferior function, in Gnostic terms the sinfulness and impurity that must be washed away by baptism.

— **Carl Jung**[3]

As the True Self comes forth out of the shell of the False Self, the water gives way to the ground below. The ground, which was obscured by the water, is revealed to have always been there. But it only shows itself to the one who will risk dying to find it. It is a journey inward to the very ground of your being. You must first walk into the dark abyss before you know for yourself that there is a ground to stand on.

The parting of the Red Sea provides the assurance that, beneath the water, there is solid ground. If you approach the threshold and refuse to return to the slavery of the False Self, the path to healing will reveal itself. You might feel certain of your imminent death, as the Israelites did, but somehow life will open up and there will be a way out. You have to be willing to go in without that certainty. *But you need the knowledge of this myth to have the faith that the ground will meet your steps. The power of the myth gives you the courage to trust.*

The crossing of the Red Sea leads to salvation for Israel (meaning, "the one who struggles with God," which is all of us). But this crossing delivers them into the wilderness for forty years before reaching the Promised Land. The initial phase, after crossing the water's threshold, is a complete disorientation and solitude. It begins a purification process of severing the attachments to one's identity that are found in family, society, religion, or any idea of the False Self which must be detached from in order for the seed of the True Self to germinate and grow. The False Self can then be dissolved into a finer energy and merge into wholeness with the True Self. The shell becomes one with the ground, from which the new life grows. This purification process is also reflected in Jesus's forty days in the desert after coming out of the baptismal waters of the Jordan River.[4]

> Everyone who becomes conscious of even a fraction of his unconscious gets outside his own time and social stratum into a kind of solitude. But only there is it possible to meet the "god of salvation."

— Carl Jung[5]

The color red is also important here in this mythology:

> And, to the alchemist, rubedo or reddening was the last stage of the long process of making gold or, psychologically, integrating the personality. It meant nothing less than bringing spiritual realization into full-blooded reality, lived out fully in everyday life.

— Edward F. Edinger[6] (1922–1998)[7]

The *Red* Sea symbolizes the new blood that now animates the new creation. The whole individual now stands on solid ground, having integrated all the opposites, so that there is no conflict between the True and False Selves. The Whole Self reenters the world to revitalize it. This is the process of Incarnation: the divine spirit and body becoming one flesh. This new life is like a tree firmly rooted in the ground, providing shelter, protection, fruit, oxygen, beauty, and goodness for humanity and the world.

NINETEEN

WORK OUT YOUR OWN SALVATION

You divided the sea by your might; you broke the heads of the dragons in the waters.

— Psalm 74:13 (NRSV)

WHEN I WAS ABOUT six years old, I remember feeling a darkness inside of my heart. I recall pounding my fist against my chest and saying over and over again, "Satan, get out of my heart!" Even though the evangelical church would later convince me that Satan was lurking around outside of me—that I needed to be saved *from him*—as a child, I seemed to instinctively know where "the Enemy" was: *inside my heart.* I got "saved" soon after that in an attempt to expel Satan from within me. I was told that he'd been displaced and that Jesus now lived in my heart. Psychologically, this theology turned my attention outward and convinced me that the darkness was outside of myself. God and Satan were opposites and couldn't be in the same place. For many Christians who had this same experience, when things go badly for them, Satan becomes the scapegoat. He is always seen to be outside of the Christian, plotting to attack. It never occurs to many believers to look for the source of their suffering within.

Unfortunately, in most evangelical and fundamentalist churches, the mythological symbols have been stripped not only from the stories, but also from the architecture. However, if you have ever been to an old cathedral, you've probably noticed some unsightly creatures on the exterior of the church. The structure itself was designed to call you forth into a mystical journey of death and rebirth.

Notre Dame Gargoyles, Paris, France, 1993

Notre Dame Gargoyle overlooking Paris, France, 2016

Notre Dame Gargoyles, Paris, France

The church symbolizes the Divine Mother, her interior being the womb that swallows us for metamorphosis. The belly metabolizes the False Self and rebirths the True Self. Whether consciously or unconsciously, each time you enter a church, you are symbolically participating in the psychological and spiritual rebirthing processes.

> The temple interior, the belly of the whale, and the heavenly land beyond, above, and below the confines of the world, are one and the same. That is why the approaches of and the entrances to temples are flanked and defended by colossal gargoyles: dragons, lions, devil-slayers with drawn swords, resentful dwarves, winged bulls. These are the threshold guardians to ward away all incapable of encountering the higher silence within. They are preliminary embodiments of the dangerous aspect of the presence, corresponding to the mythological ogres that bound the conventional world, or to the two rows of teeth of the whale. They illustrate the fact that the devotee at the moment of the entry into the temple undergoes a metamorphosis. His secular character remains without; he sheds it

as a snake its slough. Once inside he may be said to have died to time and returned to the World Womb, the World Navel, the Earthly Paradise. The mere fact that anyone can physically walk past the temple guardians does not invalidate their significance; for if the intruder is incapable of encompassing the sanctuary, he has effectually remained without. Anyone unable to understand a god sees it as a devil and is thus defended from the approach. Allegorically, then, the passage into a temple and the hero-dive through the jaws of the whale are identical adventures, both denoting, in the picture language, the life-centering, life-renewing act.

— **Joseph Campbell**[1]

As we have now seen repeatedly, hell illustrates the threshold one must cross to enter heaven. The outer shell, the False Self, returns to dust in the belly of the earth, so that the True Self can be born. Indeed, both heaven and hell are revealed to the person crossing the threshold to be different stages of one progressive process. To the unconscious person, the purifying fiery passage into the belly is experienced as dangerous and deadly. The fire is *experienced as hell*, symbolized by the exterior gargoyles of the church. The same fire is experienced by the enlightened heart to be eternal and life-giving. The fire is *experienced as heaven.* The fire itself never changes.

We see this passage in countless motifs: the mouth of the whale, the Red Sea, the Garden of Eden's cherubim with the flaming sword. We must face and slay our terrifying personal demons and dragons who guard our interior temple in order to enter the Paradise of the inner sanctuary.

And what is experienced inside the temple?

Complete silence.

I remember my first real encounter with the threshold. A few years prior to my personal metamorphosis, I had gone through an intensely stressful season at our church. The anxiety from this situation exceeded my ability to cope, and that anxiety started manifesting physically in my body. One night, my family and I went out to eat for dinner, and as I was walking out of the restaurant, I heard what sounded like a vacuum in my ear. It suddenly felt clogged, much like what can happen on an airplane. My hearing was reduced by about fifty percent.

I didn't think much about it. But, a few hours later, my inner ear started hurting so badly, it brought me to tears. I struggled in pain throughout the night. The next morning, I awoke to a complete warping of sound in my ear. The experience was disorienting, and all the sounds I heard seemed like they were being filtered through distortion, making everything sound "out of tune."

I got to the doctor as quickly as possible. She diagnosed me with an ear infection and gave me antibiotics. I felt so much better and the pain quickly subsided. However, my hearing did not come back, and I noticed an unpleasant, high-pitched ringing in my ear. About a week later, I saw an ENT who ran several hearing tests. Afterwards, he came into the room and sat down. "This isn't good. You have nerve damage in your ear. We need to start steroids now. It's good you came in early, because there's a chance we can reverse the damage, but it's not guaranteed." "What about the ringing?" I asked. "It may be permanent," he responded. I was stunned.

When I left the ENT's office, I found myself in an emotional frenzy. I quickly filled my prescription and began my course of steroids. While my doctor warned me that the steroids might cause me to feel a little wired, their effect was like pouring gasoline on the fire of my raging nervous system. That night, my husband assured me that everything would be OK. We turned out the lights, and I rolled over to go to sleep.

As I laid in my bed in the dark quiet, the ringing became louder and louder. It sounded like it was coming from some place deep inside my body. My instinct was to jump out of my skin. But I couldn't escape. Suddenly, my body became a warzone from which I could not run. As I grasped for a solution, the possibility that this could be my permanent condition overwhelmed me.

The silence was the loudest thing I'd ever heard. *The silence was deafening.* And I experienced my first panic attack.

That night in my bed, I experienced a terror that shook me to my core. I didn't know at that time what was happening spiritually, or that there was another side to this. But during that panic attack, I approached the threshold, and my inner dragons breathed fire. The most terrifying demons were not outside of me. They were within. The cherubim with the flaming sword were guarding the gate to Eden.[2] I was not yet ready to cross the threshold, and the guardians made sure I didn't. Like the wedding guest in Matthew 22, I was not yet wearing my "wedding clothes" (that is, my mind was still wearing duality, not standing naked), and so I was tossed back into the *outer darkness*.[3] As we saw in Chapter Five, *Rethinking Adam and Eve*, the dualistic mind cannot enter the Garden or wedding chamber where the *two (the opposites) are one flesh*.

However, for me, this was the beginning of reconciling the paradox of reality: I soon came to yearn for silence. Yet, it also eluded and terrified me.

Eventually, I realized that the more I could calm my nervous system, the quieter the ringing became. *There was a direct correlation between the stillness of my mind and the volume of the sound in my head.* I started recognizing the ringing as a messenger. *I had to make friends with the terrifying threshold guardians.* These inner demons were a part of me. My "enemies" were within. They became my teachers whom I befriended. They pointed me to my unhealed wounds. My mind was beginning its approach into non-duality. I was gathering "the bad as well as the good" for the wedding (Matthew 22:10). I was beginning to reconcile the opposites into the Ark.

I hope you're beginning to see the parallel themes in all these metaphors.

A person who believes he has an enemy (such as Satan) outside of himself has not yet turned inward to face himself. His outward enemies are a projection of what he can't yet face inside of himself. The projections reflect the inner, denied parts of himself back to himself.

> And the heart itself is but a small vessel, yet there also are
> dragons and there are lions; there are poisonous beasts and all
> the treasures of evil. And there are rough and uneven roads;
> there are precipices. But there is also God, also the angels, the

life and the kingdom, the light and the Apostles, the treasures of grace—there are all things.

— **St. Macarius the Great of Egypt** (c. 300–391)

Translation:

> If you want to find the devil, look in your heart.
> If you want to find God, look in your heart.
> If you want to find hell, look in your heart.
> If you want to find heaven, look in your heart.

Everything you're hoping for or afraid of is inside you. The gargoyles outside of a cathedral are the precise representation of the temple exterior, guarding what is precious inside, which is the sanctuary of your heart.

> *. . . work out your own salvation with fear and trembling.*

— **Philippians 2:12b** (KJV)

TWENTY

GO INTO YOUR CLOSET & CLOSE THE DOORS

How many people have you come across who claim to spend hours in prayer—but, curiously, the voice of God is consistent with the tenor of their own egoic agendas and desires?

The False Self is essentially a concept of the mind. It develops as a survival adaptation in response to our True Self threatening our attachments to our caregivers and/or environments. In the documentary *The Wisdom of Trauma,* Dr. Gabor Maté explains this from a psychological and biological point of reference:

> As a child, we have two fundamental needs. One need that's with us in infancy, and it's non-negotiable, is attachment. And so the other need then is authenticity. Authenticity, therefore, is the connection to ourselves...because without authenticity, without a connection to our gut feelings, just how long do you survive out there in nature? So, authenticity is not some new-age, pseudo-spiritual concept. It's actually a survival necessity. What happens when, in order to survive or to adjust to your environment, you have to suppress your gut feelings? You have to suppress your authenticity?[1]

— **Dr. Gabor Maté**

Our two fundamental needs as humans are attachment and authenticity. However, attachment is the non-negotiable of the two, at least initially. Practically, what this means is that *when our authenticity threatens our attachment, we will sacrifice our authenticity.* Our True Self, our authentic Self, is buried, and a False Self is developed, in order to maintain attachment to our caregivers and our environment. This is a natural psychological and biological response, necessary for survival. As children, we *must* maintain attachment, because we are completely dependent on others in order to survive. Our brains and physiology then become dependent on maintaining this False Self, because its dissolution is too threatening to the attachments we depend upon. However, the consequence of losing connection with our authentic True Self is traumatic. This disconnect is what the word "sin" refers to. Again, the Greek meaning of sin, "to miss the mark", is in reference to the disconnect between the True Self and False Self. This state of sin, *or loss of connection with the True Self,* is the root cause of our addiction, mental illness, unhealthy behaviors towards ourselves and others, and perpetual suffering. The price of this inevitable disconnection is unspeakably high.

The first essential task of a good religion is to reconnect us with our True Selves. This is often approached through prayer. Unfortunately, in evangelical and fundamentalist religions, we are taught to pray to a deity who is outside of ourselves. I was taught a lot of things about prayer: what to say, what not to say, how to "make it personal," how to try and listen. There is no concept of the True Self and False Self, or a recognition of this fundamental disconnection, within evangelicalism. There is no recognition of the divinity within the secret places of the heart.

> *But thou, when thou prayest, enter into thy closet, and when thou hast shut thy door, pray to your Father which is in secret.*

> — **Matthew 6:6a** (KJV)

The closet of the soul is the body; our "doors" are the five bodily senses. The soul enters its closet when the mind does not "roam" among the things of this world and the affairs of this world, but stays within—in our heart. Our senses become closed and remain closed when we do not let them be attached to external sensory things. In this way, our mind remains free from every worldly attachment; and, by secret mental prayer, unites with God its Father.

— **St. Gregory Palamas** (c. 1296–1357 or 1359)[2]

There are many traditions that approach prayer practices in the way Jesus and St. Gregory Palamas described above. It wasn't until my nervous system all but imploded on me that I was forced to admit that the ways I was taught to pray were woefully inadequate and completely useless for getting me through my situation. I was praying in the wrong direction.

While working to calm my nervous system, I discovered some practices that helped me begin to "close the doors." I began a meditation and yoga practice. Meditation and yoga are essentially prayer practices, if they are utilized in a way that stills your mind and reconnects you with your body and emotions. They are two of many pathways to silence. Some other examples are prayer chanting or repetitive prayers. Prayer is body-based. Its purpose is to bring your mind, body, heart, and soul into alignment, so that your entire being can be united with God.

The first step in these prayer practices is to still the mind and allow the practitioner to relax their identification with their thoughts. The False Self is a product of the mind, and the unconscious person is completely identified with their own thoughts. Through consistent practice, a person will actually begin to observe their own thoughts, eventually realizing that their inner being is separate from the voice in their head. This is the first step in recognizing the False Self as a mistaken identity, and the existence of the True Self as distinct from the mental construct created in the mind unconsciously over time.

Once I started to gain some space from and awareness of my thought patterns, I realized that "I" was not my thoughts. So, prayer really wasn't a conversation between my brain and God. The key was to get my brain out of the way so that my very being could commune with a mysterious Presence that is sensed in silence—what I now call God.

At first, I could feel my True Self at a particular point deep within me. As I continued my practices in silence, my mind, body, and nervous system slowly began attuning themselves to this point of stillness. My False Self had revolved around the axis of my mind, which was rooted in fear. My True Self revolved around the axis of my spiritual heart, which was rooted in the love of God by its very nature. By going into my body and closing off the closet "doors," I practiced bringing my awareness inward from my external senses, away from my mind, and down into my heart. Eventually, this silence that I first encountered at a particular point deep within began to expand outward from that point into my whole body, and eventually beyond my body. It is still a particular point deep within, but also emanating from infinite points beyond that center.

My inward tonality matches the tonality I experience emanating from objects in nature, such as trees, plants, water, mountains, etc. The energy emitted from all things natural, including your soul, is the same. The task in prayer is to still your mind long enough to perceive this energy which is abstract, yet palpable.

Silence is God's first language.

— **St. John of the Cross** (c. 1542–1591)[3]

As I said before, there are many wisdom traditions that teach and empha-size this pathway to silence. The goal in these practices is to lead a practitioner to the threshold of the "inner sanctuary" and prepare for the crossing into silence. Perhaps if I had approached the threshold in this intentional way, my experience would not have been as tumultuous. But my experience was a merciful pathway for me. I came away with the wisdom I needed for my particular life. The terrifying silence became the inner sanctuary of sublime peace.

Be still and know that I am God.

— **Psalm 46:10a** (KJV)

Nave inside Wells Cathedral. Wells, Somerset, England, UK

TWENTY-ONE

IN THE WORLD, NOT OF IT

There is something in every one of you that waits, listen for the sound of the genuine in yourself. And if you cannot hear it, you will never find whatever it is for which you're searching. And if you hear it, and then do not follow it, it were better that you had never been born . . .

You are the only you that has ever lived. Your idiom is the only idiom of its kind in all the existences. And if you cannot hear the sound of the genuine in you, you will all of your life spend your days on the ends of strings that somebody else pulls . . .

The sound of the genuine is flowing through you. Don't be deceived and thrown off by all the noises that are a part, even of your dreams, your ambitions. All these things that you don't hear the sound of the genuine in you. Because that is the only true guide that you will ever have. And if you don't have that, you don't have a thing . . .

— **Howard Thurman** (1899–1981),[1] 1980 Baccalaureate Address, Spelman College[2]

IN EVANGELICALISM, THERE IS an emphasis on being "in the world and not of it." I'll begin by explaining what this phrase actually means, and then contrast it with how fundamentalist groups use it to keep their followers trapped as part of "the world."

This phrase, "in the world and not of it," actually describes one who has withdrawn from society long enough to find their True Self and to recognize the sound of their genuine voice. Not simply their audible voice, but what could be called the internal compass or inner knowing. Only you have access to this genuine voice and can discern how it communicates with you from within.

In an effort to avoid social rejection, beginning in childhood, a person must deny parts of their authentic self. In order to maintain attachment to parents, family, friends, a church community, and society, people repress the parts of themselves that aren't socially acceptable and that threaten those attachments. Those "unacceptable" parts of ourselves vary depending on the environment, but the strategy is the same. Each of us "reads the room" to determine which parts of ourselves are acceptable and which parts will sever our connections to the ones we love and hope will accept us. The term "the world" here is referring to this covert contract that requires conformity to gain acceptance. As children, acceptance is a basic survival need. There is no choice except to become "of the world," to enter into this relational contract, and it happens before our brains can even make conscious decisions. To be "of the world" means to reject oneself (or parts of oneself) to maintain connection to others.

However, within the evangelical church and other fundamentalist religions, being "in the world and not of it" is used to keep people trapped in this covert contract. It manifests as tribalism. There is no awareness of the True Self. The emphasis is on conformity to the rules of the group. This requirement to conform in order to maintain attachment to the church community, or family of believers, actually keeps people "in the world", or in this covert contract of conformity. It keeps people trapped in a system where they cannot know, accept, or reveal who they truly are. To do so would result in the rupture of relational attachments. Especially as children, a rupture like this could be life-threatening, because we are dependent on those in our environment for basic survival. As adults, although we can now survive on our own, relational ruptures still feel terrifying to our nervous systems which were programmed in childhood for survival. These ruptures can *feel* like life-or-death, regardless of if they really are life-or-death. So, naturally, we continue to repress our authentic selves. This continued state of self-repression, for the sake of attachment to the group, is an act of self-harm and violence towards the True Self.

Tribalism is an addiction that creates a feeling of safety for our nervous systems. To be "of the world" is to be controlled by this addiction. Christianity was supposed to break us from this addictive pattern, not encourage it. For many Christians, addiction to the tribe has become a socially acceptable form of numbing the anxiety that the emergence of the True Self creates for the nervous system. Your True Self might cost you your tribe. That is a terrifying proposition. Howard Thurman brings the seriousness of this dilemma to the forefront and echoes Jesus when he states: *". . . if you hear it (the True Self) and then do not follow it, it were better that you had never been born."*

> For what does it profit a man to gain the whole world and forfeit his soul?

> — **Mark 8:36** (ESV)

Spiritually speaking, "the world" is our animal impulse for safety, domination, and power, and the systems that feed and support those animal impulses. The impulse of the tribe is to crush the enemy (working as a proxy for "god") to secure the safety and power of the present and future "Promised Land." To be "of the world" means to be a slave to these animal instincts. It is to deny or repress who you genuinely are for the sake of connection with others. Institutions, filled with people who are unconscious of their True Selves, generally gravitate towards dehumanization through uniformity. Institutional Christianity is no different. It's not that there should be no organized religion. But organized religion that lacks awareness of this gravitational pull towards the animal instincts will inevitably devolve into toxicity. Only the True Self can distinguish the animal instincts from the sound of the genuine in oneself. The work of a Christian, then, is bringing the brain and nervous system into alignment with the True Self. True Christianity is less about adopting beliefs and joining a tribe, and more about converting your brain and nervous system to a new way of living that is in harmony with your innate True Self, *which is Christ in you, the hope of glory.*[3]

> I'm startled or taken aback when people walk up to me and tell me they are Christians. My first response is the question "Already?" It seems to me a lifelong endeavor to try to live the life of a Christian.

— **Maya Angelou**[4] (1928–2014)[5]

Most Christians today are "of the world." They adhere to the system of tribalism. Non-Christians are seen by the group as "lost" or "in the dark." Non-believers are a threat to the tribe. This fosters a feeling of separation from fellow humans in differing tribes. Members of the church community must repress whatever parts of themselves that the group deems unacceptable.

Jesus overcomes this tribalism and lives from a place of compassion, love, and solidarity with all other humans. To be "in Christ" is to see the essence of God in yourself and all others. It is to see the True Self and recognize the sound of the genuine within yourself and others. This is a major psychological shift. It requires the death of the False Self that finds identity within the tribe. To believe like Jesus believed is to know that you came from, are sustained by, and will return to God. It is only the mind's construction of the False Self that divides people into categories and perceives separation from God.

> *There is neither Jew nor Gentile, neither slave nor free, nor is there male and female, for you are all one in Christ Jesus.*

— **Galatians 3:28** (NIV)

To be "in the world and not of it" does not mean that you belong to the correct tribe or believe the correct theology. It recognizes that most people function from the lower animal instincts of the False Self, not from their higher human capacity for compassion and love, which is the natural outflow of the True Self.

You are from below; I am from above. You are of this world; I am not of this world.

— **John 8:23** (NIV)

Here, Jesus uses "below" to refer to those functioning out of the False Self, which only has access to animal instincts that promote and find safety in tribalism.

To be "in the world and not of it" means that you exist among those functioning from their animal instincts; however, you identify with your True Self which originates in God, and you recognize the authentic soul in everyone else. This reveals a fundamental connection between you and all of creation. So there is no need to be part of a tribe, because humanity is your tribe and you are already at home. Others may not see God in you, but you see God in them, and that is what compels you to love them. Being "in the world and not of it" is ironically the exact opposite of the tribalistic impulses of fundamentalist church groups, which see outsiders as "lost" and require insiders to conform. The unity that is sought is actually the uniformity of many gathered False Selves.

There is in every person, that which waits, waits, waits, and listens for the sound of the genuine in himself. There is that in every person that waits, and waits, and listens for the sound of the genuine in other people. And when those two sounds come together, this is music God heard when he said, let us make man in our image.

— **Howard Thurman** (1899–1981), 1980 Baccalaureate Address, Spelman College[6]

You are simultaneously tribeless and at home with people of every tribe. You are in the world, but not of it.

Twenty-Two

HATE YOUR MOTHER & FATHER

If anyone comes to me and does not hate father and mother,
wife and children, brothers and sisters—yes, even their own
life—such a person cannot be my disciple.

— **Luke 14:26** (NIV)

WHY DID JESUS SAY such an extreme thing? As a Christian, aren't I supposed to strive not to hate anyone? This verse always perplexed me until I recognized my True Self.

Jesus speaks directly to overcoming our relational attachments to pursue true authenticity. During my own process, I had a distinct moment of knowing that I was going to lose people in my life. It wasn't until I was convinced that denying my authentic identity would kill me—either slowly through mental and emotional *dis-ease* (lack of ease) or quickly through suicide—that I resolved that I would no longer betray myself in order to maintain attachment to a person or group. Up until that point, I could not tolerate the distress of others in order to do what was right for me. But finally, the rejection of my True Self became more painful than rejection from others.

In evangelicalism, you are taught to sacrifice yourself for the sake of others. This constant self-sacrifice is encouraged as evidence of righteousness and devotion to God. Sacrificing for others can indeed be a good and healthy thing, if one has healthy boundaries, a sense of their True Self, purpose, and truly altruistic motivations. Self-sacrifice can also be an unhealthy means of seeking approval, manipulating others, and pridefully denying your own needs. In evangelicalism, the word "sacrifice," in practice, encouraged people to dissolve their personal boundaries, repress their intuition, or "forgive quickly" for the sake of keeping the peace with family and other Christians.

Once I discovered that God had been hiding within me the whole time in the innermost chamber of my being, sacrificing my True Self, who was in union with God, was no longer the moral high road I once thought it was. I began to observe which "self" was making sacrifices and to what end. I began to see the betrayal of my True Self as a betrayal of God. I had been sacrificing the sacred for a false sense of belonging and security. I was a hypocrite.

> Woe to you, teachers of the law and Pharisees, you hypocrites! You are like whitewashed tombs, which look beautiful on the outside but on the inside are full of the bones of the dead and everything unclean. In the same way, on the outside you appear to people as righteous but on the inside you are full of hypocrisy and wickedness.
>
> — **Matthew 23:27–28** (NIV)

Evangelicals extrapolate Jesus's sacrifice on the cross as a mandate for perpetual suffering and self-sacrifice. Because Jesus suffered on the cross, many Christians see suffering as a badge of honor, and allow all sorts of abuses to continue in their own lives and the lives of others. Unfortunately, and (mostly) unconsciously, the Church often perpetuates abusive situations under the guise of love and forgiveness. However, as I began to look back at Scripture, I noticed Jesus living a life with extremely solid boundaries. Over and over again, when he was threatened or mistreated, he fled. He rebuked people. He let people walk away. He never sacrificed his authenticity for the sake of attachment to others.

Once I discovered Christ within me, experiencing this life as my True Self, I had a moral imperative to choose authenticity over attachment. This is not to say that this was easy. It was not. Relational ruptures are painful. But I knew that any relationship with someone who devalued my True Self could never bring the intimacy we both actually desired.

The proximity of the relationship does not diminish the importance of protecting and honoring yourself. In fact, the closer the relationship, perhaps the more important it is for boundaries to be in place.

> *Then Jesus entered a house, and again a crowd gathered, so that he and his disciples were not even able to eat. When his family heard about this, they went to take charge of him, for they said, "He is out of his mind."*
>
> *. . . Then Jesus' mother and brothers arrived. Standing outside, they sent someone in to call him. A crowd was sitting around him, and they told him, "Your mother and brothers are outside looking for you."*
>
> *"Who are my mother and my brothers?" he asked.*
>
> *Then he looked at those seated in a circle around him and said, "Here are my mother and my brothers! Whoever does God's will is my brother and sister and mother."*
>
> — **Mark 3:20–21; 31–34** (NIV)

Our cultural conditioning reflects the tribalism that is wired into our biology. This especially holds true in family units. But Jesus cuts right through this by instructing us to *hate* our family in order to follow.

He's not using the word "hate" here in a malicious way. He's not instructing his followers to wish ill-will on their family, harm them in any way, or stoke resentment. Quite the contrary. He's using the *energy* of the word to emphasize the importance of living an authentic life, even if it costs you relationships. The intensity of the word "hate" is needed, not to encourage harm to anyone, but to overcome our biological impulse to betray ourselves in order to "keep the peace" in our familial relationships. Sometimes, the energy of a righteous anger is what's required to untether us from attachments that no longer serve us, and to propel us on to our own authentic path.

Your True Self will no doubt be a threat to some people. Questioning the tenets of a religion, setting personal boundaries, and pursuing *your* destiny will be frightening to many people. Jesus is telling the truth: there is no room to compromise your True Self for the sake of relational attachments.

> *Then Jesus said to them, "Only in his hometown, among his relatives, and in his own household is a prophet without honor."*
>
> **— Mark 6:4** (BSB)

In many cases, it will be those you love the most who will reject you. Choose yourself (and, by extension, Christ in you) anyway. This is what Jesus did, even when his hometown of Nazareth and family rejected him. He was not safe in his hometown, but he was home wherever he went. His home was within. How could he be anywhere else but home? So it is with you.

In fact, intimacy in relationships is *not possible* with people who do not know or accept who you truly are. Relationships sustained by the dishonesty of the False Self are not *real* relationships. You've possibly experienced this loneliness—being in many relationships, but not feeling truly known. You actually fear that if you were to be known, the relationship would break.

Once you know your True Self, this feeling of loneliness becomes more transient and dissipates. You commune with God at all times just by living your authentic life. You "pray without ceasing" by being fully present. Fully alive.

When authentic relationships do come along and last, you experience the joy of true intimacy. I remember the season when I was seriously questioning my evangelical beliefs. I had already let go of many of them and I knew that

I could never go back. My husband, Jared, was the music director at a large megachurch, and our beliefs had always been the same. For the first time in our relationship, I questioned if our marriage could survive my rapidly shifting beliefs. In a sobering conversation with my husband, Jared, I asked frankly, *"If I become a Buddhist or something weird, are we going to be OK?"*

To be clear, I don't think Buddhism is weird. But, as an evangelical, in my ignorance, I used to. I certainly knew that there was a visceral reaction to other faith traditions within evangelicalism. So I asked Jared the question in this very crass way in order to communicate that I was going to follow my authentic journey wherever it took me. I couldn't promise a return to Christianity, and I needed him to know that.

He looked right into my eyes and said with the sincerest voice, "We are OK."

After over a decade of being married to this man, I was shocked that this was the most loved I'd ever felt. This unconditional love for me had always been true for him, but I realized for the first time that he loved the *real* me and that there were no conditions on that love. I didn't have to be anything, Christian or otherwise, for him to love me and want to be in a relationship with me. He loved me for *me*. I experienced the real intimacy I longed for. I no longer had to fear that my True Self would threaten our attachment. That is the kind of relationship we all want. I didn't know what I had until I had the courage to show up authentically. The acceptance and love from Jared were there, but my False Self could not receive it.

You must first establish that intimate relationship with your True Self, and then you will be able to cultivate real intimacy with others. That's what Jesus is saying. Don't settle for fake intimacy with yourself, others, or the Divine.

Twenty-Three

ORIGINAL SIN

What is blasphemous is to believe and feel 'I am a being apart from God's being. I am a self unto myself, a temporary, finite self, separate from all others and from God.' That is the original sin, the root cause of all other so-called sins. It is a departure from the Garden of Eden.

— **Rupert Spira**[1]

TOTAL DEPRAVITY. BROKEN. INHERENTLY evil. Original sin.

In the modern Christian religion, these are some of the words used to describe why we as humans behave badly. For many, the doctrine of original sin is the scapegoat for "sinful" behavior. We need an explanation for the evil we see in the world, and this is the go-to answer. However, the term "original sin" is not found in the Bible. "Original sin" is not a concept in Judaism; therefore, it would have been foreign to Jesus. Fr. Richard Rohr likes to point out that the church seems to have glossed over Genesis 1 and 2, where we and all creation are called "good...good...good...good...good...very good."

The doctrine of original sin was largely developed by St. Augustine[2] and introduced by him several centuries after Jesus. In brief, it mostly came out of his failure to completely repress his sexual desire. With this idea, he was attempting to explain the reason for "sinful" sexual human behavior. Keep in mind that he considered sexual behavior to be sinful *even within marriage,* albeit acceptable for procreation. He considered sex within marriage, for pleasure, to be sinful.

> It is, however, one thing for married persons to have inter-
> course only for the wish to beget children, which is not sinful:
> it is another thing for them to desire carnal pleasure in cohab-
> itation, but with the spouse only, which involves venial sin.

— **St. Augustine** (c. 354–430)[3]

Augustine later wrote that that sin of sexual intercourse in marriage with-out procreative purposes can be cleansed by acts of charity and almsgiving.[4]

About 1,000 years later, the doctrine of original sin was formally adopted by the Catholic Church and became part of the official church teaching. This doctrine, of course, infiltrated Protestantism as well. To be blunt, we allowed a well-intentioned man with a very distorted and unhealthy view of his sexuality to shape the way we view ourselves. It has distorted the way we view humanity.

Despite all of creation, including humans, being declared "good" in Gene-sis, the doctrine of original sin misidentified the reason for unhealthy human behavior, by declaring that humans were inherently *bad*. Being convinced of one's inherent badness is a source of shame and self-loathing, and is a roadblock for healing. *Complete healing assumes that someone was originally whole. Originally not broken.* A belief that one is inherently broken from the beginning makes healing elusive. Healing requires a *return* to a healthy and whole state. One cannot return to a state that never existed. The concept of original sin implies a place of brokenness in which complete healing is never fully achievable, because it never existed in the first place. By being convinced that we are broken, it is assumed we were never whole, and thus we do not seek to heal.

A more helpful concept is: *Inevitable Sin*. As we have seen, it's inevitable that the False Self will form a protective shell around the embryo of the True

Self. It's inevitable that our brains will do this unconsciously and we will lose our awareness of who we really are.

Psychology explains that when we are wounded, our brain literally rewires itself in ways that protect us from pain. We are not conscious of this wiring—even as it drives our feelings, the chemicals in our brains, our coping mechanisms and, yes, our habits, addictions, and behaviors. *Yet, as Christians, we have been conditioned to feel as if we are broken, when, in fact, our biology is functioning exactly as it should.*

A friend of mine, who is a counselor, introduced me to an ingenious term that I think the church (and society) should adopt: *generational trauma.* We don't pass on generational *sin*; we pass on our unhealed traumas, which leads to self-forgetting, or "missing the mark." None of us escape trauma. Some of it is large and some of it is small, but no one comes out unscathed. Perhaps the biggest and most inevitable trauma of all is the loss of connection with our True Self.

The word "sin" compels us to problem-solve and manage behavior. The word "trauma" awakens us to the internal disconnection, so that we can work to heal it. We are all created "good . . . very good" (Genesis 1:31), but we must awaken to our individual traumas in order to heal. *Pain and trauma that is not healed will be transferred.*

Who you are—your True Self—is *good.* When you accept and truly believe that about yourself, you can then begin to look at the roots of your behaviors and addictions and ask: "why?"

The word "sin" means "to miss the mark." It doesn't mean "to disobey God." By sinning, we've simply forgotten who we are. Behind every behavior we label as "sin" is a wound that needs to be healed. When you address your traumas and begin to heal, you'll see the Fruits of the Spirit begin to flow naturally, because they have always been inside you. This is not the fruit of original sin. It's the fruit of original goodness. Love, joy, peace, patience, kindness, goodness, faithfulness, gentleness, and self-control are the natural fruits of the Tree of Life, which is birthed from the seed of the True Self.

At the risk of drawing one too many theological inferences from Disney movies, the 1995 movie, *The Lion King*[5], illustrates this concept well. Simba, the young lion cub, is heir to his father Mufasa's kingdom. Mufasa's brother, Scar, kills Mufasa, and tells young Simba that his father's death was his fault. Believing this, Simba internalizes shame and guilt, and he flees. He not only flees his geographical home, but he flees from his true internal identity. He believes this lie about himself—as we all did—that we are inherently bad, and it is our badness that causes the pain we experience.

In an unexpected mystical encounter years later, Mufasa appears to Simba as a spirit in the clouds. His father tells Simba that he's forgotten who he is. He instructs Simba to look inside himself to remember who he is: the son of a king. Simba, remembering his original blessing, then "dies to [his False] self" and returns to his home. He returns to the Garden of Eden. *The process of "death to self" looks less like denying yourself of needs, and more like remembering who you always were.* **Returning to Eden is a journey that happens within.** Simba's true identity never changed. However, his loss of awareness of his True Self led him to identify with a distorted identity. This fueled a feeling of being "lost"—both inwardly and outwardly. It created much chaos, neglect, and harm for himself and the others he was responsible to care for. I'm sure most of us can relate.

Much like a seed, each person needs to be nurtured in order to grow into their inherent beauty. We don't have to bend and shape trees for them to become beautiful. We give them what they need, and they bloom on their own. This is the gift of salvation. By realizing the truth of who you are, as fundamentally good and belonging in nature, the True Self is freed to fulfill its destiny as the Tree of Life that bears good fruit.

TWENTY-FOUR

THE EYE OF THE NEEDLE

Jesus's teaching about how difficult it was for rich people to be saved always perplexed me. He says it's easier for a camel to pass through the eye of a needle. This seems to imply that salvation for a rich person is nearly impossible. Historically, most of the Christians in America that I knew were relatively rich by the world's standards. Jesus wasn't talking about us, right? Again, this metaphor did not come into focus for me until I understood the True Self and False Self.

The only motivation of the False Self is self-preservation. Since it knows it can be destroyed, it fears annihilation. Therefore, it is inevitably violent towards the True Self and others. It is narcissistic and self-deceiving. Its survival depends upon us identifying ourselves with it, and so we remain addicted to the passions of *anger, pride, vanity, envy, greed, fear, gluttony, lust,* and *sloth*. These passions defend against the revelation that the False Self is not our true identity. There is something more that is hidden deep within us, but to access it, we must encounter the wounds that created the False Self in the first place.

These passions, or *sins,* are native only to the False Self, not to the True Self. Therefore, the True Self can observe the passions of the False Self and identify what needs healing. Wherever these passions, or sins, show up, there is a wound to heal.

Again, I tell you, it is easier for a camel to go through the eye of
a needle than for a rich person to enter the kingdom of God.

— **Matthew 19:24** (NIV)

When Jesus uses the terms "rich" and "poor" in Scripture, he is referring to a person's spirit. "Blessed are the poor in spirit, for theirs is the kingdom of heaven."[1]

To be "poor in spirit" means not to be weighed down by baggage. Baggage is the heavy defenses we accumulate over our lives in response to our wounds. You know you have it by noticing what makes you burn with anger, envy, greed, pride, judgment, etc. The origins of our reactions are our wounds. When left unacknowledged and unhealed, these reactions become our automatic defenses—our *baggage*.

As we have seen, the True Self is seated in the inner sanctuary. There is no baggage here. There is silence and peace. So, when we encounter baggage, we must offload it in order to enter again into the inner sanctuary.

Why does Jesus use the camel in this metaphor and not another huge animal—perhaps an elephant?

Jesus is describing the process that must be undertaken to become poor in spirit—which means your spirit is free of baggage. Dating from possibly the 9th century, a myth has circulated about a gate in Jerusalem called the Eye of the Needle. The historicity of the gate is debatable, but the symbolism in the story is illuminating.

At night in ancient times, the main gate to the city would close. They didn't want enemies to be able to rush into the city at night, so when travelers arrived on their camels, they could only enter through a very tiny gate called the Eye of the Needle. One would have to stop and unload all of the baggage on the camel. It was a long, arduous process.

"Eye of a Needle" in a gate in Nazareth

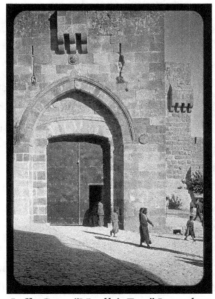

Jaffa Gate, "Needle's Eye," Jerusalem

A "rich" man is one who is carrying a lot of baggage within. He is identified with the False Self. A "poor" man is one who has healed his wounds—becoming a light and free spirit—not easily offended, not clinging to anything, and nimble enough to bend and move freely through the walls he encounters.

I find it compelling that the cross of Calvary is located *outside* the gates of the city. When Jesus tells us to carry our cross, we can see that our crucifixion (the psychological healing process) will happen *outside* the gates of heaven. Once the process of dying to ourselves—unloading our baggage—is finished, our spirits are then "poor." We can slip through the gate. We can then resurrect, like Jesus, inside the city—clinging to nothing and free to move through walls with ease.

In evangelicalism, you were most likely told that you entered the kingdom by praying a prayer of salvation—*sincerely*. This is a fundamental misunderstanding of the Bible and lacks spiritual wisdom. You enter by becoming poor in spirit. You enter by unloading your baggage.

> *Its gates will never be closed at the end of day because there is no night there.*

> **— Revelation 21:25** (NLT)

For a person who has crossed the threshold into the sanctuary, it is possible to move in and out. The "gates will never be closed" (Revelation 21:25). An encounter with the True Self can never be taken away. Once the seed begins to germinate, there's no reversing the process. But the process of salvation is ongoing and the pace will vary from person to person. The False Self does not simply fall away instantaneously, but you no longer identify with it. Once the threshold has been crossed, confronting your baggage, your demons, no longer feels life-threatening. You work with it to bring yourself closer into alignment with your True Self in God. When you notice baggage, you go within to explore the wound and heal it. Fear and pain may still be present, but not to the degree that they were before crossing the threshold.

The psychological wounds are healed one by one so that the spirit can flow ever more efficiently and with clarity. The mind, body, and spirit can increasingly exist in greater harmony with one another.

When there is complete identification with the False Self, a person's psychology is mostly working in resistance to their spirit. This creates a lot of *dis-ease* inside the body and, by extension, the environment. As psychological healing continues and baggage is released, the spirit becomes more and more "poor," allowing it to move through the body and out of it freely. The True Self can never be destroyed, so there is nothing to fear or resist. The more we come to realize this, the more our spirits can flow with greater and greater ease, passing through the Eye of the Needle into the kingdom of God.

TWENTY-FIVE

JESUS STRIPPED OF HIS GARMENTS

Now is the time to loosen, cast away
The useless weight of everything but love.
For he began his letting go before,
Before the worlds for which he dies were made,
Emptied himself, became one of the poor,
To make you rich in him and unafraid.
See, as they strip the robe from off his back
They strip away your own defences too,
Now you could lose it all and never lack,
Now you can see what naked love can do.

— **Malcolm Guite**, Excerpt from poem *The Stations of the
Cross, Poem X: Jesus is Stripped of His Garments*[1]

SEVERAL TIMES IN THE story of Jesus, garments are used to symbolize defenses or baggage. We see this intimately in the story of the Last Supper and
again on his journey to crucifixion.

*Jesus, knowing that the Father had given all things into His
hands, and that He had come forth from God and was going*

back to God, got up from supper, and laid aside His garments;
and taking a towel, He girded Himself. Then He poured water
into the basin, and began to wash the disciples' feet and to wipe
them with the towel with which He was girded.

— **John 13:3–5** (NASB 1995)

By removing his garments—first his outer clothing and then the towel around his waist—symbolically, Jesus is naked. He's making himself completely vulnerable and exposed. He's demonstrating what is required to become poor in spirit. Our outer garments represent the defenses of the False Self and the outer forms it identifies with: our race, our status, our successes, our possessions, our power, our pride, etc.

In removing his garments, Jesus is demonstrating his identification with his True Self and the knowledge that he came from God and will return to God. This is our ultimate reality as well. Like Jesus, we come from God and will return to God. Underneath the garments of our religion, politics, wounds, and false pride is our naked self—the image, the likeness, and essence of God. This place of naked emptiness is filled only with love.

One of the most unhelpful messages I received in evangelicalism was that Jesus did something in my place. It was a trade, so that I didn't have to endure what he endured. We didn't share the same fate. We praised him because he did it, and now we don't have to. This message is a thief of true life.

You might be wondering, "Doesn't the Bible say he paid my debt?" Jesus's death on the cross isn't a payment that satisfies a debt owed to a separate, Fatherly entity looking on from above. Rather, in the body of Jesus, God fully absorbs our accumulated pain that we project onto him in order to rid ourselves of the anxiety the pain causes us. Instead of continuing this cycle of transferring pain to another, Jesus absorbs the pain fully. He recycles the painful energy that is deposited into him and converts that energy into love.

Jesus demonstrates his love for all people through this process in two ways. First, he stops the transfer of "payments" for pain. The pain transferred to him no longer has anywhere else to go. His body is the end of the line, where he accepts the responsibility of allowing suffering to transform pain into compassion. Secondly, his willingness to do this reveals to us the ultimate solution to our own suffering: do the same.

God demonstrates through Jesus that our sins are not held against us. However, until we undergo the same psychological, emotional, and spiritual process as Jesus, we are slaves to the sin of the False Self and are not free. The gift of salvation is attained through your own internal crucifixion. It's your False Self that has to die. Not another person. Not Jesus. Jesus's death reveals the truth of what inside of you needs to die and how. He reveals our psychological need to transfer pain to others because the False Self cannot hold it. This is called *scapegoating*. When we stop scapegoating our pain, our False Self begins to die and to be recycled into compassion. We sacrifice our False Self and trust it will be resurrected into love. Our "debt is paid" when we submit to the same process that Jesus submitted himself to. Jesus doesn't replace you on the cross. He mythologically and metaphorically demonstrates how to submit to it yourself. Your debt is paid by *you*, or more specifically, *Christ in you*.

Jesus was a master teacher. He taught through myth. *His very life became a life-regenerating myth.* The details of the historicity of Jesus's life are not what is most valuable for spiritual transformation. It's the myth that his life offers that has the potential to awaken us to our deepest power and truth about ourselves and our place in the cosmos.

Jesus's journey means nothing if it's not your inner journey and transformation. His suffering does nothing for you if you aren't allowing your own suffering to transform into more expansive Grace. He doesn't take the place you deserve. *(No one deserves to die a brutal death in the first place.)* He asks you to follow him on a journey he's been on. He goes first, so you can follow.

Evangelicalism reinforces learned helplessness. It's like Jesus showed us how to build a house by going first, building his, and giving us the blueprint. But then, instead of following the blueprint and building our own house, we just marveled at the house Jesus built and worshiped it while freezing in the cold.

"I can't, but Jesus can" is not the message. The message is: Jesus can and did, so I can too, and he shows me how.

> *I am the way and the truth and the life. No one comes to the Father except through me.*

— **John 14:6** (NIV)

This verse should be taken to mean that no one can realize their True Self apart from the process that Jesus demonstrates of dying to the False Self. Your idea of who you *think* you are must be crucified in order to come into your innermost sanctuary—the hiding place of God. Jesus assures me that I can die to my False Self. I can be stripped naked of my defenses. I can carry my cross. I can be buried completely hopeless. I can trust this is the only way to resurrection and the realization that I am a child of God alongside Jesus.

Jesus doesn't build your life for you. He gives you the blueprint and invites you to follow it. To pick up your own cross and carry it. To become like Jesus is to allow the Word to be made Flesh in your body. Your flesh! Through you, the Word of love will dwell among us.

> *Then Jesus said to his disciples, "Whoever wants to be my disciple must deny themselves and take up their cross and follow me.*

— **Matthew 16:24** (NIV)

As Malcolm Guite writes in his poem, to follow Jesus is to drop the useless weight of everything but love. To lose all your garments until all that's left is naked love.

To follow Jesus is to become who you truly are. To follow Jesus is to bring your *real* life into *this* life. It is to follow your own authentic path, which can only be done from a place of love, because your True Self is grounded in love.

TWENTY-SIX

PAUL (THE TRUE SELF) WAS HIDDEN WITHIN SAUL (THE FALSE SELF)

When I was a child, I spoke as a child, I felt as a child, I thought as a child. Now that I have become a man, I have put away childish things. For now we see in a mirror, dimly, but then face to face. Now I know in part, but then I will know fully, even as I was also fully known. But now faith, hope, and love remain—these three. The greatest of these is love.

— 1 Corinthians 13:11–13 (WEB)

MOST OF US TAKE this passage to refer to periods of time— childhood versus adulthood. But Paul is talking about the process of psychologically maturing. He "became a man" on the Road to Damascus. He came into contact with his True Self. In Galatians 1:15–16, Paul says that "God revealed his Son *in me . . .*" on the Road to Damascus. The True Self had always been there, in him, but he was not aware of it.

Notice that Paul was already physically an adult, Saul, when this inner realization happened, but he still had the mind of a child. The same is true for many adults now. When he uses the word "child," he's not talking about physical age. He's referring to his False Self. As we have seen already, the False Self is constructed by the mind in childhood, but remains into adulthood unless it is brought into consciousness and confronted. Some adults remain in this "childish" state until their physical death. As my friend used to say, "Some people live to age 80, and some people live to age 10 . . . 8 times." It's true.

When we turn to look inward now, we may not be able to see our True Selves at all. But the first step is acknowledging that it is there in the first place. Paul uses the mirror metaphor to depict the psychological process of examining yourself and distinguishing between the True and False Self. When you look in a mirror, as Paul illustrates in 1 Corinthians, there are always two separate selves, but only one is *real*. The other is an illusion. However, the illusion is what we see at first. We only see what we look like on the outside. Our external projected self is the illusion, or False Self. At first, we identify completely with the image we see in our reflection. The awakening is realizing that who you really are is not the image in the mirror, but rather the True Self which is seeing that image.

In Greek mythology, Narcissus was known for his outer beauty. One day, he decides to get a drink from a pool of water and sees his reflection for the first time. He falls in love with his False Self—his external image of himself. This is where we get the word *narcissism*. It is completely identifying with the False Self and falling in love with this reflection, protecting it at all costs. Narcissus eventually kills himself out of sorrow and frustration, because he cannot touch the object of his desire—which is his True Self. The False Self is a reflection of the True Self, keeping Narcissus looking in the wrong direction. It's so close to the real thing, but not quite it. Narcissus's external image is adored and celebrated by everyone, including himself. His reflection *seems* so real, but grasping it is elusive. His reflection is a distorted picture of what he really wants, not the real thing. Narcissus can't let go of grasping at the reflection that almost satisfies. Other versions of the myth say that he drowns trying to touch it. He never realizes what is behind his reflection—his True Self. It is the False Self that must be exposed as illusionary for the True

Self to be realized. We must sacrifice what is most precious to us—who we think we are and what we think we want—to discover the True Self behind the reflection.

We cling to the image of the False Self as reality. But it is elusive. However, our True Self can only be known by looking in the mirror at our False Self. We have to *first* see and acknowledge that it is the False Self staring at us in the mirror. *It is only then that we can make the split and recognize that the Self staring back at us is separate from our True Selves.* In 1 Corinthians 13:12 above, Paul describes his awakening with the mirror and says he can partially see his True Self. It is like looking at a reflection in water that is rippling, making it difficult to see the image. You can see it is there, but the image is not clear. The False Self, the external image, is acknowledged, but there is a split, and he can now view two separate entities—The False Self being a shattered reflection of the True Self. As the mind begins to heal and becomes still and silent, the reflection in the water becomes more and more clear. Paul says, *"For now we see in a mirror, dimly, but then face to face"* (1 Corinthians 13:12a). Eventually, when the water is completely still, it perfectly reflects the True Self, which is love. *"Now I know in part, but then I will know fully, even as I was also fully known. But now faith, hope, and love remain—these three. The greatest of these is love"* (1 Corinthians 13:12b–13).

Paul affirms that his True Self has always been there. He just didn't see it until now. *He had to awaken to what was already there. He didn't have to pray a prayer to accept his salvation or ask Jesus into his heart. He woke up to what had always been there, that he had not yet seen until then.* His True Self, his "Son in me", his true nature, his true reflection was always love. He says he will come to fully know himself, even as he has always been fully known (1 Corinthians 13:12b). As he gradually saw his reflection more and more clearly, he realized that he was looking at love through the eyes of love. Love was looking at itself. The two became one.

Paul's Road to Damascus was the death of his False Self, Saul. Paul was always his True Self. He realized who he truly was. His essence was always love. *Paul was always buried within Saul.* This is what it means to be saved! It is a revelation of your true identity. I Am. In the mythological pattern of his death and resurrection, Jesus revealed to Paul the meaning of his awakening on the Road to Damascus. Saul was crucified so that Paul could be resurrected.

Salvation is not an exit ticket to get into the party in heaven after this life. It is the death of your False Self, leading to the revelation of your True Self. *The realization that you are already at The Party! Right now!*

TWENTY-SEVEN

THE WELLSPRING OF LIFE IS WITHIN

The Kingdom of Heaven is not higher but aliver; it is right here, just on the other side of that 'terror we can just scarcely bear'; the only thing lacking to embrace it is the depth of our hearts.

— Cynthia Bourgeault[1]

REAL, AUTHENTIC LOVE *SEES*. Like the mirroring Paul describes, real love is an accurate, particular, precise love. I noticed this quality in my encounter with the transgender woman on my front porch. During the conversation, I slowly began recognizing her as a vessel of Christ. In my hesitation to trust her and receive her help, there were some moments of going back-and-forth in conversation in which she repeatedly demonstrated that she saw *me*. I had never met this person before, but somehow, she knew my most intimate feelings and experiences. As I began to describe my darkest moment in hell, she disclosed to me that she had experienced the same depths. My deepest panic, my deepest despair, she knew personally. Until that moment, I was so ashamed of the way I was falling apart minute by minute. Although the people around me were trying to be there for me, I couldn't seem to get anyone to really understand the depth of the crisis. I felt so alone in my experience. Until then. I knew this woman had been exactly where I was. Suddenly the fear and shame dissipated, and I knew Christ was with me in hell. Christ had come to find me in the pit!

The woman articulated my past to me and why it was affecting me in this way. She pointed me in the precise direction I needed to go. I had expected to be taken to a hospital. I knew I needed help right then. The woman told me she would take me there, but that it wasn't going to solve what was happening internally. "Do you have a counselor you can go to?" I did. But I was scared it wouldn't be enough. It would normally take a few days to get in, and I couldn't wait any longer for help. Besides, I'd been in counseling for years, yet here I was, having what felt like a complete nervous breakdown. Still, my husband got on the phone with the counselor's office. Much to our surprise, the receptionist said, "This never happens, but someone just canceled at the last minute, and there's an opening in a couple of hours." I looked back at the woman on my porch and then at my husband who was holding the phone. I agreed to see the therapist, and that appointment was the beginning of unearthing and healing my unacknowledged trauma. I hadn't been ready to look at myself and do the work until that moment when I hit rock bottom. The woman stepped into my house and pushed her hands up under my diaphragm to show me how to calm future panic attacks. Though my body was still shaking, my soul felt seen and safe. Saint Sophrany of Essex once said, "You may be certain that as long as someone is in hell, Christ will remain there with him." I now can assure you that this is true. I owe that certitude to the experience of Christ meeting me in this unexpected transgender body. In all of my searching for God outside of myself, I had overlooked God. God showing up on my doorstep was an external picture of ultimate reality. My search for God "out there" was like sniffing around for my nose.

I recognize the qualities of my encounter in the story of the woman at the well. Jesus comes to her in her ordinary routine. She doesn't have to go anywhere special. And, like me, the woman goes toe-to-toe with Jesus, until he asserts that he really does see and know the particulars of her life and pain. It's a knowing that does not just sympathize with a story, but validates the particular details and reflects back with precision an understanding of the pain and suffering.

Jesus tells the woman that "the spring *within her* will well up unto eternal life" (John 4:14). A spring of water comes from an aquifer deep in the ground. It literally appears "up there" once there is so much water in the aquifer that it pushes its way up and spills out on top of the land. The picture Jesus paints here is that heaven/eternal life originates and emerges from within us. But, to access the source of Living Water, we have to dig deep. The well next to the woman is a picture of her heart, where she will find what she's looking for. Heaven comes up out of the deeply unconscious mind, buried under the layers and layers of dirt. Excavating our deepest pains, wounds, and longings requires courage to dig deep and a faith that there is Living Water to be found underneath it all. This is what the myth promises.

Most of us were taught that heaven was a place to escape to. If we believe the right thing, one day—later—we can evade our suffering. But, that's the exact opposite of the Way that Jesus reveals. Instead of avoiding suffering, he tells us to get to the bottom of it...to keep digging down...down...down...until we hit something *real*. With all the biblical talk of wells and springs, how did we miss that the source of life clearly wasn't up there, but down here? I'm afraid it's so deep within us, that in looking out and beyond, we've overlooked God completely.

The bottom of your heart, hidden in Christ, is the wellspring of life from where heaven will emerge. It's not—*at first*—higher. At first, it's deeper, fuller, aliver, and wider. Only after it is all those things does the Living Water push up from within to include higher.

> *Christ with me,*
> *Christ before me,*
> *Christ behind me,*
> *Christ in me,*
> *Christ beneath me,*
> *Christ above me,*
> *Christ on my right,*

Christ on my left,
Christ when I lie down,
Christ when I sit down,
Christ when I arise,
Christ in the heart of every man who thinks of me,
Christ in the mouth of everyone who speaks of me,
Christ in every eye that sees me,
Christ in every ear that hears me.

— **St. Patrick's Breastplate**, Old Irish Prayer attributed to
St. Patrick

If the only direction you look to find God is up, you will never find what you're looking for. Jesus goes on to tell the woman at the well that you do not worship God in a physical place ("this mountain nor in Jerusalem"), but in your own Spirit, and in the knowledge that heaven is within you. It is your living reality. You first return home, deep within yourself, to discover that home is everywhere, because anywhere you go, there you are.

"Woman," Jesus replied, "believe me, a time is coming when
you will worship the Father neither on this mountain nor in
Jerusalem . . . God is spirit, and his worshipers must worship in
the Spirit and in truth."

— **John 4:21, 24** (NIV)

TWENTY-EIGHT

PARABLE OF THE HIDDEN TREASURE & THE PEARL OF GREAT PRICE

The kingdom of heaven is like treasure hidden in a field. When a man found it, he hid it again, and then in his joy went and sold all he had and bought that field.

Again, the kingdom of heaven is like a merchant looking for fine pearls. When he found one of great value, he went away and sold everything he had and bought it.

— **Matthew 13:44–46** (NIV)

ONCE AN UNDERSTANDING OF the True Self and False Self is established, it's hard to unsee the purpose of Jesus's parables. The True Self is the treasure. The True Self is the "Pearl of Great Price." Before you can even begin to look for the treasure in a field, you have to know it's there in the first place. I don't know how many fields I've seen in my life, but I've never looked at one and thought, "I'm certain there's treasure buried in that field." The state of sin is our obliviousness to the treasure buried within us, underneath the surface. It's the complete lack of awareness that a treasure even exists in the field—within you! Before someone goes searching for a treasure, they must at least have a suspicion that the treasure exists.

The purpose of myth—the purpose of Jesus's parables—is first to bring awareness to a treasure that you were unaware existed. If all Jesus really wanted was for everyone to say a prayer sincerely so they could go to heaven when they die, then he adopted a pretty poor sales pitch. Hopefully, by understanding the function of myth, the purpose of these parables is opening up to you. Even if you don't know what the treasure is exactly, the knowledge that it is there may be enough for you to start digging.

Something interesting about the discovery of the treasure or the pearl is that, upon finding it, the men went away and sold everything. You may recall that when God revealed Christ *within* Paul (Galatians 1:16), he retreated for three years (Galatians 1:18). Once one is born again, or saved from the False Self, there is a period of time where one must withdraw from society in order to "sell their possessions," or detox from the addictions stemming from their false identity. From a psychological perspective, these addictions are known as *narcissistic supply*. Narcissistic supply includes the relationships, societal status, reputation, possessions, roles, and power a person has used to feed the image of the False Self and make that identity "rich." The False Self is rich with desire, identifications, regrets, resentments, self-loathing, pride, vanity, envy, greed, fear, lust, appetites, and expectations.

A purification period of isolation is needed to wean oneself off of this addiction to narcissistic supply. As a person becomes firmly rooted in the True Self, which is grounded in God, the attachments to external identities begin to loosen. This period of withdrawal is not just spiritual and psychological, it is physical. As you start drawing on your authenticity for safety and security, your brain slowly begins to rewire itself and your nervous system. Your body eventually no longer needs narcissistic supply to regulate itself. This process can take years, even a lifetime. Eventually, you learn that, when your nervous system is triggered, you can work with it. You allow your triggers to become pointers to what still needs to be compassionately examined within you. After a period of detox, instead of avoiding triggers, you use them as teachers.

Slowly, as you gain mastery over your mind and nervous system, you are able to "purchase the whole field." The "field" is your entire body and life resurrected out of your True Self. The price that is paid is the sacrifice of your False Self and its addictions.

We see this detox process, this period of starving all attachments to the False Self, reflected in the few days that Jesus is dead in the tomb between crucifixion and resurrection. It is a time of grief as the old falls away and the previous form dies. When one awakens to the treasure (or pearl) within, there are often feelings of guilt and shame for the behavior of the False Self. There can also be great regret for time that was lost living an inauthentic life. It is the crucifixion process that metabolizes guilt, shame, and regret and transforms that energy into love and compassion for oneself and others.

In the next chapter, Jesus warns about the danger of initiating this process too soon. We will see how it's necessary to sin and to struggle before you can awaken to your True Self. In fact, in many of the world's great spiritual traditions, students traditionally were not allowed to study spirituality until the age of thirty-five. Jesus himself was not initiated into the fullness of his path until around age thirty. There is wisdom in this timing.

We cannot really come to know God except through our suffering and inadequacies, which take time to accumulate and then prepare us to let our False Selves go. Jesus on the cross represents suffering as the path to liberation. We are released from regret, guilt, and shame once we understand that suffering is the portal through which we are freed. Suffering, paradoxically, becomes the grace through which we are saved from ourselves and come to love the world as Jesus does.

> Grace transforms our failings full of dread into abundant, endless comfort . . . our failings full of shame into a noble, glorious rising . . . our dying full of sorrow into holy, blissful life . . . Just as our contrariness here on earth brings us pain,

shame and sorrow, so grace brings us surpassing comfort, glory, and bliss in heaven ... And that shall be a property of blessed love, that we shall know in God, which we might never have known without first experiencing woe.

— **Julian of Norwich**[1]

TWENTY-NINE

PARABLE OF THE WEEDS

Jesus told them another parable: "The kingdom of heaven is like a man who sowed good seed in his field. But while everyone was sleeping, his enemy came and sowed weeds among the wheat, and went away. When the wheat sprouted and formed heads, then the weeds also appeared."

— **Matthew 13:24–26** (NIV)

IN MY EXPERIENCE OF evangelicalism, the explanation I was given for this parable is that the "weeds" represented unbelievers who would be thrown into hell. *No.* This dualistic explanation is both shoddy theology and dehumanizing to those outside the "Christian tribe."

The Parable of the Weeds is adjacent to the Parables of the Hidden Treasure and the Pearl of Great Price. This parable illustrates another layer of complexity of the human heart and psyche. Back in Chapter Three, *The Anatomy of a Seed,* I wrote this: *It is important to note that the embryo, or True Self, cannot survive without the outer shell, or False Self.*

The treacherous journey from the growth on the tree, to the ground, through the brutal elements of nature, and finally burial in the ground would not be possible without the shelter of the outer shell. The embryo would never be able to complete its necessary journey without this protection. Likewise, the flourishing of the True Self would not be possible without the protection of the False Self. It is only once the True Self is ready for *rebirth* that the False Self no longer serves a purpose and must be buried and die. This is the process of *dying to (False) Self.*

Jesus's Parable of the Weeds emphasizes the necessity for both the True Self and the False Self to become firmly established. The human loses awareness of the True Self (*falls asleep*), making it possible for the False Self to establish its defenses and addictive patterns (*sowing the weeds*). Most of us are probably aware of at least some of our unhealthy behaviors, but we are unaware of their origins. We assume we were "born this way." The origins of our behaviors are often elusive to us, until we bring our unhealthy patterns into our conscious awareness and begin to investigate them.

> *The servants asked him, "Do you want us to go and pull them up?"*
>
> *"No," he answered, "because while you are pulling the weeds, you may uproot the wheat with them. Let both grow together until the harvest. At that time I will tell the harvesters: First collect the weeds and tie them in bundles to be burned; then gather the wheat and bring it into my barn."*

— **Matthew 13:28b–29** (NIV)

The natural impulse of humans—which has, to a certain extent, corrupted much of religion—is to circumvent the process of allowing the weeds to grow. Couldn't we skip all the suffering caused by the False Self? Couldn't God extinguish all the pain of the human experience? This parable offers the deeper wisdom: cutting short this process is detrimental to the flourishing of the human psyche and soul. The process must be allowed to unfold with patience and precision.

Religion is often used as an attempt to inhibit the growth of "weeds" through behavior modification. This strategy is misguided. Religion as behavior management is actually a defense mechanism, a system of repression that keeps us in denial that the False Self exists and is running the show.

Historically, Christianity is prone to shaming the defense mechanisms of the False Self. Its focus has been on pulling up the weeds as fast as possible, instead of allowing the weeds that are there to grow until both the True Self and False Self are intact enough to withstand the process of burning.

The man in the parable instructs his servants to allow the weeds to grow. First of all, it is the shell of the False Self that provides the True Self with safety and security in this first phase of life. The human psyche requires this step, or else it cannot move forward to dismantling the shell that has served it. If a solid sense of False Self, or ego, is not firmly established, the human psyche will persist in trying to complete that first step.

I offer a personal example of what this parable is getting at. Within the evangelical church, there is often a large emphasis on service. This might be in the form of volunteering at the church, or perhaps going on a mission trip to another country. Any kind of participation in a service activity is applauded and seen as positive. I often signed up for these sorts of service opportunities. I even committed to overseas missionary work after an emotional session at a youth camp...*when I was twelve years old!* All of the elders in my church experience affirmed these sorts of decisions. They were viewed as "good fruit" by the church and by me.

The problem is, much of what I committed to was not in alignment with my True Self. My False Self was searching for the affirmation of belonging in the tribe. It was searching for personal identity through affiliation with these church groups. I was seeking to prove to God how serious I was about obeying Him and winning as many souls as I could for His kingdom. I wanted to be a standout child of God.

Did I *really* want to leave my family and friends to be a missionary in another country? Probably not. But the invitation had been presented, and the "gospel" was at stake. This was life-and-death! Somebody needed to accept the mission, and so I did. In my eagerness to prove my devotion to God and the church, I committed to so many service projects that they completely drained my energy and eventually sucked the life out of me. This desire to prove myself and gain belonging within the group was a "weed." But it was celebrated as "good fruit." This was all unconscious, of course. But it is an example of how two people, doing the same thing, could have very different motivations. For one, a certain behavior may reflect a weed. For another, the same behavior could be wheat. Personally, I've had to learn to examine my motives closely when I am invited to serve. Am I doing this altruistically? Or am I searching for belonging and significance through an external source?

This personal story is not an indictment of all service activities. It's an illustration of the wisdom in not being too quick to uproot the weeds. Before the wheat and the weeds have had time to grow, they are often indistinguishable. I spent a lot of time in my life calling weeds "wheat." I devoted myself to a lot of things in order to satisfy the longing of my False Self to feel special, unique, and accepted.

Conversely, I repeatedly stifled the wheat in my life, believing it to be a weed. That wheat could've been boundaries on my time and energy. It could've looked like saying a guilt-free "no" to activities that weren't right for me—even if they were marketed as "good for all."

Another personal example in my life of wheat mistaken as weed has been depression. Almost universally, depression is viewed as something negative, especially within the evangelical church. It was an "attack from the enemy," and it felt like a failure on my part when I could not overcome it. I resisted it and would try to combat it. How could depression be anything but a weed to get rid of? However, what I have come to discover is that, for me, depression is a sign that I have fallen asleep to some part of myself. There is some treasure I've buried deep in the field that is calling out to me. The only way for it to get my attention has been through depression, which forces me "down." Now, when I become depressed, I can find the courage to turn towards the dark hole inside of me and look for the buried treasure—some piece of my authentic self that I hid to protect.

As difficult and unpleasant as depression feels, it has served an extremely important purpose in my life. If I'd never been depressed, I would have left parts of my True Self buried and abandoned. What a tragedy! In embracing my depression as a messenger, I have uncovered my wheat, which is my expressive spirit, inquisitive mind, intuition, and strength, all of which were born out of my sensitivity, but often unwelcome in my environment. This wheat was unwelcomed in church and society, and so I tried my hardest to bury it. Depression forced me to turn inwards and dig deep into the field to recover these lost treasures. In each instance, once the depression has served its purpose, it has dissipated.

In evangelicalism, I was taught that the "wheat" referred to Christians and the "weeds" referred to unbelievers. On Judgment Day, the weeds, or unbelievers, would be burned in hell. Beyond being lazy, toxic theology, this reading of the parable further feeds the False Self's need to see itself as "chosen" and special while others will be left behind. It is a distraction from the wisdom in the parable: mainly that the field is *you*. It is your heart and life. You are full of good seeds. But while you've been unconscious, weeds also grew. Both must be allowed to grow so that when you are mature, you can accurately identify and uproot the weeds. Weeds that are too small will simply tear off aboveground, leaving the roots to grow deeper. It is actually easier to spot and pull out weeds that have been allowed to grow. Then the wheat and the weeds can be properly sifted through. Then, only the weeds will be burned.

THIRTY

THE PASCHAL MYSTERY (THE CHRIST MYSTERY)

CHRIST IS THE ONE story, the one pattern, the one mystery of the universe—revealing itself in infinite forms.

The many myths throughout the Bible point to this ultimate mystery and search for truth. The stories seek to help us turn back inward to ourselves, to discover that we've carried the map of the universe within us all along. *The truth sets you free,* because it has always been right there inside of you. Realizing this, you can finally exhale and feel at ease in your body and in the world. The truth has always been exactly where you are—hidden both in you and in nature—although you must first discover it within yourself before you will see it anywhere else. Nature is finally your home, and you can relax into it. This is perhaps most poignantly revealed through the pattern of the life of Jesus, also known as The Paschal Mystery.

The Paschal, or Christ, Mystery is a theological term that refers to the birth, life, death, resurrection and ascension of Jesus. In this one person, the Christ Mystery is contained and fully revealed. It unlocks the ultimate mystery of the universe since the beginning of time and space: life, death, rebirth. This Christ Mystery has been unfolding in every piece of matter from the beginning. It transcends time and space, while also being made manifest in all transient forms. We see it in every part of nature, and we too are a part of nature. It is the substratum just beneath the surface of what we can perceive with our senses.

Jesus is meant to reveal the Christ Mystery—not just in himself, but in everyone and everything. Every death gives way to something new and beautiful, if we can let go and trust the process. The mystery that Jesus reveals is *the one* story of the universe. In the Christ Mystery, all external forms eventually dissolve back into the One. The dissolution, at first, feels tragic. But it is in the dissolution that we discover that who we are is not an impermanent, external form, but the permanent presence that is animating the external form. In other words, we are not our incarnation; we are the presence that is animating this incarnation. This revelation—that our true identity is not in our external form—is liberation. Instead of identifying as the body, which will lose its form, we are affirmed as "the body of Christ." Our finite form, our particular incarnation, has always been a small yet integral part of the larger whole. We are a cell in the body of God. This unveiling ushers in an immediate illumination of our connection to everyone and everything. The boundaries of separateness between God, ourselves, others, and the entire scope of creation are eliminated. The most fundamental part of every piece of the universe is the same.

> The move from seeing the "Body of Christ" as a group of people who believe a certain way to experiencing the "Body of Christ" as the entire universe is the "truth that will set you free."
>
> **— Michael Gungor**[1]

If you picture a tree, it is easy to see that the tree is actually the sum of all its parts. One part alone is not the whole tree. But the tree would not exist without each part. The tree is one, but it is also many. Our mistake is believing that we are somehow separate from the body of God. By ourselves, we are not God. *But God also does not exist without us.* We are a part of the whole. There is no "reaching" God. The limbs do not "reach" the tree. The roots don't "reach" the tree. By their very nature, these parts are a part of the tree. By our very nature, we are a part of God. *God would cease to be "all in all" if God did not include us.*

Death is "defeated," in that it is revealed to be only a step in the evolutionary cycle of form. One way to loosely picture this is imagining water as a solid, liquid, or gas. Water itself is not these forms. Rather, water is the name we give to clusters of H_2O molecules. We are like these water molecules that are constantly shifting forms. When we identify exclusively with the solid form, an ice cube, then it is certainly tragic when the ice cube breaks or melts. The death of the form feels devastating. But, by identifying as the water itself, we understand that it is simply the form of the water, not the water itself, that changes. There is no longer reason to resist or fear death if it is merely a transition to another form.

> *Jesus said to her, "Do not cling to me, for I have not yet ascended to the Father; but go to my brothers and say to them, 'I am ascending to my Father and your Father, to my God and your God.'"*

> **— John 20:17** (ESV)

Jesus emphasizes the futility in identifying with form in his words to Mary at the tomb: *Don't cling to me.* The wisdom here is that the form you try to cling to will remain elusive. It is only by releasing your attachment to forms, or non-attachment, that Christ's presence reveals itself to have always been right here. You discover that you have, and have always had, what you're looking for.

For many of us who grew up with a very literal interpretation of the Bible, literalism and historicity have become an idol. Either Jesus's death and resurrection were historical events—or bust. You may or may not believe the story of Jesus as a historical event, but regardless, the wisdom revealed in the story is the same. Arguing the historicity of a life like Jesus can often end up being sideways energy for both believers and non-believers. The purpose of myth and religion is to reveal these mysteries inside of you and to ground you in the overarching mystery of the cosmos. The symbolic truth that the story of Jesus reveals is eternally true. It was the pattern of the universe before his life, during his life, and after his life. The story of Jesus simply *reveals what has always been true and accessible to every human being who has ever lived.* The living myth contained in the story of Jesus holds the key to liberation for all, regardless of one's belief in its historical accuracy.

Early in my journey out of evangelicalism, I met with a friend named Candi, who I suspected might be on a similar path as me. We had both been leaders in our church. She was a well-known worship leader who had been through her share of tragedy in life. We met for dinner and spent hours unpacking our journeys. I laugh a little bit remembering this, but towards the end of the evening, I felt timid about asking her this question, because it felt so consequential. Finally, I worked up the nerve.

"Do you believe Jesus literally rose from the dead?"
Momentary pause.
What Candi said next blew my mind.
"Does it matter?"

Wow.

I had never even considered that this was a possible answer. "Does it matter?" was the perfect answer. Sure, people have been arguing over this for centuries. But I didn't have to spend my energy thinking about it anymore. I no longer had to stake my faith on my belief in a literal event. The wisdom revealed in the story was enough for me to spend a lifetime contemplating and applying. I could be uncertain about my belief in a literal resurrection and still be enraptured by the Christ Mystery. I had already experienced death and resurrection myself, and I'd come to understand that it's our own journey that is really the point of all this. Transformation came when I acknowledged not just Jesus's wounds, but my own. Perhaps this story was more like a mirror I was meant to see myself in.

I know for me, as a recovering evangelical, that literalism became an idol. I realized that the story of Jesus was true, regardless of if it was a historical event. In fact, the more I treated it as a myth, the more I came to recognize the Paschal Mystery in countless other myths and as an ever-present reality that the entire universe was saturated in. The Jesus myth was a reflection of the Christ Mystery happening all around me, in me, and through me. I saw this pattern in everyone and everything else as well. We live in a sacramental universe which both hides and reflects the ultimate truth about who we truly are. Christ was all in all. *Christ is all that matters, and he lives in all of us (Colossians 3:11). Therefore, we all matter. Everything matters.*

The gate of heaven is everywhere. When we idolize the Bible as literal history, we mistake the gate for the place it leads us to. Jesus is a gate. The rock Jacob dreamed of his ladder was a gate. Moses's burning bush was a gate. The transgender woman on my front porch was a gate. Anything that awakens your consciousness to the presence of Christ is a gate. The gate lets you enter, but you are meant to continue past the gate. *"Don't cling to me,"* Jesus said after his resurrection. Don't cling to a form of Jesus that you can picture concretely in your mind. If you nail him down, you kill him. You kill the life of the story. In letting literalism go, the living spirit in the story becomes available to your life right now. Let Jesus ascend and evaporate into God, becoming one with the source of all life.

This mystery manifests in all, through all, as all. It is the mystery that is the One; it is only the temporal forms of the One that change. Myth, including the story of Jesus, identifies your True Self, like Jesus, with the unchanging One through which you live and move and have your being (Acts 17:28). Your form was birthed from this One, it is sustained by this One, and it dissolves back into the One. You are the offspring of God (Acts 17:28), just as Jesus. His story is your story. This is eternal life. This is the Christ Mystery.

For in him we live and move and have our being. As some of your own poets have said, "We are his offspring."

— **Acts 17:28** (NIV)

The most sacred, riveting, enrapturing moments in my life have been those in which I've felt, "I don't know anything, but I'm fully here right now with everything that I am." I'm standing at the edge of my life looking at the vast mystery of it all, just thinking:

"*Wow.*"

THIRTY-ONE

EAT MY BODY; DRINK MY BLOOD

Jesus said to them, "Very truly I tell you, unless you eat the flesh of the Son of Man and drink his blood, you have no life in you. Whoever eats my flesh and drinks my blood has eternal life, and I will raise them up at the last day. For my flesh is real food and my blood is real drink. Whoever eats my flesh and drinks my blood remains in me, and I in them.

— **John 6:53–56** (NIV)

GOOD RELIGION IS MEANT to facilitate rituals that remind us of our oneness with the whole and with all things. This is not simply a philosophical reality but also a physical one. This ultimate reality is always at work, whether we acknowledge it or not. The purpose of myths and rituals is to shift our awareness towards the understanding of reality *as it actually is,* not as we *perceive* it to be. Of course, each person lives by their own subjective reality, depending on the needs of the False Self. But our subjective reality does not influence *actual reality*. It is our task to identify our subjective reality as distorted and to align our perceptions with ultimate reality, so they flow in harmony together. To bring our inner nature into accordance with Nature itself.

In instructing us to eat his body and drink his blood, Jesus is being pretty frank about the interconnectedness of all things.

In the womb, it is the mother's physical body that creates the baby's body.

It is her nutrients that *become* the baby's body.

Once the baby is born, it is her milk that becomes the baby's body.

Later, it is apples, oranges, chicken, beef, and vegetables that become the child's body.

Within a few hours, whatever food you put in your mouth will literally transform into your human body.

Life feeds on life.

It is in the death of life that life can continue.

And one day, our bodies will go into the ground and feed the soil from which new life grows.

All of life is recycling energy into different forms.

In Luke 8, there is a story about a woman who suffered from chronic bleeding. She touches the hem of Jesus's robe, and immediately Jesus feels the discharge of energy, healing the woman.[1] The woman simply touched an object that Jesus had touched, and his energy transferred to her. Jesus's energy was contained within the robe. The energy from Jesus was able to transfer to the woman because her defenses were not blocking the flow. Her true, authentic self made itself vulnerable and open to receiving. We can infer from this story that any object that Jesus touched contained his energy, but only those who were *poor in Spirit*, or emptied of their baggage, could be filled with it. Christ's energy is always present in the material world, but it cannot be received if it is blocked by the shell of the False Self.

Because of the way gravity holds the earth's atmosphere together, all of the molecules on earth are more or less recycled amongst everyone on the planet. In fact, at any point in time, at least one atom in your lungs can be traced back to any figure in history.[2] To be clear: a molecule of oxygen in your lungs, at some point, passed through the physical lungs of Jesus (or any other given person from the past you could think of). Imagine knowing that you touched something touched by Jesus. Well, you have! You have that molecule infused with Christ in your lungs right now. In a very real, physical way, Jesus's body is creating your body.

Jesus's blood saturated the ground beneath it. His flesh fell to the dirt as it was ripped off. His flesh and blood became soil. The soil was soaked with Divinity. The plants and vegetation that grew from the soil were infused with Divinity. The food eaten from the ground was thus an extension of Jesus's Divine body. When you eat that food, you are very literally eating the Body of Christ. Your body becomes what you eat. You are the Body of Christ. We are all feeding off of one another, and we are all infused with Christ. This is the ever-present reality. The only shift needed is your awareness of this. Once you become aware that you are already *in Christ*, you can welcome all of life as Divine. Everything is revealed as sacred.

From a psychological perspective, just as humans physically need blood flow for life, the blood of Christ represents the "lifeblood" of psychological energy needed to realize the full potential of the True Self. In pouring wine from the cup, Jesus is illustrating the psychological energy that will be poured out of the container of the False Self for the regeneration of the True Self.[3]

> The notion that, by eating the flesh, or particularly by drinking the blood, of another living being, a man absorbs its nature, or life, into his own, as one which appears among primitive peoples in many forms . . . The most notable application of the idea is the rite of blood brotherhood, examples of which are found all over the world. In the simplest form of this rite, two men become brothers by opening their veins and sucking one another's blood. Thenceforth their lives are not two but one . . . In later times we find the conception current that nay food which two men partake together, so that the same substance enters into their flesh and blood, is enough to establish some sacred unity of life between them . . .

— **William Robertson Smith**[4] (1846–1894)[5]

Like grapes being crushed to release wine, it's the crushing of the body (the False Self) that causes the blood to flow, or vital life energy to be released. It is this blood being extracted from the False Self which "washes" or releases the mind from guilt and shame. Once the container of the outer shell, or flesh, has been emptied, the energy that was once used to hold the False Self together is released from the bondage of that container and available to nourish the True Self.

This process is depicted symbolically in the engraving, *Christ in the Wine Press,* where we see the cross bearing down on Jesus. This motif is also sometimes called the mystical winepress in Christian iconography. We see Jesus's body becoming the grapes in the winepress, which are then crushed into wine. His body represents the False Self containing the vital life energy. The False Self must be crushed for the psychic energy to be extracted and able to flow, becoming available for the regeneration of new life.

Christ in the Wine Press by Hieronymus (Jerome) Wierix, c. before 1619 (Metropolitan Museum of Art, New York)

Once a person experiences the vitality of the flow of their own life energy, they recognize this life energy as the basis for all substances, including bread and wine. All food you consume is a communion with the blood of Christ, or this *spirit of life*. All conscious interactions—with people, things, air, laughter, nature, everything—become communion with Christ. Your life becomes one with every other life, reinforcing and fusing our shared identity and uniting individual forms into "one body." Everything in life is animated and saturated with this same spiritual energy. Everything is "one with the Father," extending out from the same source, like branches from a tree. The only thing that's missing is our awareness of this reality.

Extraction of blood, or psychological energy from the False Self, is what brings awareness of this reality, and that psychological process is what Jesus is foreshadowing at the Last Supper. It is from our own personal cups, or individual forms, that we pour out our blood for the "payment of sins." This means that the more repression of the True Self there has been, the more energy must be extracted from the False Self; the more "blood" must be "spilled." The spilling and drinking of your own blood represent the means of your fusion with God. While the suffering of the False Self is largely cyclical and unproductive, this conscious suffering is meaningful. This voluntary sacrifice of the False Self is the suffering that brings peace and regeneration of life. In *Ego and Archetype*, Edward F. Edinger explains that "... *Christ sacrificed himself in order to extract or make manifest his spiritual essence...*" [6] The spiritual essence of Christ is the Holy Spirit, which was released by the death of Jesus's body and spread out "to the ends of the earth."[7] We, too, must make the voluntary sacrifice of our False Selves in order to release the spiritual essence of our True Selves into the world.

Communion is not a sentimental remembrance of a one-time event 2,000 years ago. It is an active participation in eating, swallowing, digesting, and transmuting the physical body of Jesus. Every cell and molecule has been in-fused with Christ and is perpetually recycled on the planet. This meditation gives way to the realization that all of creation has been infused with Divinity since the beginning of time. Christ is incarnate in all. It is the renewing of your mind, aligning with this knowledge, that transforms your entire being into the likeness of Christ, revealing the mystery of your very existence.

> *For God wanted them to know that the riches and glory of Christ are for you Gentiles, too. And this is the secret: Christ lives in you. This gives you assurance of sharing his glory.*

— **Colossians 1:27** (NLT)

Each of us are not the entire One, but also not apart from the One. We are all one body. We are all one family. The universe is the Body of Christ, and you've always been a part of it. There is nothing to escape, other than the idea that you have ever been separate from God. The bread, the wine, Jesus's body, and our bodies are one body. To become "like Christ" is to become aware of what already is, and then to willingly participate in that reality. As Fr. Richard Rohr puts it, "A mature Christian sees Christ in everything and everyone else."[8]

Christ was fully illuminated in Jesus. Christ is what draws us to Jesus. Christ is present in every atom of creation. Christ is hidden in all physical matter, including you. Christ is present in all, and fully revealed in the beating and bleeding heart of Jesus.

> *Through him all things were made; without him nothing was made that has been made... He was in the world, and though the world was made through him, the world did not recognize him. He came to that which was his own, but his own did not receive him.*

— **John 1:3; 10–11** (NIV)

THIRTY-TWO

FATHER, SON, & MOTHER SPIRIT

As verily as God is our Father, so verily God is our Mother.

— **Julian of Norwich**[1]

BY AFFIRMING BREAD AND wine as a physical extension of his body, Jesus is affirming the presence of God in all of nature. Christ is the One. But we discover the One expressing itself through the endless manifestations of form in nature.

In Chapter Seven, *The Two Become One Flesh*, I discussed the word for Spirit: *Rúach* (spirit) and *Rúach Hakodesh* (spirit-the-holy) are feminine nouns. The Bible reveals Jesus as being not only filled with this feminine Spirit, but also supported and held by feminine figures—whereby we come to understand that Mother Nature herself is the hiding place of God.

Most of the women mentioned in Jesus's story are named Mary, although there are others. In the context of myth, these feminine figures represent archetypes of the feminine nature of God. In different contexts and roles, we see women not just serving Jesus, but mothering him—from birth, through death, until resurrection. They are not just nice trimmings on the Jesus story. They are essential in ushering Jesus through his entire journey of self-realization.

It is Eve who hides the True Self in the womb of the False Self, so that the embryo can survive its fall from unitive consciousness. *Mother God protects.*

It is Mary who carries Jesus in her womb and births him. *Mother God bears all things.*

It is Mary who breastfeeds baby Jesus. *Mother God nurtures.*

It is Mary who raises Jesus as a child. *Mother God guides.*

It is Mary who searches for Jesus in Jerusalem. *Mother God pursues.*

It is the Holy Spirit who descends upon Jesus. *Mother God fills.*

It is women who help Jesus as he travels. *Mother God sustains.*

It is Mary who anoints Jesus for death. *Mother God initiates.*

It is women who cry for Jesus on the road to Calvary. *Mother God pleads for you.*

It is Mary who accompanies Jesus at the cross. *Mother God suffers with you.*

It is Mary who stays at the cross. *Mother God never leaves or forsakes you.*

It is Mary who holds Jesus's dead body in her arms when he is taken off the cross. *Mother God grieves for you.*

It is Mary who oversees Jesus's burial. *Mother God watches over you.*

It is Mother Earth who swallows Jesus for three days. *Mother God holds you in her womb.*

It is Mary who keeps vigil at the tomb. *Mother God tethers you with her love across space and time.*

It is Mary who prepares spices to anoint Jesus's dead body. *Mother God dignifies you.*

It is Mary who first recognizes the risen Christ. *Mother God sees you.*

> *But the fruit of the Spirit is love, joy, peace, forbearance, kindness, goodness, faithfulness, gentleness and self-control. Against such things there is no law.*

— **Galatians 5:22–23** (NIV)

It is our own True Self that bears this distinctly feminine fruit of the spirit. It is also the discovery of Mother God in nature that allows us to trust the process that is unfolding within us and beyond us. We can finally trust that creation is good. We can relax in the certitude that we are held by a loving Mother. Any true experience of God will eventually yield to this revelation. We can even trust in death as a return to the womb of God. There is simply nowhere we can go that she is not holding us inside her.

In 2015, Christian music singer Chris Tomlin released a worship song called "Good Good Father."[2] It was a wildly successful song and reflects the nearly-exclusively father-driven picture many evangelical churches hold of God. But the coexisting reality of God as Mother has remained, albeit largely unacknowledged. It's simply been relegated to the individual and collective unconscious. But we cannot heal ourselves as individuals, nor our societies, until we embrace the entire Trinity of God, three in one: Father, Son and Mother Spirit. This is the model for all of reality, operating in every cell, every atom, and every particle which we cannot yet measure. It is in embracing this reality *as it is* that ushers us into the fullness of life. It is from Mother God that the Christ child is born. It is in her that we see the masculine child held in the womb of the feminine mother. The Christ child is then birthed into the womb of Mother Earth. The physical and spiritual are brought together in an infinite cycle of consummation between masculine and feminine, birthing us from one ever-expansive womb into the next. Heaven and earth forever becoming the One. When we finally say "yes" to this reality, as Mary, we discover the femininity of our own souls as well. The two (body and soul) become one again.

*A Quiet Moment by Timothy P. Schmalz. Located at
Ignatius House in Atlanta, Georgia*

THIRTY-THREE

THE KINGDOM OF HEAVEN IS WITHIN YOU

. . . for He has prepared us to become fully human [Anthropos].

— **The Gospel of Mary**, Chapter 5, Verse 3[1]

IN HER BOOK, *THE Meaning of Mary Magdalene*, Cynthia Bourgeault illuminates the sacred symbol of the *Anthropos* represented by Jesus. She gives a modern translation for the Greek word *Anthropos,* which is often translated as "human." However, it carries more weight than simply "human" or "humanity." Although it is a gender-inclusive word, it goes beyond androgyny. Bourgeault translates *Anthropos* to mean "fully human" or a "completed human being."[2] It includes both the masculine and the feminine in itself, but is beyond simply the bringing together of the opposites. Jesus, representing the *Anthropos*, symbolizes the fully complete human being—the highest potential for individuals and humanity.

Jesus said to them, "When you make the two into one, and when you make the inner like the outer and the outer like the inner, and the upper like the lower, and when you make male and female into a single one, so that the male will not be male nor the female be female . . . then you will enter [the kingdom]."

— **Gospel of Thomas**, Saying 22[3]

Jesus is the picture of a masculine body infused with a feminine Holy Spirit. He is the picture of a perfect integration of all the opposites, both personally in a finite human body, and cosmically in an infinite spirit. By bringing together the vertical with the horizontal in a cruciform reconciliation, his cross gives way to a circle—the symbol of completion. He is the picture of the One, out of which the opposites arise and within which they are contained.

I am the Alpha and the Omega, the First and the Last, the Beginning and the End. "Blessed are those who wash their robes, that they may have the right to the tree of life and may go through the gates into the city."

— **Revelation 22:13–14** (NIV)

In the very beginning of Genesis, we find God introduced as the One that includes the opposites, both masculine and feminine:

In the beginning God (Elohim [masculine]) created the heavens and the earth. Now the earth was formless and empty, darkness was over the surface of the deep, and the Spirit of God (Rúach Hakodesh [feminine]) was hovering over the waters...

Then God said, "Let us make man in our image, in our likeness..."

And the Lord God said, "The man has now become like one of us, knowing good and evil."

— **Genesis 1:1–2; 26a; 3:22a** (NIV)

In the beginning, the opposites are contained *within* the One God. "Our" is contained in the One God. The opposites are born out of the One, and also contained in it. To the uninitiated, the opposites—male and female, conscious and unconscious, heavens and earth—*appear* to be in stark contrast with each other. But Jesus, on the cross, reveals this perception to be flawed and incomplete. What has appeared as opposite and incompatible is reassembled in an integration of the opposites within his finite body and the universe as well. Leonardo Da Vinci depicts this in his famous drawing of the *Vitruvian Man*:

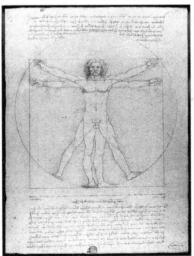

Vitruvian Man by Leonardo Da Vinci, c. 1490

Creator of one of the most famous and iconic images in the world, Da Vinci posited "the human body to be an analogy, in microcosm, for the workings of the universe."[4] He envisaged the great picture chart of the human body he had produced through his anatomical drawings and *Vitruvian*

Man as a *cosmografia del minor mondo* ("cosmography of the microcosm"). He believed the workings of the human body to be an analogy, in microcosm, for the workings of the universe. He correlated the symmetry of the human body with the symmetry of the universe.

> For you must realize that earth unfolds its properties and pow-
> ers in union with Heaven aloft above us, and there is one
> Heart, one Being, one Will, one God, all in all.

— **Jacob Boehme**[5] (1575–1624)[6]

This symmetry is precisely reflected in the image of Jesus. A human in-cluding, yet beyond, gender; reflecting and transmitting the divine truth of the universe. This is what it means to be "fully human." All the knowledge and wisdom of the universe can be discovered inside of you.

The kingdom of God is within you.

— **Luke 17:21b**

Adam and Eve were not created separately, but instead Eve was taken out of Adam. The entire creation myth is about separating opposites from within the One. The light and dark were pulled apart from each other. The sky was pulled out of the water. The land was pulled out of the water. The vegetation was pulled up from the land, the animals were pulled up from the dust of the earth, and so on. This myth depicts the many coming out of the One, and the individual and cosmic yearning to realize our oneness.

The symbol of Jesus is quite satisfying to the psyche, but most do not understand why, because they see Jesus as something separate and beyond themselves, rather than a reflection of themselves and their deepest yearning to be whole and part of the One. In falling in love with Jesus, what we actually love is Christ within us, pulling us towards our final destiny—a realization of ourselves as the Anthropos, fully human. Crucified, yet alive. Finite, yet infinite. Particular, yet universal. Our nature at one with God's nature.

The "kingdom of heaven" is not something lying "above the earth" or coming "after death." It does not have a yesterday or a day after tomorrow, and it will not arrive in a "thousand years." It is an experience of the heart. It is everywhere and it is nowhere. [Edited excerpt]

— **Friedrich Nietzsche**[7] (1844–1900)[8]

PART III

CREATING HEAVEN ON EARTH

THIRTY-FOUR

CARRY YOUR CROSS

WHAT DOES "CARRY YOUR cross" actually mean? With a broader mythical understanding of Jesus, it is easier to make sense of his teachings.

> *Then he said to them all: "Whoever wants to be my disciple must deny themselves and take up their cross daily and follow me. For whoever wants to save their life will lose it, but whoever loses their life for me will save it. What good is it for someone to gain the whole world, and yet lose or forfeit their very self?"*

— **Luke 9:23–25** (NIV)

The "self" Jesus is referencing at the end of this passage is the True Self. The "life" a person seeks to save is the life identified with the False Self. It is that life, created through identification with the False Self to survive and maintain attachment in the world, that must be crucified to make way for eternal life to flow from the True Self. The True Self is who is "in Christ." To save your life is to let your True Self become fully human, at one with God.

Atonement, or "at-one-ment", with God refers to the process of acknowledging the ways in which we have betrayed our True Self. Our true nature is love, which is rooted in God. Our True Self is an extension of the great "I Am." To carry your cross is to consent to the process of bearing your specific wounds and allowing them to transform you. *It is your individual psychological healing process.* In Western Christianity, the nearly exclusive focus is on the suffering of Jesus. But carrying your own cross requires that you turn inward and fully experience your own sufferings. This process is about you, allowing your suffering to transform you and release you from the addictions that bind your True Self from coming forth into the flesh.

Beginning very early in our lives, we experience psychological, emotional, and relational wounds. The wounds inflicted are often unintentional. They are not necessarily caused by someone or something that happened. The wounds sometimes develop in response to our environment simply not mirroring or "seeing" who we really are on the inside. The function of the False Self is to protect us from the pain of those wounds.

We usually associate the word *narcotic* with drugs. For instance, a dentist may narcotize a tooth before filling a cavity. A narcotic dulls pain and puts a part of the body to sleep. The False Self's psychological process of "putting oneself to sleep," or narcotization, is essential for survival. Psychological numbing is how children cope with overwhelming pain. But it also numbs us to the awareness of our True Selves and leads to addiction. To feel the pain of one's wounds in full before one is ready can completely overwhelm the nervous system. The crucifixion process requires you to allow yourself to feel the full impact of your own pain. It is consenting to allow your wounds to pierce your heart. This is what transforms your heart from stone to flesh. There is no escaping the pain now. There is no more stone to protect it. You finally let go of your defenses and allow your heart wounds to bleed.

Jesus did not take your place on the cross. He "saves" you, in that he clarifies what you must do to save yourself. He clarifies, for your mind, your "at-one-ment" with God and everyone else. This correction in perception illuminates the personal path you must walk to align your outer life with the truth of your newfound inner reality.

Fully experiencing your own personal pain brings one into solidarity with the suffering and pain of others. How can we have compassion, or "suffer with" others, if we cannot feel our own pain? Our crucifixion involves not only experiencing our own pain, but also looking at those suffering on the crosses to our right and left. One who is on their cross always finds themselves suffering along with others. Compassion is dying on our own cross and suffering alongside others on their crosses. Compassion completely equalizes humanity. There is not one who escapes this pain. *But we can only suffer our own pain. Others must bear their own suffering.* We finally see that the only way out is *through,* and somehow "suffering with" the other becomes the plot. In being fully present with ourselves and others, in staying with the pain, we become fully alive, because we're present with the totality of life—the light and the dark.

I should mention that this psychological healing process can be extremely intense. Feeling your pain and "dying to self" necessarily involves fear and grief. Many of us have been conditioned to avoid grief. It is natural to try to avoid pain. If we aren't accustomed to allowing our pain, the anxiety of that process can be overwhelming to the nervous system. The process involves detoxing from the personal addictive defenses that have numbed you from your pain. It is often advisable to walk through this process with the support of a professional therapist. Part of the healing is working to recognize when you need help and learning to receive it. Offering compassion to yourself may look like allowing trusted people to support you on your journey, as you slowly learn to tolerate more and more of your own pain without numbing yourself through defense mechanisms.

Carrying your cross is the process of "fixing your pipes" psychologically, so that the spirit of God can flow freely through your heart. The Greek word for "repent" is *metanoia,* meaning "to change your mind" or to go beyond the mind. As we have already seen, the "mind" is the False Self, which must be firmly established before it can be changed. With very few exceptions, the process of metanoia can only happen after the False Self is firmly established in adulthood. A tree can only grow out of a firmly established seed. The intersection of the horizontal and vertical beams of the cross is right at the point of the human heart. In the *Acts of Peter* (which is one of five early Christian texts recounting the lives of the apostles), while Peter was being crucified, he explained parts of the cross from which he was hanging, including "the nail which holds the cross beam to the upright in the middle." This nail is "the conversion and repentance [metanoia] of man."[1]

Your individual suffering intersects with the suffering of all. You no longer look up at Jesus suffering from the foot of the cross. You *look out from the cross* through the eyes of Christ. You become the temple through which God sees, hears, loves, and heals the world. By allowing your personal suffering to transform you, you participate in the suffering of Christ—which is the suffering of the world—because it is Christ who suffers in all who suffer, which is everyone.

THE ENNEAGRAM

I will not go into great detail on this, but I have found the Enneagram to be one of the most useful tools available to identify your specific "cross." In brief, the Enneagram is a system that identifies nine "types" of people. Each person emerges from childhood with one of the nine types of personality structures, or False Selves. Each type has a "core wound" resulting in the disconnection from the True Self. The core wound fuels the specific "flavor" of suffering created by each of the nine types. The suffering distorts that type's perception of reality, leading to their "sin" and predictable addictive behaviors. The addictions are the False Self's attempt to reconnect with the True Self and live out of that authentic essence. This can never be accomplished from the dualistic perspective of the False Self. It is a compulsive attempt to achieve something that almost works, but never quite does, thus fueling the addiction.

The Enneagram also identifies the specific gifts and hidden essences of each type. The person who has done the psychological work of carrying their cross and dying to the False Self will embody the specific gifts and reveal the essence of the True Self associated with their type. The Enneagram serves as a road map for the individual: first, to first identify and observe how the False Self is operating within; second, to work to psychologically separate from the False Self; and finally, to recover and integrate the True Self and embody its gifts.

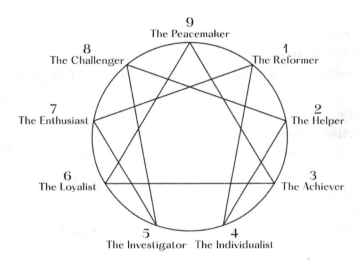

Type One: *The Reformer*
Addiction of the False Self: *Anger leading to Resentment*
True Self Expression of Essence: *Divine Integrity, Perfection, Brilliance*

Type Two: *The Helper*
Addiction of the False Self: *Pride (Self-denial) leading to Flattery*
True Self Expression of Essence: *Divine Will, Compassion, Humility*

Type Three: *The Achiever*
Addiction of the False Self: *Vanity leading to Deceit*
True Self Expression of Essence: *Divine Hope, Truthfulness, Creativity*

Type Four: *The Individualist*
Addiction of the False Self: *Envy leading to Melancholy*
True Self Expression of Essence: *Divine Beauty, Depth, Equanimity*

Type Five: *The Investigator*
Addiction of the False Self: *Avarice (Greed) leading to Stinginess*
True Self Expression of Essence: *Divine Understanding, Transparency, Non-Attachment*

Type Six: *The Loyalist*
Addiction of the False Self: *Fear leading to Cowardice*
True Self Expression of Essence: *Divine Faith, Trust, Courage*

Type Seven: *The Enthusiast*
Addiction of the False Self: *Gluttony leading to Planning*
True Self Expression of Essence: *Divine Joy, Wisdom, Sobriety*

Type Eight: *The Challenger*
Addiction of the False Self: *Lust leading to Vengeance*
True Self Expression of Essence: *Divine Truth, Power, Innocence*

Type Nine: *The Peacemaker*
Addiction of the False Self: *Sloth leading to Indolence (psychological laziness; self-erasure)*
True Self Expression of Essence: *Divine Love, Harmony, Right Action*

A more detailed explanation of the Enneagram is beyond the scope of this book. However, I've found it to be a valuable tool to bring specificity to what can seem like an abstract concept: the specific characteristics of one's True Self and False Self. Resources that expound upon the Enneagram in much more detail include: *The Wisdom of the Enneagram* by Don Richard Riso and Russ Hudson, *The Enneagram: A Christian Perspective* by Richard Rohr, *The Instinctual Drives and the Enneagram* by John Luckovich, *The Spiritual Dimension of the Enneagram* by Sandra Maitri, and *Keys to the Enneagram* and *Facets of Unity* by A.H. Almaas. There are other resources as well, but I have personal engagement with these works. You can also read more about the types online at EnneagramInstitute.com[2] and Enneagram mer.com.[3]

"Carrying your cross" is specific to you and your individual psychological wounding. The Enneagram brings precision to the texture and features of the True Self and False Self, and provides a map of the "Road to Calvary."

It is a tool for bringing clarity and can help you identify your False Self, so you can begin the process of moving beyond its constraints—in other words, *metanoia*.

THIRTY-FIVE

FORGIVENESS IS TRANSMUTING ENERGY

Does *FORGIVENESS* FEEL LIKE a loaded word to you? In my estimation, the concept of forgiveness is poorly understood. It is often manipulated to perpetuate toxic situations and relationships. It's important to bring clarity to what forgiveness is, and what it isn't.

Perhaps the most essential task in detaching from the False Self is forgiveness. There is a misconception that forgiveness is "letting it go," but that's not accurate. Forgiveness involves transmuting energy. I'm using the word *transmute* instead of *transform* for a specific purpose. *Transmute* specifically implies a transformation to something *higher or more precious*—such as, in the metaphorical process of alchemy, converting lead to gold. It's not correct to say that the lead is "let go of." In fact, the energy of one substance is taken and transformed into a new substance. Energy—whether physical or psychological—cannot be created or destroyed. What is "let go of" is attachment to the form that contains the energy.

Another misconception about forgiveness is that it has to involve reconciliation. This is also untrue. Reconciliation is a restoration of a relationship. The work of reconciliation is separate from forgiveness. It is not a prerequisite for forgiveness at all. Reconciliation should only be on the table if, first, the perpetrator of the hurt is no longer engaging in harmful or abusive behavior; and, second, the victim wants to reconcile the relationship. As demonstrated by Jesus, he forgave many people who he did not reconcile with. His life was marked by strong boundaries. The pressure to reconcile can actually be an impediment to forgiveness, if it means that a person must continue subjecting themselves to harm.

The purpose of forgiveness is to release you into internal freedom. Sometimes the process of your forgiveness is a catalyst for others to heal; sometimes not. But the main purpose is *your* personal transformation, and that's where the focus should be. *You are not responsible for any other person or their healing.*

Unforgiveness is sometimes necessary when harm and abuse is ongoing. It allows a person to defend against the harm. In order to forgive, it is usually necessary for a person to be out of harm's way. It is difficult to feel your pain when you are still in survival mode. Physical, emotional, and psychological distance creates the space needed to stop defending oneself from harm and to sift through the pain it caused.

Unforgiveness, however, requires a significant amount of energy. Maintaining anger and resentment requires your body to generate an energetic response each time the offense or offending person comes to mind. It may even be a seemingly-unrelated trigger that reminds the brain of the offense. An example might be resenting someone for a past humiliation in public. One might feel rage toward one's child when he throws a fit in public. In reality, the child is simply immature and overwhelmed by emotion. The child is dealing with that overwhelm in the only way they know: by crying and screaming. However, this may unconsciously trigger the parent's unresolved feelings of humiliation and anger, rooted in a past wound, which are then directed towards the child. Strong emotional reactions that are out of proportion with the present situation are often signals of unresolved wounds and unforgiveness. These types of emotional reactions require a lot of energy from the body.

Each person has a fixed amount of energy available to them in their bodies. However, when the False Self is intact and maintained by unforgiveness, a significant amount of available energy is spent replaying the story of the offense, consciously or unconsciously (as demonstrated by the example with the parent and child). You may spend a lot of mental energy consciously ruminating about a person or situation. Or you may actively try to avoid thinking about the person or situation at all. Sometimes it is both. You may obsess over a relatively small offense from an acquaintance, while avoiding confronting the real injury inflicted by a loved one or life circumstance. Rumination and repression consume a substantial amount of energy.

The key to forgiveness is in knowing that you can only heal what you're willing to feel. When it comes to forgiveness, pain is going to surface, and you must be willing to feel your pain all the way through, until your anger gives way to the grief underneath it. As demonstrated by Jesus on the cross, with forgiveness, something must die. Grief follows death. So, you must consent to experiencing grief.

You must also consent to feeling your shame if you're forgiving yourself. This process is not quick, easy, or painless. But it is essential. You can't just "get over" your pain or leave it in the past. You have to bring it into the present, feel it, and work your way through it. Forgiveness is like a surgery with no anesthesia. You are both the doctor with the scalpel and the patient on the table. *It's going to hurt.*

Even if we understand the need to bring up past wounds to heal, it's often difficult to access the emotions underneath our anger. Here are just a few suggestions to help you begin to feel your emotions and bring them to the surface. These take practice: meditation, mindfulness, yoga, journaling, making lists of grievances against a person, going to therapy. EMDR therapy is particularly effective in helping to access buried emotions from the past and reprocessing the feelings in a healthy way. More and more mental health counselors are becoming trained in EMDR.

Emotional pain cannot just be left in the past. It is an energy that buries itself deep into our cells. It causes *dis*-ease in the body, and often outwardly manifests with physical symptoms. Through the grief process, this energy is transformed into love and compassion. All of your cells respond to this, and your body becomes lighter, more at ease, and more luminous.

What I'm describing is actually physiological. Grief leads us to the point of futility—the point at which our brains register that what we are trying to hold onto or do is impossible. Only when our brains register futility can we experience the disappointment and sadness that follow, and then our brains can adapt. This process is described by Dr. Gordon Neufeld and Dr. Gabor Maté in the book *Hold On to Your Kids*:

> Futility must sink in for the energy shift to occur, the shift that leads to acceptance, from frustration to a sense of peace with how things are. It is not enough to register it intellectually, it must be felt deeply and vulnerably, in the very heart of the limbic system, at the core of the brain's emotional circuitry...
>
> One of the most obvious signs of futility sinking in is the eyes watering...
>
> When futility registers emotionally, signals are sent to the lacrimal glands resulting in the eyes watering. These tears are different from the tears of frustration...
>
> The tears of futility are set off by different neurological circuitry and are psychologically unique. They feel different on our cheeks. They are accompanied by a shift in energy: a healthy sadness, a backing-off from trying to change things. Tears of futility actually bring a release, a sense that something has to come to an end. They signal that the brain truly apprehends that something is not working and must be let go of...
>
> But if tears of futility never come, adaptation will not occur. Whether our eyes water or not, the most common feelings of futility are sadness, disappointment and grief.

> **— Dr. Gordon Neufeld and Dr. Gabor Maté**[1]

When someone is emotionally stuck in unforgiveness, instead of feeling sadness and disappointment, often there is sarcasm and contempt, an inability to move from mad to sad. Unfortunately, our culture often sends the message that tears are shameful. Humans will do almost anything to avoid feeling grief and shame.

> When we stop crying, it's as if the brain's capacity to process emotions—normally quite flexible and responsive—becomes rigid. It loses its plasticity, its ability to develop. Without futility, as without satiation, maturation is impossible.

> **— Dr. Gordon Neufeld and Dr. Gabor Maté**[2]

Forgiveness is the portal through which spiritual rebirth can happen. It is the point at which resentment is transmuted into compassion. A grievance is a grief that you're holding onto. In order to forgive, you must let go of your grief—that is, grieve. As Christ demonstrates on the cross, the point at which you forgive, when you allow your grievance to empty from your body through grief, is the point at which you die to yourself and are buried. This is when spiritual rebirth (resurrection) happens. A seed must be buried and die in the ground to give birth to new life. So it is with us.

Although reconciliation in a relationship is not always possible (especially if that person will not respect the boundaries you've set), you will know you have forgiven the person who hurt you when you no longer resent them and you feel peace about the past. You will know, when you feel compassion and empathy for that person, and can recognize the depth of their own pain that they projected onto you. Oftentimes, we not only need to forgive others, but ourselves. Forgiving yourself allows you to offer love, kindness, and compassion to yourself as well.

> There is nothing that cannot be forgiven, and there is no one undeserving of forgiveness.

> **— Archbishop Desmond Tutu**[3]

"Father, forgive them, for they do not know what they are doing" (Luke 23:34) is the posture of a person, Jesus, hanging from a cross, who understands that people inflict their own pain on others in an attempt to expel it from their bodies. It is the posture of someone who understands that pain, not transformed, is instead transmitted—because energy cannot simply cease to exist. It can only change form. It is an understanding that we are all victims of other victims in one way or another. This knowledge allows the heart to open to compassion for the suffering of all victims—ourselves and others, including perpetrators. Forgiveness does not eliminate responsibility or accountability for harm done. It does extend unconditional compassion to all. Perpetrators have experienced their own victimization. It is essential to acknowledge the whole scope of an individual and to allow their entire story to exist in the light. We must have the courage to look into the dark, keep our eyes open, and have the humility to withhold judgment. I have personally found that those who have forgiven the greatest atrocities are the least judgmental.

Compassion is the heart's most natural state, and therefore, compassion allows the body to use energy most efficiently. Aligning yourself with love transmutes the energy of unforgiveness, utilized to keep the False Self intact, into the energy of compassion, which services the flourishing of the True Self. Unforgiveness can be visualized as lead; compassion as gold. It is this golden energy that grows the True Self from an embryo into a Tree of Life. Our energy is no longer used to nurse old wounds. It is now efficiently channeled to nourish the growth of our True Self. This is the fullness of life. It's the harnessing of all your energy for your good, the good of others, and the good of the world.

Jesus did not die to do this work for you. He died to show you that this was possible for every human, because *he was human*. His final message on the cross was that forgiveness for the entire world is the last gate into heaven. Not one resentment will be able to slide in. You must die the same way you were born: free of resentment, free of guilt, free of shame, full of compassion and love. This is how you are "saved by the cross."

What is a follower of Jesus but one who seeks to die with nothing but love left in their heart? Offering the mercy of forgiveness to myself first, for the dreadful pain I've caused myself and others. Then for all, even those who've caused me tremendous pain. And finally, to forgive life itself for the anguish of suffering, which I cannot blame on anyone. I wish to die with no record of wrongs in my heart. I wish to have let it all go, and to have let the lightness of grace and peace lift my soul to eternal rest. I wish to travel lightly in this life, holding onto nothing, especially the heavy load of resentment. I must surrender to my own sacrifice on my cross, laying at the altar my offering—the parts that I used to build my personal prison—until all that's left of me is love.

> To avoid being angry with individuals, you must pardon the whole mass, you must grant forgiveness to the entire human race.
>
> — **Seneca**[4] (c. 4 BC–65 AD)

THIRTY-SIX

THE WORD MADE FLESH

And the Word was made flesh and dwelt among us . . .

— **John 1:14** (KJV)

JUST AS CHRIST WAS present in Jesus, Christ is present in all flesh. When we live out this realization, the *Word is made flesh*. The Word dwells both among those who can see and those who cannot.

The intersecting beams of the cross can be imagined as representations of your true nature as one beam and Nature itself as the other. Imagine each beam having a hole through its center. Once these holes are brought into alignment with each other, a nail can be perfectly slid through both holes, connecting the two beams in an intersection of the X- and Y-axes. The nail creates the Z-axis. The holes of the X- and Y-axes must be perfectly aligned before the nail of the Z-axis can fasten them together. The nail, then, represents a manifestation of the divine principle, which expresses itself through your life. The light enters through that point in the center. This is the *Word made flesh*. The Divine can now achieve its full incarnation in you. You become an instrument of God—a living temple. Your presence, by itself, brings forth the presence of God. You make visible the Source, which is otherwise invisible. Your life becomes a microcosm of the macrocosm, like Da Vinci's *Vitruvian Man*. You function as a mediator, or bridge, between two worlds.

VIVE ✲ JÉSUS!

VOILÀ CE CŒUR QUI A TANT AIMÉ LES HOMMES

IL N'EST QU'AMOUR ET MISÉRICORDE!

VENEZ TOUS A MOI....
Vous qui êtes fatigués et affligés
et je vous soulagerai *Math XI.28.*

Partout où cette image sera exposée et honorée elle y attirera
toutes sortes de bénédictions ... N S.à la B Marg. Marie.

IMP.TURGIS & FILS. PARIS

Catholic Holy Card depicting the Sacred
Heart of Jesus by Turgis, c. 1880

The Sacred Heart of Jesus, one of the well-known Catholic devotions, illuminates this principle. It illustrates the long-suffering love and compassion of the heart of Christ towards humanity. The lance pierces through the center of the heart. The ever-burning fire is generated by the source of our existence. The True Self is the portal for the eternal fire, which burns off the illusions of the False Self. It is Christ which is the *Word of God*. Christ, the Word, is the "undifferentiated yet everywhere particularized substratum of being."[1] This Word was transmitted through the person of Jesus, and this symbol represents the complete self-realization of sacred humanity. In order to realize this ultimate truth in your own life, it is essential to recognize the eternal omnipresence of Christ as having manifested fully in the particular, temporal person of Jesus. Jesus Christ is a *particular* manifestation of the *eternal* Christ. Jesus Christ represents those two realities respectively.

In evangelicalism, one is often encouraged to "become like Jesus." The problem here is that, in striving to imitate Jesus, one often divests from their own particular incarnation. You become "like Jesus" by realizing *your True Self*. Likewise, your True Self becomes a *particular* manifestation of the *eternal Christ*. Your body is the instrument of potential, through which Christ transmits love and expression in the world. Every human is fundamentally sacred and carries this seed of potential for complete realization of the True Self. However, it requires the consent of the individual for the process of realization to unfold. It is through individuals that give their "yes" to this path that the vital energies of the Divine come forth into the world. It is through our True Self that the Divine flows into the domain of the human psyche and pierces through the comprehensions of the mind, or False Self, which ardently resists this process for fear of annihilation.

Redemption consists of a return to identification with your True Self as Christ, and letting Christ animate your life. Jesus was completely self-affirming and demonstrated how we can have the courage to affirm our True Selves as well. The True Self understands Christ to be the source and natural trajectory of all forms, like a seed to a tree. Understanding this truth elevates everyone and everything, rather than certain individuals, to a sacred status, worthy of reverence. A mother adores all her children. The redeemed, therefore, become extraordinary in their ability to fully inhabit the ordinary. *They are like a burning bush: to the untrained eye, just a part of the background of life. To those who can see: quietly ablaze.*

There is nowhere to go to seek God any longer, for God is right here in the fullness of this moment. God is the source generating this very moment and all the forms of life in it. Our shared fundamental identity with Jesus in no way diminishes Jesus. The love we feel for him is now felt for all of creation, and we sense the presence of that love in every form. Loving every member of the one family increases, not diminishes, our love for Jesus.

We also revere Jesus and any other human who has walked the arduous path of self-realization. We hold these individuals in high esteem as role models that reflect our divinity to us, and that inspire us to realize our true nature and our highest potential. Identity in Christ does not curtail the work.

The Word must be *made* flesh. Christ must be made manifest in the world through your True Self. There is no shortcut to becoming who you are. There is no shortcut to a seed becoming a tree. The path must be walked, and no one else can walk it for you.

Our own sacred spiritual heart, at the intersection of our cross, is the portal through which God comes down and the human ascends. The mythological picture of Jesus on the cross represents both God and Man dying for one another. In this cruciform intersection of heaven and earth, God is now lowly, and Man is now raised. They sacrifice themselves to one another, so that each may live together as one. "Why hast thou forsaken me?" is the agonizing realization that God was not "up there", but *in here. In our hearts.* Resurrection is the lifting of the consciousness to understand that we were always *in here with God,* too. It is Christ who suffers this agonizing passion within us. It is Christ who bears the pangs of this birth of new realization in our bodies. In us, through our crucifixion of consciousness, the Word becomes fully flesh.

God will become visible as God's image is reborn in you.

— **St. Bernard of Clairvaux** (c. 1090–1153)[2]

THIRTY-SEVEN

JESUS IN DISGUISE

Seeking the face of God in everything, everyone, all the time,
and his hand in every happening; this is what it means to be
contemplative in the heart of the world. Seeing and adoring
the presence of Jesus, especially in the lowly appearance of
bread, and in the distressing disguise of the poor.

— St. Mother Teresa[1]

IN THIS QUOTE, MOTHER Teresa eloquently illustrates the paradox of seeing through "the eyes of Christ." The people she served clearly were not literally Jesus of Nazareth. But they *were* literally Christ. We are all one, but we are differentiated within the One. Mother Teresa saw every*one* as the One, or Christ as *All in All* (Colossians 3:11).

The task in the first half of life, when our psyche is constructing the False Self, is to solidify a sense of separation, so that our False Self can remain intact and protect the precious seed that it carries within. In order to do this, we must "self-forget." We must remove our awareness of Christ within, and instead project that awareness onto an object outside of ourselves. That outside object becomes a deity, to which we transfer our love and sacred devotion. The moment Jesus asks God, "Why hast thou forsaken me?" represents the moment where the psyche retracts its projection onto an outside deity, and that energy returns to its original, rightful place within the human. The man on the cross realizes his divinity, and the "deity in the sky" (the projection) realizes his humanity. The False Self realizes the Christ within, and the True Self realizes it must walk the path of death and resurrection. Once again, this is the Christ Mystery, which represents the absolute truth of every living thing and the pattern that all creation follows.

Practically, we rightly recognize the divinity of Jesus first, so that we can later recognize the divinity in all. We fall in love with Jesus first, so that we can later fall in love with Christ everywhere. We need to love the particular first, so we can love the universal later.

Mother Teresa clearly saw people in this way. By saying she saw Jesus in everyone, she recognized the fundamental truth about reality: Christ is hidden within all matter. By referring to Christ as "Jesus," she makes this ultimate truth immediate and urgent. There are no longer hypothetical questions about how one should act if one encountered Jesus. Everyone *is* Jesus. When someone suffers, it is Christ who is suffering within them. For the person who realizes this, there is a knowing that, when they help someone, they are comforting Jesus who is suffering within. Even if that person seems to be unredeemable, we know that their disguise is not their true identity. Beneath the disguise is the embryo, the True Self waiting until the right moment to be born.

> *For I was hungry and you gave me nothing to eat, I was thirsty and you gave me nothing to drink, I was a stranger and you did not invite me in, I needed clothes and you did not clothe me, I was sick and in prison and you did not look after me. They also will answer, "Lord, when did we see you hungry or thirsty or a stranger or needing clothes or sick or in prison, and did not help you?" He will reply, "Truly I tell you, whatever you did not do for one of the least of these, you did not do for me."*
>
> — **Matthew 25:42–45** (NIV)

The reason those in the verse ask, "Lord, when did we see you...?" is because they have not yet recognized Christ within themselves; therefore, they cannot see Christ in everyone else. They are under the illusion of separation, believing Christ and "mere humans" to be different.

The *least of these* is firstly your True Self, whom you must first learn to love. Jesus instructs to "love your neighbor *as yourself*." It is impossible to love your neighbor until you learn how to love yourself—your True Self. It is first *you* who needs your compassion. It is your True Self who first starves and thirsts for your love. It is your True Self that is locked in prison and needs freedom. It is first ourselves that we must learn to love, so that we can properly recognize Christ within others, and then love our neighbor purely and properly. If we fail to do this, the "help" we give to others is actually a prideful inflation of the False Self—an attempt to think of itself as good, powerful, and not needing anything.

Compassion means "to suffer with." For someone who has recognized the Christ within, there is a connection and solidarity with the suffering of humanity. All suffering is the suffering of Christ; therefore, to ease the suffering of another, to comfort Jesus in his time of need, becomes the highest honor in life. No, you cannot carry his cross for him. But you can comfort him, feed him, sit by his side—and that is enough. Just a little comfort, love, and peace makes the pain bearable. There is no need to escape pain anymore. You accept it as essential to the experience of life and enter into it, knowing that you will find Christ in it and it will transform you. It is consenting to bear the pain itself that releases the transformative healing power. As you yourself surrender to your suffering, Christ finds you there, and it becomes a mercy that opens your heart to the compassion of God.

> I picked up a man from the street. He was eaten up alive with worms and nobody could stand near him he was smelling so badly. I went to him to clean him and he said, "Why do you do this?" And I said, "Because I love you."

> — **St. Mother Teresa**[2]

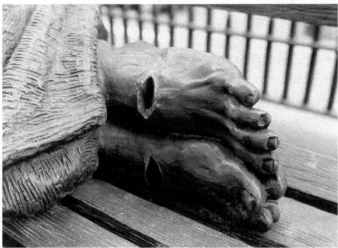

Homeless Jesus by Timothy P. Schmalz. Located at the Holy Rosary Cathedral in Vancouver

Surely Mother Teresa demonstrates what it means to have a "relationship with Jesus." It's not asking Jesus to come into your heart, as if he weren't already there. Rather, it is finding him within your heart. It is, first, a relationship with your True Self, and second, with everything else. It is all the same infinite, primordial substance in disguise. Once this is realized, there truly is nowhere to go to "find God." God is everywhere. The idea of "searching for God" seems as naive as a child in utero searching for its mother. You can imagine the sad irony of a child, in the womb, suffering because it believed that it had lost its mother—when, all the while, it was inside her...and her body was inside the child, providing the nutrients for its growth through the umbilical cord.

> God is the Mother,
> and the Father,
> and the egg,
> and the sperm,
> and the multiplying cells,
> and the child,
> and the nutrients,
> and the umbilical cord,
> and the birth,
> and the mercy of Mother and child meeting one another,
> and the life force that propels it all forward.

It is a proper relationship to the mythology of Jesus that grounds us in this ultimate reality. . .or if you'd like—*God.*

THIRTY-EIGHT

THE TRINITY

The letters of the name of God in Hebrew... are frequently mispronounced Yahveh. But in truth they are unutter-
able...This word {YHWH} is the sound of breathing. The
holiest Name in the world, the Name of the Creator, is the
sound of your own breathing.

That these letters are unpronounceable is no accident. Just as it
is no accident that they are also the root letters of the Hebrew
verb "to be"...So God's name is the name of Being itself. And,
since God is holy, then so is all creation.

— **Rabbi Lawrence Kushner**[1]

FOR OUR MODERN MINDS, the metaphor of a mother conceiving, growing, birthing, and nurturing a child illustrates a more accurate picture of the Trinity than the traditional version which lacks a feminine archetype. Perhaps it is necessary to imagine God as an object (frequently a man in the sky) in earlier cognitive development. The brain is designed to separate things into categories and assign specific characteristics to those categories. But inevitably, this leads us to understand God as someone distinctly different from and separate from us, onto whom we then project all kinds of characteristics.

But, in order to become mature human beings who can heal ourselves and the world around us, it is imperative that we come to understand more accurately the nature of God. While it is true that we will never *fully under-stand* this mystery, it's false to assume that we cannot understand it at all. We can. We can grasp layer upon layer, and come into a deeper understanding of ultimate reality, but only if we are willing to lay down our pride and admit that we were wrong about what we thought we knew. By knowing nothing, by *unknowing*, we can begin to understand.

As we come to realize Mother Nature as the hiding place of God, we can begin to see that the entire universe—the stars in the sky, the fish in the sea, the trees, the rocks, the oceans, *everything*—is a temple of God. We know that everything exists in connection to every other thing. Every object in the universe reveals the principle of the Trinity—the dynamic relationship of God to God's self.

Everything that exists came into existence through this trinitarian, dynam-ic energy. Individual objects only exist in relation to other forms, connec-tions, and developmental processes. God is revealed in material form, in that the lifeforce underneath the material form is a dynamic thrust of birth, life, and death. This threefold process is at work in all time and space. God as three-in-one is not so much a noun as a verb. The personifications of Father, Son, and Holy Spirit are not to be understood as literal nouns, but rather, symbols to help our brains understand the creative thrust to life propelling the entire cosmos.

The very structure and substance of the universe is not so much made up of individual static objects, but rather, the energy of love—yearning for connection, desiring unity, and moving towards expansion. And we each are a part of that. The Trinity is the picture of the movement of this energy, pulsing through and propelling all things into being. God is not so much a being. God *is Being*. God is not a dancer. *God is the dance.*

When we think of God as creator, our minds are trained to think of an old man in the sky who made an object and then left it to itself, perhaps like an engineer building a robot and then setting it loose. But a more accurate picture is that of a juggling act. In order for the creation to come alive, there must be a juggler, objects for him to juggle, and the intentional, coordinated energy of tossing the objects. In this picture, the creation requires multiple related objects to be propelled forward by intentional energy. The entire juggling act is the creation. God is the entirety of the threefold process: beginning, middle, and end. God is also the movement and relationship between the objects driving the creation forward—each object, of course, being the totality of this same process. (In fact, each object is itself the culmination of atomic and subatomic particles in relationship to one another.)

Music is another good metaphor for this trinitarian principle of creating. Music requires a musician, an instrument, and an intelligent effort to produce sound. The creation of music, then, is many different components all working in harmony together. The creation is much more like a participatory process, not a separate, static object. *When we speak of "God's creation," we are actually naming the ongoing cooperative movement of life itself. Creation is God manifesting God.*

God is reality itself. The Trinity offers us a way of understanding this reality as fundamentally loving. To trust God is to trust life itself. It is to trust that you are truly a part of this loving reality. That you belong here. That you are a manifestation of this divine love. That is the ultimate act of faith. Science is continually giving us a more accurate picture of how reality works—the interconnected relationship of everything. *Faith is believing that this reality is not cold; it is loving and meaningful.* This faith is what gives you the courage to take a step forward, trusting that when you step, life will move towards you. But you have to take that first step before you can experience for yourself that this is true—and that step is always beyond your boundaries and comfort zone. You can't know it's true from someone else telling you. You have to find out for yourself. You have to ask the universe to dance and then begin dancing, believing that when you put your hand out, someone or something will be there to take it and dance with you, just like any good parent would.

In full vulnerability, writing this book is an act of faith for me. I'm writing it now because I trust this trinitarian nature of God. I trust that if I dance, the universe will dance with me. I'm taking the first step with no guarantee that anything will come of it. I'm writing from my truest, most authentic place, and trusting that these words will find their way to you in a magically ordinary way. That, at just the right time, these words from my heart will find their way to you, and you will know they were written for you.

God is no longer a man in the sky. God is the threefold dynamism of love: generating all things, folding itself into all things (including you and me), and unfolding from all things in an ever-expanding revelation of itself. God is three-in-one: unity in distinction that propels itself forward.

> When God laughs at the soul and the soul laughs back at God, the persons of the Trinity are begotten. When the Father laughs at the Son and the Son laughs back at the Father, that laughter gives pleasure, that pleasure gives joy, that joy gives love, and that love is the Holy Spirit.

— **Meister Eckhart** (c. 1260–c. 1328)[2]

THIRTY-NINE

THE SECOND COMING OF CHRIST

> The eternal mystery of the world is its comprehensibility...The
> fact that it is comprehensible is a miracle.

— **Albert Einstein**[1] (1879–1955)

I REMEMBER LYING IN bed on Christmas Eve when I was a little girl, maybe six or seven years old. I couldn't sleep because I was so excited about Santa coming to my house. I knew I needed to go to sleep, but the anticipation was keeping me awake. Suddenly, I started hearing what I was certain was thumping on my roof. The reindeer had landed, and I'd heard them! My heart started racing and I squeezed my eyes shut, lying as still as I'd ever been, trying not to breathe too loudly. I can still feel my head pressed against my pillow and my body curled up in the fetal position. My eyes were closed, but all my other senses were heightened. I began to hear noise in the hallway. I heard Santa lightly put something in the stocking on my door and quietly go back downstairs. I continued lying there, frozen, until the house was still for quite a while and I was pretty sure he was gone.

At that time, there was nothing anyone could have done to convince me that Santa wasn't real. I'd heard him! The next morning, I found a candy cane in the stocking on my door, and I came downstairs to find potato chips strewn across the kitchen floor. Santa explained in his note that the reindeer were hungry and had come inside for a snack. I couldn't believe this happened. But I had proof! I'd heard all the sounds, I'd seen the candy cane and the mess in the kitchen, and I even had a written account of it all. Magic was real.

A couple years after that, on Easter Sunday, I received a beautiful stuffed bunny in my Easter basket from the Easter Bunny. That evening, we phoned my Granny to wish her a happy Easter, and she asked me if I liked the bunny she sent. A bit confused, I looked at my mom and asked, "I thought that bunny was from the Easter Bunny?" A somber look fell over my mother's face, and she simply said, "I'm sorry, hunny." I went upstairs to cry. It didn't occur to me until later that night in bed that perhaps Santa and the Tooth Fairy shared the same origins as the Easter Bunny. I came downstairs to confirm my fears about Santa, and later about the Tooth Fairy—returning to my bed to cry each time.

In the days after, as I analyzed all the implications of this news, I questioned the reality about which I had been so sure. If those magical moments with Santa weren't real, maybe God wasn't real. No, I decided—the grownups wouldn't lie to me about that. None of them actually believed in Santa, but they really seemed to believe in God. Now it felt silly to think that Santa was always watching me and working from the North Pole, but I was still certain that God was a real man, watching me and working in heaven—up there somewhere. Santa was just a myth. But I was certain the man in the sky was real.

The maturation of my faith reminds me of my evolving childhood understanding of Santa Claus. Young minds often need hyperbole in order to make sense of their reality. "Real" often can only mean "literal" for a child. However, even as an adult, my brain persisted in this childlike state. As Paul described, "I understood as a child, I thought as a child" (1 Corinthians 13:11). Remember that Paul's childlike thinking didn't mature until he was an adult on the road to Damascus! Our spiritual task involves a psychological maturation in adulthood, as Paul describes.

In my evangelical upbringing, the Second Coming of Christ was presented in a very literal way. Like a child, I once believed that *the magic*, in the form of Jesus, would swoop in out of the sky, much like Santa Claus. I truly believed that this was not only possible, but an inevitable certainty. Once I discovered that Santa was not a literal man, the idea of a literal Santa seemed preposterous. From a deeper, eternal perspective, however, I was wrong. The "Santa myth" was a container for a truth that was *more deeply real even than historical fact*.

St. Nicholas was a historical man. He lived in the third century and became the patron saint of children. One of the best-known legends about him describes a father with three daughters in Nicholas's village, who became so poor that he had no choice but to sell his daughters into slavery or prostitution. Nicholas heard of the poor father's plight, and one night he went to the house in secret. He threw a purse full of gold coins through a window in order to provide a dowry for the eldest daughter to be married. He did the same for the second daughter, when the time came for her to be married. When it was the third daughter's turn, the poor father stayed awake and discovered it was Nicholas who was giving them the money. The father was overcome with gratitude, but Nicholas asked that he be kept anonymous until after he died. Over the years, the stories of St. Nicholas's generosity towards children spread. The legend eventually evolved into what we know today as Santa Claus.

I now realize that the magic that I experienced as a young child *was* real. The spirit of St. Nicholas was deeply real to me, and that spirit was transmitted to me through myth. As a child, I naively attributed the source of that spirit or "magical energy" to a literal Santa that didn't exist. But I was mistaken when I let my awe and wonder die along with my belief in a literal Santa. What I experienced as a young child was the eternal spirit of Christ that emanated from St. Nicholas across time. The reality of that experience was true in the deepest sense. It didn't matter what I believed to be generating it. I was participating in the eternal Christ Mystery, which is always active, alive, and now. The spirit of Santa shows up every time a parent loves their child so much that they surprise them with gifts of love. That love is pure magic. It is real. In fact, it's the *only thing* that's *really real*. Santa does not physically come every year. He is a personification of a palpable, eternal spirit, manifesting in the pure love of our own hearts and homes.

The same holds true for Christ. In evangelicalism, you are trained to accept some version of a belief that the historical thirty-three-year-old Jesus will come galloping in on the clouds one day. Although our brains may need to imagine it this way to begin with, the myth is meant as a container for a deeper truth. The spirit of Christ comes again every time a person realizes that this very existence is "magic." That this very universe is the body of Christ. We are all a part of Christ and sustained by Christ. Ultimate reality itself is the miracle that is generated and sustained by love. *There is nothing but Christ. Every thing is Christ. God is revealed through Christ to be in harmony with the natural world.* Your entire being is raptured in this aliveness. Christ is the pulse of existence. The Second Coming is when your perception of heaven and earth intersect in a collision called "Christ." Christ comes again. In a literal sense, a historical Santa or Jesus flying through the clouds is absurd. As a representation of a living, breathing truth, there is nothing more real.

This principle is depicted well in the life of St. Francis, who has often been called "a second Christ." He is even said to have experienced the phenomena of the stigmata (bodily wounds corresponding to the wounds of Christ such as the hands, wrists, and feet). St. Francis emphasized an interconnectedness with all of nature and would spend time preaching to animals. This was depicted by the Italian artist Giotto, painted around 1295–1300.[2]

St. Francis of Assisi Receiving the Stigmata by Giotto, c. 1300,
Paris

A subtle interpenetration of your spirit with the spirit of those "unseen existences," now so deeply and thrillingly felt by you, will take place. Old barriers will vanish: and you will become aware that St. Francis was accurate as well as charming when he spoke of Brother Wind and Sister Water; and that Stevenson was obviously right when he said, that since:

"The world is so full of a number of things,

I'm sure we ought all to be happy as kings."

Those glad and vivid "things" will speak to you. They will offer you news at least as definite and credible as that which the paper-boy is hawking in the street: direct messages from that Beauty which the artist reports at best at second hand. Because of your new sensitiveness, anthems will be heard of you from every gutter; poems of intolerable loveliness will bud for you on every weed. Best and greatest, your fellowmen will shine for you with new significance and light.

— **Evelyn Underhill**[3] (1875–1941)[4]

This is truly what it means to be "raptured." To realize you've been in heaven the whole time and never knew it. Everything you've been looking for is inside of you, and that includes God. The fact that we can better and better understand the mystery in which we are living does not diminish its miraculous quality. The fact that Santa didn't defy the laws of nature and fly through the sky, but rather that my parents loved me enough to give me gifts anonymously, does not make this situation less magical. The very plausible and logical explanation of the event makes it no less wondrous. On the contrary: the ordinary is miraculous! Love was right there with me the whole time, and it still is. The ordinary is ablaze with meaning. This precious moment, here and now, is generated and sustained by love. That reality was revealed by Jesus in 33 A.D., and it is revealed again every time a human becomes conscious of this ultimate truth. The awe and wonder I experienced as a child came from within my own soul. The Second Coming of Christ is the recovery and expression of the True Self in its full essence in the ordinary, physical world, bringing new life and regeneration to one's personal life and the lives of those around them.

FORTY

THE KINGDOM BELONGS TO CHILDREN

A CURIOUS DETAIL IN the Adam and Eve myth is often overlooked. In Genesis 2:21, the text says that ". . . God caused the man to fall into a deep sleep." *The story never says that Adam woke up.*

By understanding God as the trinitarian thrust of the universe, we can see the energy of life constantly moving towards expansion in all living things, including our individual and collective consciousness.

> *But Jesus called the children to him and said, "Let the little children come to me, and do not hinder them, for the kingdom of God belongs to such as these."*

— **Luke 18:16** (NIV)

Adam's state in the Garden, before God created Eve, represents the state of unitive consciousness experienced by children. The True Self—the experience of which Jesus calls *"the kingdom of God"*—experiences itself as one with God, a part of the whole of reality, and an extension of the Tree of Life. This is the conscious state of a child. Of course, the child is not aware of this. There is no past or future for the child. They simply experience life here and now in their bodies, which are always conscious of the present moment. Contrary to the mind, the body is the place that is always present. This is the Garden. It could be said that a child is always "playing with God." They are completely present to the presence of God, or reality itself. They are fully immersed. Everything they experience is accepted completely and responded to accordingly. There is no "good and bad," "pleasurable or painful." Life just *is*. Because of this state of consciousness, children are trusting and vulnerable. They embody and live out their true essence, even though they are not aware that this is what they are doing. Their awareness and reality are one.

As a seed falls from a tree, it takes with it a piece of the True Self (represented by the embryo within the seed). God putting Adam to sleep symbolizes this phase of development. We've seen already that this stage, being asleep in our consciousness, is what drives our growth. The shell of the False Self is the vehicle that protects the embryo within and allows it to be propelled forward. It's not Adam who chooses to sleep. He does not choose to "sin," or to lose contact with his True Self. It's God who puts him to sleep. It is the nature of reality to move us forward into growth. Although we come to identify completely with the outer shell of the seed (the False Self) in our sleep, it is our True Self inside that yearns to realize itself and grow out of the shell.

When Jesus instructs his followers to "become like little children," he's ushering them into the next stage of growth. He's instructing you to awaken from your sleep, recover your authentic self, and begin to let it grow. Of course, at this stage in our growth, we don't start acting like little children, irresponsible and unaccountable for our actions. No. "Becoming like a child" means unlearning the conditioning of your mind, the belief that you must be inauthentic to adapt to and survive in your environment. It's recovering your trust in life and your willingness to be truthful and authentic, which is necessarily vulnerable—*like a child*. It's synthesizing your knowledge with your faith to conclude that all of creation is fundamentally good, and moving forward in a meaningful progression towards wholeness.

In our state of unconscious sleep, we behave from a deep place of fear. When we wake up to our true nature, we recover our childlike faith in life that it will meet us where we are. We expect to look for love, and to find it. We play, and trust that life will join us in our playing. We are free to be who we really are and always were. The "world" (i.e., the False Self and societies constructed by False Selves) will not understand this way of being. But it's okay. You're playing with God, and you know what it's taken you to get here.

> First the fall, and then the recovery from the fall, and both are
> the mercy of God.

— Julian of Norwich[1]

Waking up to the True Self, the inner child, is a profound experience. For me, there were feelings of elation, but also of immense sorrow. Much like birthing a child, it is extremely painful. But it's a pain that I know belongs and is purposeful. This feeling of purpose in the pain does not make it easier. Rather, it gives me the fortitude to stay with it and to allow it to finish its work. Like Jesus, I surrender to it. I'm allowing myself to hang on my cross until that process finishes its work in me. This is an ongoing process. It was the Jesus myth that gave me the faith to do this. I am no longer trying to escape my pain or numb it through compulsive behaviors. I no longer view pain as a curse that doesn't belong. Life is painful. It is beautiful and joyous, but it's also tremendously harrowing.

I've learned that I can bear what initially seems like unbearable pain. The allowing of the pain in my heart frees me from suffering and expands my heart space. Suffering isn't defined as the mere existence of pain; it is the *resistance* to pain. When I began allowing myself to embrace *all* of life, the joys and the sorrows, I found that everything I experienced was transient. If I could courageously permit myself to feel it all, I found that the feelings moved through me more quickly. I no longer felt stuck in my suffering. I no longer had to cling to happiness like a lifeboat. The waves of experience came and went, but I was anchored in the peace of my True Self. That peace is predominantly what I now experience. I still feel the waves of my emotions, but they are typically not as volatile or intense as before. The recovery of my True Self, my eternal soul begotten of God, was the treasure buried in the field. It was a mercy to find it and to discover I had been carrying the treasure inside myself all along.

The kingdom of heaven is a way of seeing and being in the world. It's a view of objective reality as good and beautiful. It's an openness to whatever is happening in this moment and a trust that you will be sustained, come what may. Therefore, it is not necessary to fret over the future, because you are so grounded in this trust. Jesus recognized that children inherently viewed reality in this way. When they need love, help, connection, or sustenance, they ask, because they trust that those needs will be met. The kingdom of heaven is a recognition of reality as fundamentally *loving* and *loveable*. It responds when one asks for help from the sacred place within.

The kingdom is what the False Self imagines heaven to be, but believes it must wait until after physical death to experience. The reason we can imagine this reality is we have a distant memory of experiencing ultimate reality this way long ago. Trust in this reality was broken very early, and you fell from this trusting state of consciousness. But nonetheless, you possessed this basic trust at the very beginning, and that is why you long for a return to what you once had. This childlike trust in reality is what Jesus instructs us to find and recover. In the kingdom of heaven, the dualistic mind—order and disorder (the Tree of Knowledge of Good and Evil)—is synthesized into a higher unitive consciousness, symbolized by the Tree of Life and the cross of Christ. In the kingdom of heaven, life's paradoxes are yielded to and affirmed.

When you approach reality with the same openness and trust as a child, you can affirm this way of seeing the world for others who can't yet see it. You can give children a somatic imprint that will help them to remember this loving reality when they inevitably "fall asleep" like Adam. This is why good, responsive parenting and nurturing environments for children matter. Adults must strive to mirror reality to children in the way Jesus does.

When children approach Jesus for a loving connection, he welcomes them. That's it. He doesn't tell them a scary story about burning in hell after they die to coerce them into believing something about him. He confirms their trust in a reality that is fundamentally loving. Like Jesus, we can affirm to children that they are good, that they belong, that they are loved just as they are, that they are safe and will be provided for. They can trust that, when they need help, they can ask and we will respond. Their big feelings will not threaten their relationships to the ones they love and depend on. This mirroring sustains a child's basic trust for long enough to develop the confidence to flourish. When a solid trust in reality is laid as the foundation, a child can then begin to explore and make mistakes, trusting that there is a safe haven to return to and solid ground on which to stand and fall.

Jesus's affirmation of children's trust is an invitation for adults to protect that trust. When adults use the trust of children to tell them frightening stories about God, they abuse their power. When adults tell children that they are inherently bad and cannot be with God (or their families) unless they believe the right things and say the right words, they abuse their power. The twist is: it's nearly impossible to mirror children in a way that reflects the kingdom of heaven, unless we ourselves believe that reality is a loving thing, infused with God. Unless we ourselves can relax into a basic trust in life as inherently good, beautiful, and trustworthy, we can't affirm our children's inner knowing of this reality.

> *If anyone causes one of these little ones—those who believe in me—to stumble, it would be better for them to have a large millstone hung around their neck and to be drowned in the depths of the sea.*

— **Matthew 18:6** (NIV)

If we introduce God and the world to our children out of fear for their eternal souls, we become a stumbling block for our children to find the kingdom, which is here, now, and within them. Our fear becomes their fear, and they can no longer trust themselves or God. "On earth as it is in heaven" requires our participation in co-creating this loving reality with our children.

Have you ever thought about the fact that Jesus never tried to convert children? His message to children is: *I love you. I love you. I love you. Come to me. You belong.*

You don't have to convert a child into believing that it belongs to its mother. The child inherently belongs, and it's self-evident to both mother and child. Jesus is always speaking *to adults* when he says to become like children in order to enter the kingdom. How can a child be converted to a child? All we accomplish when we "convert" children is that we instill in them a toxic belief that they don't belong in the family that they indeed belong to. Heaven is a child's birthright.

Conversion as an adult is the realization that heaven is your birthright. You belong. You've always belonged. You're in. A person doesn't cease to be a part of a family just because they've stopped *believing* they're part of the family. The task *for adults* is to believe that you've always belonged as you authentically are. There's nothing to say or do. No prayer to pray. No performing to affirm your worth. No ticket needed for entrance. Only the realization of what's always been true. Children inherently know this.

Churches often lead children to believe that they aren't in the family (that they indeed are in). And that, to be in the family (that they're already in), they have to say or do or believe something. In evangelicalism, I was told that if I didn't believe as taught, I'd be punished forever in a cosmic fireplace. This is psychological abuse and has caused religious trauma in many people, myself included.

Jesus's work was to awaken *adults* to their preexisting, unconditional place in the family from the start. His warning about psychologically damaging children—about causing them to stumble into the belief that they don't inherently belong with God—is stern. Repentance is for *adults* who've forgotten their place in the family of God. This *metanoia* ("changing your mind") is to happen after you're psychologically developed enough to endure the grief process that accompanies the loss of the False Self, and have the ability to generate the self-compassion required to navigate the process of recovering the True Self. Then, you can productively move forward into a new, life-generating reality.

FORTY-ONE

THE PRODIGAL SON

THE STORY OF THE Prodigal Son illustrates quite poignantly the inherent place we have in the eternal family of God from the beginning. Forgetting one's identity and place in the family is quite a different thing to resolve than being told that you are not even part of the family. The latter creates an attachment wound that is considerably more difficult to heal and overcome. It interrupts the natural process of development and understanding of God. It confuses a person's relationship to themselves and to nature.

In the story of the Prodigal Son, it is not the father who sends the son away for doing wrong. The father never turns his gaze away from the son, even as the son turns away. And upon the son's return, we find the father is already facing towards the son, as he has always been.

> *So he got up and went to his father. But while he was still a long way off, his father saw him and was filled with compassion for him; he ran to his son, threw his arms around him and kissed him.*

> — **Luke 15:20** (NIV)

The son's single step of faith towards his home was met with a father rushing forward. Throughout the whole journey from home to wandering and back again, *the father never turns his face away from his son.*

In evangelicalism, believers are taught that the Father required Jesus to be tortured and killed, in order that humanity might return to the Father. They are taught that the Father cannot look at them in their state of sin. Brian Zahnd points out that it's as if the father in the Prodigal Son story saw his son coming, but demanded the torture and death of an innocent person to appease his wrath before he could turn towards his son and embrace him.[1] I hope you can see the psychological damage this would cause the son to know that, in order to return to his father, someone else had to die. This psychological burden is what the evangelical dogma lays on its followers. Believers, including children, are told that they deserve to be tortured and die, and that it is their fault that Jesus died in this brutal way. This narrative is an inaccurate, toxic rewrite of the Prodigal Son story.

It is actually the son, by leaving everything he knows, who completes the developmental process of self-actualization: solidifying his False Self, falling asleep to his True Self, coming to the end of the False Self, dying to his old reality and illusionary identity, and finally discovering his True Self at home where he started—only now he has the wisdom to understand the journey of his life as it comes full circle. He completes the cycle of self-forgetting, self-remembering, and self-actualizing. He fulfills his destiny.

The other brother is asleep as well. But he never deviates from the "world's" expectation of him (the False Self and systems of religion and society). He does what he's supposed to do and obeys the rules set for him. In objective reality, he's at home with the father, but his subjective reality is not conscious of it. Heaven is right there, but he doesn't know it. It's his lack of perception that creates his personal hell. It is the Prodigal Son who has the courage to seek his destiny and is rewarded for it.

Although we will all fall asleep to our True Selves, it is essential that we instill in our children the truth that they inherently belong in our families and in the family of God. The goal is *not* to save our children from the dangers of an external hell. The goal is to give them the courage to find and face their own demons. It is to make their lives so loving and warm that, when they find themselves asleep in the cold, they begin to feel their own fire within, and they can surrender to and generate a love that warms them again. For the Prodigal Son, salvation was not an acceptance into a family from which he was separated, but a remembrance of and return to a family to which he'd always belonged. Salvation is an experience of the transcendent, but it is also imminent. It's imperative that our children know that they come from love, they belong to love, and will return to love. The Prodigal Son acquires this wisdom through the fulfillment of his own journey in a pattern named by Fr. Richard Rohr: away from order, through disorder, and finally to reorder.[2] He always had what he was looking for. But still, one must first seek to find. The journey cannot be transmitted on behalf of another. The adventure must be taken for oneself. It is not enough to simply believe in the Way; one must actually walk the Way.

> *For we also have had the good news proclaimed to us, just as they did; but the message they heard was of no value to them, because they did not share the faith of those who obeyed.*

> — **Hebrews 4:2** (NIV)

Forty-Two

I AM THE WAY, THE TRUTH, & THE LIFE

What if "the Way, the Truth, and the Life" was a path of radical inclusion instead of religious exclusion?

The story of the Prodigal Son reveals the significance of Jesus's often misunderstood saying, "I am the way, the truth, and the life. No one comes to the Father except through me" (John 14:6). The wisdom of the Prodigal Son reveals that "*the Way*" is your own way. Any path laid out before you must be someone else's, not yours.

Homing pigeons are a fascinating species. These birds have the ability to find their way back home from hundreds, even thousands, of miles away. Scientists theorize that these pigeons rely on their senses, sensitivity to the earth and sun's magnetic fields, and their own internal compasses to find their way back. Much like these pigeons, we will find ourselves scattered in different directions, searching for the way back home. The way in which we find home is different for each individual. Not everyone is beginning from the same position. Some are farther away than others. The terrain is different. The experiences and encounters will be different. *The Way* that Jesus refers to is the discovery and navigation of your own path. It is the Word, the spirit of love, which lights the path. Like the internal guidance system of homing pigeons, that Word is inherently within each of us from the beginning. *The Way* is not a prayer to accept Jesus into your heart. It is the very love within you that illuminates the journey you must take. The Prodigal Son and the other brother had two very different paths. It is foolish to assume that two people will discover their True Self in the same way.

The other brother is much like many religious people. By believing they already possess "the truth," they fail to go find it. This was my general experience in the first half of my life. A Baptist preacher had handed me the "the truth" when I was seven years old. What else was there to look for? Just adhere to the religious rules (i.e., try to avoid "sinful behaviors"), and do my duty as a Christian by sharing this "good news" with others. Chances are, if you've had "faith" figured out since you were a child, there may be some unknowing that needs to happen. Who are you without your familial role? Without your religion? Without your customs? Without your career? Without possessions? Without your opinions and beliefs? Who are you when all these outer garments are stripped off? As J.R.R. Tolkien so wisely said: *Not all who wander are lost.*[1]

Spiritual rebirth is the discovery of the face you had before you were born. The face you had before you did anything "right" or "wrong." It is an encounter with your True Self—your eternal soul—which was hidden in God (Mystery) in the center of your being (the Garden of Eden) before you "ate the apple" and your mind split into duality (good and bad, right and wrong, saved and unsaved). It is the mind that creates categories and labels. The mind, Adam, is what "names" everything and then attempts to control what it has labeled and judged. It is our creative life force within us, Eve, who pulls us on the journey of inner knowing. Spiritual rebirth is to go all the way back and discover who you were before you created and accepted your labels.

Jesus is not a trade or a substitute payment. Jesus cannot be reborn for you. A belief in a doctrine about Jesus doesn't magically make you reborn. The biblical myths can show you how to journey towards the center of yourself, where the Tree of Life resides deep within you. But you must decide to take this inward journey. You must consent. Like Mary, you must say "yes" to the labor process. At the right time, the Christ child is born within you.

The way, the truth, and the life are within. We realize this by walking through our individual journeys of death, resurrection, and rebirth, just as Jesus demonstrated. Through this process, we are stripped of all external identities, until all that's left is the face we had before we were born. This is the recovery of your soul and authentic self, which can now come forth into the world, bestowing on fellow humans your divine light, which was begotten in the darkness—birthed in the womb of your heart.

FORTY-THREE

A NEW EARTH

Then I saw "a new heaven and a new earth," for the first heaven and the first earth had passed away, and there was no longer any sea.

— **Revelation 21:1** (NIV)

WE'RE CONDITIONED TO THINK of the Promised Land, heaven, a New Earth, as places and conditions off in the future. But the Promised Land is found in our own bodies. Heaven is here. The sea of the unconscious mind is no longer a darkness to be feared. A New Earth is created when we walk out our life in the awesome awareness that our lives are meaningful and that we belong here. Your True Self, your treasure, has always been with you. But are you aware of it?

It is the world—the system that sees itself as chosen and others as excluded—that is passing away. It is the world that divides humanity into winners and losers, the world that values believers and diminishes unbelievers, the world that sees itself as good and others as evil, that is passing away.

Apocalypse does not point to a fiery Armageddon but to the fact that our ignorance and our complacency are coming to an end... The exclusivism of there being only one way in which we can be saved, the idea that there is a single religious group that is in sole possession of the truth—that is the world as we know it that must pass away. What is the kingdom? It lies in our realization of the ubiquity of the divine presence in our neighbors, in our enemies, in all of us.

— **Joseph Campbell**[1]

Emmanuel, "God with us," is an ever-present reality of which we become aware. It is our level of awareness that changes, not the reality. We don't invite Jesus into our hearts; we realize God has been with us all along. We invite God, perhaps in the form of Jesus, to make us more aware of this truth.

The problem has never been that you were separated from God. The problem is that you are separated from yourself. Jesus reveals that God is already within the body. The body is always in the present moment. The problem is that your mind is not. Your mind is in the past or in the future, but not here in the present. Your body is here. God is here. Love is here. But your mind is not. Jesus is the picture of God and humanity existing together in the body, which is here. Jesus saves by making the mind whole and undivided, able to perceive and experience the heaven which is at hand.

A more peaceful world, both internally and externally, requires our co-operation. The Promised Land is the body in harmony with nature. Before you can get to the Promised Land, you must consent to the journey. The unconscious waters of the Red Sea, or the sacrificial blood of Christ, must be met consciously and voluntarily. This submission to our own psychological and spiritual crucifixion and resurrection is free will. It is entirely up to each one of us to make our own journey to the Promised Land and co-create a New Earth with God. Making peace depends on each of us, so the speed at which we surrender to this process is determined by us.

The free will, or consent, that is needed to realize the kingdom within is a consent to grief. The recovery of the True Self necessarily requires the death of the False Self. Grief always accompanies death. The death of the illusions, expectations, relationships, dreams, identities, and hopes of the False Self at first feels like a never-ending abyss. Walking into this is courageous, but it is also delicate and sacred work. It is important that it not be forced on anyone. A person must be free to live their own life.

For those that choose their adventure, their *Way*, faith is cultivated by the trusting that there will be a *Way* for them. As we make peace with the paradoxes of our lives and reconcile the opposites, we ourselves return to our wholeness and move forward in our individual purpose. We become a piece of the New Earth: healed, living in and from the kingdom of God, bringing fresh life to revitalize a withering world.

Each person possesses both heaven and hell within. Is it possible for you to explore all that is within you without judging it, allowing it all to be there together? Can you explore the many mansions of your heart, including the dark dungeons, and trust that God will be found in them all? This is how we experience all parts of our existence and bring life to every dark, undiscovered place within. In God's house, there are many rooms, and God is found in every one of them. *To know God fully is to experience yourself fully*. By integrating all the parts of yourself into the One whole, you bring a new incarnation of Christ into the world: fully God and fully man. *Emmanuel—God with us*.

> *Whither shall I go from thy spirit? Or whither shall I flee from thy presence? If I ascend up into heaven, thou art there;* ***if I make my bed in hell, behold, thou art there.***
>
> **— Psalm 139:7–8** (KJV)

Once the power of myth is grasped, we are ushered into an entirely new experience of life. Exploring the wonder of life through myth connects us to our innate power, which was always there, lying dormant, all along. It is a shocking discovery. The parts of ourselves which we berated into hiding are found to be our gifts. As it turns out, all we really have to do is be ourselves—our True Selves. As Jesus reminds us:

Is it not written in your Law, "I have said you are 'gods'"?

— **John 10:34b** (NIV)

Your gift to the world is *You*. In the end, whenever that may be, we will all find what it is that we seek. And that is *Good News*.

[God our Saviour] will have all men to be saved, and to come unto the knowledge of the truth.

— **1 Timothy 2:4** (KJV)

EPILOGUE

Myth is the exact opposite of something that is untrue; actually, it is something that is so true, it is ever and always, irrepressibly bubbling up from the soil of every alphabet, every language, every time, every culture.

— **Stan Mitchell**[1]

SOMETIMES I WONDER HOW I would have received a book like this when I was a devout evangelical. Would I have entertained this book? Would I have been able to follow its logic? To be honest, it's hard to say. My conversion was so abrupt and intense. In many ways, I feel I am an entirely different person than I was before. I try to communicate in a way that would make sense to the old me, but I can only ponder how that earlier me would have received the new me. I know that the old me projected a lot of fear and judgment onto people outside of evangelicalism. I've been on the receiving end of a lot of that fear and judgment since I've left. It doesn't feel good. But I understand it. And I have compassion for myself and others who lived out of that place for so long. My own Apocalypse ushered in weeping and gnashing of teeth, to be sure. I understand why others do not want to go there.

My greatest motivation for writing this book came out of love for my children. They are growing up in the southern Bible Belt. I know they are going to fall asleep to their True Selves. And I know that they are immersed in a religious culture that purports to know the answers and offers easy but inadequate solutions to suffering. Certainty is a very potent force that's hard to pull yourself away from, especially when that need for certainty is motivated by fear.

One night, when my oldest daughter, Norah, was eight years old, she was unusually quiet and anxious at dinner. She had her fists tightly clenched together, which was peculiar. We kept asking her if she was okay. When she finally opened up, she admitted that she'd been scared to tell us.

A friend from the playground had told her that there was an angel who wanted to be better than God. So the angel fell from heaven and turned into a devil, who lived in a place down below, called hell. Apparently, Norah pointed down at the ground, to confirm where the danger was. Her friend quickly told her she couldn't point there or say the word [hell] or she might go to . . . shhh . . . *H.E.L.L.* when she dies.

Norah had clenched her fists all evening, afraid that if she opened them up and pointed the wrong way, she might go to hell.

Her instant acceptance of this story made me reflect on my own experience accepting terrifying "biblical" threats from pastors and other authority figures as truth. I saw myself in Norah, but also in her friend who had told her this "truth" with authority. I was that little girl as well, sharing the "truth" as it was told to me. I couldn't be upset with her for terrifying my daughter. Fear is viral. It has found its way to me, and I've passed it on.

Norah had never heard of the concept of hell before this, so I was surprised at how long it took my husband and me to unwind the story. We had an hour-long conversation about it, which included debunking the existence of zombies, which this friend had apparently also shared with Norah. By the end of the conversation, Norah seemed to feel at ease and confident that what her friend was sharing was made-up. But then, a couple nights later, she couldn't sleep. She was lying in bed, terrified of zombies and hell. Her mind was hooked on the "what if." What if it was true, that if she pointed down, she'd burn forever in hell?

I wonder how many of us are still living life with clenched fists? Afraid of hell. Afraid of God. Afraid to question any of it.

With Norah, it wasn't enough for me to assure her that her friend's stories weren't true. She was curled up on her bed, in the fetal position, in fear. Her mind knew, logically, that I was probably right. The hell and the zombies she was imagining probably weren't real. But her body didn't know and couldn't trust. She was frozen and terrified. I knew that I was going to have to create a felt sense of safety in her body in order for her mind to calm down.

So, I sat on the bed and held my big girl like a little baby. I asked her what she was feeling. "I feel like I'm *in* hell," she said. "Yes. You are," I replied. "This is it. Let's pretend that it's a real place. If it is, Mommy will come find you, and I'll hold you just like this." Norah started crying. I assured her that love would come to find her in hell. She finally relaxed and said that the warmth of my love was beginning to make hell feel like heaven. What a profound thing for a child to say. Exactly. She understood. But she had to know the truth in her body before her mind could accept it.

Just as it wasn't very effective for Norah simply to hear that hell, as she understood it, wasn't real, I've found that this assertion isn't very convincing for believers either. As adults, we bury the feeling of fear in our bodies. Many of us have heard some version of the story Norah heard about hell. For some of us, it was from our parents. For others, it was a pastor. A youth minister. A friend. A Halloween hell-house. The stories and illustrations have varied in their details over time, but their traumatic impact has been consistent.

Our bodies need a feeling of safety and security in order for us to explore our deepest-held fears and beliefs. My hope with this book is to offer imaginative explanations that make *more* sense. It's an invitation, not to throw away what's most precious, but to consider it from a new perspective, one that has the potential to relieve you of cognitive dissonance and to unlock the power of the stories that have gripped you. There's power when you realize that the stories speak to us not because they are historically accurate, but because they arouse our deepest potentials.

Religion is at its best when it makes us ask hard questions of ourselves. It is at its worst when it deludes us into thinking we have all the answers for everybody else.

— **Archibald Macleish** (1892–1982)[2]

My hope is that, by understanding the function of myth, you can begin to release yourself from the rules that bind you. Instead of finding security in rule-keeping and concrete beliefs, you can engage with mythological stories in a way that furthers your curiosity and understanding of yourself and others. My hope is that you can begin to exchange certainty for some mystery and adventure.

It's a thrilling experience to realize that a myth has been activated in your life. I remember the awe and wonder that I felt when I had the epiphany that my descent into hell *was the belly of the whale.* Suddenly the story of Jonah was no longer an unimaginable historical plight, far removed from me. Suddenly, I *was* Jonah, living out the mystical experience that the biblical story was conveying through allegory. The power I had transferred to a text suddenly boomeranged back into my body. I would still describe that particular event in my life as harrowing, but wow, did I feel alive in the experience of my own being. There was something that had come alive in me, and I knew almost immediately that my life was going to change. I felt my own power, my own pain, my personal joys and sorrows. I felt my own essence, and I knew for the first time in my life that I belonged and that my existence was sacred and divine. I understood the importance of living an authentic life. I began to feel peace and contentment when I was truly myself. I noticed how much my energy would be drained when I was performing for the acceptance of others. I experienced others gravitating toward me to express their deepest truths. Somehow, the authentic selves in others sensed my authenticity and were drawn to it. Sometimes, our bodies sense what is true before our brains can make sense of it.

There's a verse in Amos that's fascinating:

The LORD says, "People of Israel, I think as much of the people of Ethiopia as I do of you. I brought the Philistines from Crete and the Syrians from Kir, just as I brought you from Egypt.

— **Amos 9:7** (GNT)

In the evangelical church, the heart is hardened by being told that Israel was the only group of people who heard the voice of God. Here in Amos, the Lord admonishes Israel by saying that, as he's speaking to them, he's also been speaking to people all over the world. The Philistines were the enemy of Israel. Yet, here, we have God saying he's delivered them as well. From a fundamentalist perspective, this is very hard to reconcile.

Mythologically speaking, it makes perfect sense. The nature of God is at the very foundation of humanity; therefore, these sacred truths have been welling up through the human psyche and finding form in myth since the beginning of civilization. Stories of virgin births, great floods, creation, and sacrifices of firstborn sons appear in cultures all over the world over the span of millennia. The study of comparative mythology notes the shared elements of mythological themes and plots among different cultures—many of which had no contact with one another, but presented roughly in the same time period. Many people groups, even today, recognize shamans, whose role in the culture is to be a "link," so to speak, between the unconscious world and their society. The role of the shaman is much like the role of Jesus: as a bridge between humanity and the Divine. Their task is to revitalize their culture with "fresh blood," vital life energy extracted from the unconscious, which is then transmitted through mythological stories and symbols. This is exactly the function of Christian myth. Though the particularities of the myths may be different based on geography and culture, all of humanity is pulling this "living water" up from the same well.

When I began to understand myth, the world suddenly seemed to open up to me. When I was an evangelical, I believed that I possessed the only truth, which I needed to bestow upon the "lost." But in understanding the power of myth, suddenly the rest of the world did not feel threatening to me anymore.

I realized that I did not know what I thought I knew. I became intensely curious about the wisdom found in other faith traditions. To my surprise, I found that nearly all religions possess similar wisdom under the tapestry of their unique traditions. Underneath the dogma I found precious jewels.

When I became a student of Life, I found that she was eager to share her secret treasures with me. Christianity is my mother-tongue. But I now find the many wisdom "languages" of the world are expressing similar themes. My False Self had mistaken my language to be the essence that the language was pointing to beyond itself. A similarity would be to insist that the English word "love" was the only true love. There are many words across many languages that express love. The word *love* (English), or *amor* (Spanish), or *aimer* (French) is not literally love. They are just words, pointing to a reality beyond the word. The same is true in religion. Religious traditions are like languages: they are meant to point to something beyond the religion itself.

What a small world evangelicalism created for me. When I was able to see the unifying source beneath the diversity of world religions and mythologies, I was truly able to value and appreciate the different ways humanity has sought the Divine. I hope to hand this curiosity and wonder to my children and maybe a few others as well.

The biblical myths are true in that, if we are unconscious of them, they live us. As we become conscious of ourselves, we begin to live them. Upon awakening to this, I realized that parts of me could be found in all the biblical stories. Initially, this was a terrible revelation. While I had been conditioned to think of myself as part of the "good team," or God's chosen people, I realized that my False Self (with whom I'd identified up until that point) was more like Egypt, not Israel. My False Self worshiped the Golden Calf, not God. My False Self was more like a Pharisee than a follower of Jesus. I was unconsciously living out the roles of the oppressor—both to myself and others—all while believing I was living a righteous life.

It wasn't until I began the work of making what was unconscious in me conscious that I could accurately assess my role in the myths and begin to live into the story of liberation. I couldn't identify with Jesus in the story until I could admit that I was the Pharisee. I couldn't transform my mind until

I could accurately name and diagnose the truth of my life. Like Peter, I had betrayed God, myself, and others. Like Peter, I had denied Christ by denying my True Self. Shrinking who I authentically am was no longer the moral high ground, because it was Christ in me who I was suppressing. This realization was devastating, until I was met with the grace of this truth: I was ignorant, not evil. I now knew better, so I could do better—both for myself and others.

Think about someone who you completely despise, or perhaps a group that threatens your well-being, or its leader. I think the reason we judge people we dislike so harshly is because we feel betrayed by them. Their actions seem to fail our shared humanity. What we don't realize is that the people who betray us have also been betrayed. Because of the pain we feel after betrayal, we judge them and feel delight when they get what's coming to them. When we do this, we betray our own hearts and humanity—just like them.

Jesus reveals what holds the power to heal: compassion. The moment that Peter betrays him, Jesus looks right at Peter. Jesus's gaze reflects back to Peter two things. One, Peter has not only betrayed Jesus's humanity, but also his own. Two, Jesus sees Peter's greatest sorrow. Peter has also felt the pain of betrayal and has, in turn, betrayed himself as well. Peter's actions have nothing to do with Jesus. They have everything to do with himself. Jesus knows this. That's why Jesus doesn't take the betrayal personally or interrupt the flow of love towards Peter. Other people's actions reflect how they feel about themselves, not about us. Love knows this.

True compassion for others is first birthed from compassion for ourselves. We must recognize that we've been betrayed. We've betrayed our True Selves. And that's why we betray others. At the root of every act of violence and betrayal is a sorrow too deep for words. Jesus saw this sorrow in Peter. He turned toward him. He loved him.

In that culture, if someone betrayed you, you would cease to look at them. This communicated that they were "dead to you." Despite the betrayal, Jesus looks at Peter (Luke 22:61). Jesus's compassion, in the midst of betrayal, was the power that redeemed Peter. Jesus saw who Peter truly was behind his mask and loved him. This allowed Peter to begin the process of grieving his False Self and letting his True Self emerge. *He [Peter] went out and wept bitterly.*[3] Grief and remorse lead to the humility necessary to open the heart to compassion.

Compassion is the only attitude from which we can tell the whole truth. When someone sees the truth about themselves, they will see their greatest sorrow. We must see the sorrow of those who betray us if we truly want to help heal the world. May we offer ourselves and others the same compassion that Jesus gives to Peter. To do that, we must search and know ourselves to find that we are worthy of this compassion. So are our friends. So are our enemies. *Don't try to save the world until you have looked at it from Jesus's point of view: hanging on the cross of forgiveness for the entire human race.*

Perhaps the most difficult part of coming to terms with my False Self was the shame I felt around certain ways I had treated my children. I realized that, in many ways, I had transferred my unconscious pain and fear to them. Within evangelicalism, I believed my role as a parent was to raise good, obedient, "godly" kids. Of course, I love my kids. But I was conditioned to believe that the loving thing to do was to shape and mold them to my church's standards.

In reality, all I did was force them to perform to earn my love. I was anxious and insecure about being myself around others, so I needed my children to behave, in order to reflect to me and others that I was a "good parent." I do not feel this way anymore, and I am sorry that my children did not always feel my unconditional love for them. I am sorry that they, at times, had to suppress their essence on account of me. I wish that my illusions would have fallen away before I had children. This has been an exercise in self-compassion and forgiveness for myself. I do recognize that I did the best I could with what I knew. Fortunately, it is always the right time to say "I was wrong" and do better. It is always the right time for metanoia.

I love the relationship that I have with my children now. I love myself and have peace about my life, and this extends to my relationship with them. The more I become myself, the better I love my kids, and the freer they feel to be themselves. I now know that my primary role as their parent is to hold them in unconditional love, so that they can cultivate the courage to know and explore their authentic selves. I know that unnecessary fear and control through religious dogma directly hinders their natural growth.

Be wary of those who promise all the blessings of God with a salvation decision. The truth is that real salvation feels like a giant train wreck. It involves fear and trembling and weeping and gnashing of teeth. You're going to lose friends, disappoint people you dearly love, and be completely misunderstood. You're going to grieve the life you imagined and let it fall away. If your life is rooted in a church culture, it's possible that those who've meant the most to you are suddenly going to be afraid of you, wondering if your mind has been infiltrated by Satan.

Your salvation will be marked with pierced hands, or a wrenched hip, or a thorn in your side. You will be able to point to the wound, name it, and explain how it threads you through the eye of the needle.

Salvation is paradoxically something you wouldn't wish on anyone, and also a path you invite everyone to walk. Salvation happens when you surrender to the possibility that you might die from a broken heart, and then, somehow, by grace, you don't. You pass through the shadow of death and find out it'll all be okay. You fall into the abyss of fear, only to find there's a plush landing at the bottom of the dark hole. Suddenly, you aren't afraid anymore.

Then, and only then, do you inherit the blessings of God, which are love, joy, peace, patience, kindness, goodness, faithfulness, gentleness and self-control. Then, and only then, will you be certain of the hope you profess. Until then, faith involves trusting this process and surrendering to the death of the False Self when the time comes. Find a myth that leads you through the path of descent and is honest about the cost of walking it.

Living out my own myth has given me the confidence to tell the truth as best as I understand it, including admitting when I'm wrong. Among other things, it has given me the courage to disavow doctrines I know to be harmful, even in the face of being ostracized. While there have been losses to grieve, I have gained what I didn't have before: mainly, inner peace and security. This is my hope for you. That you would know that the peace you search for is within you; the journey of inner exploration is an adventure that will not return void. I hope that you would find love at the center of every creature and feel held in a body that loves you as well.

"What is the meaning of life?" is perhaps the question every human eventually asks. Perhaps you can suspend the certainty in unquestionable answers that you've been handed. Perhaps you can take the risk of not knowing what you think you know. You might find that the meaning of life is *you*. To have the courage to live. To be fully alive, even as you die.

What if you died fully alive? What if you looked right at death with your eyes open? Look into the void and fall face first. The myths promise you that you'll fall through fear into love. But you have to do it! You have to walk your path and live your life. Only you can do it.

> *I declare to you, brothers and sisters, that flesh and blood [the False Self] cannot inherit the kingdom of God, nor does the perishable inherit the imperishable. Listen, I tell you a mystery: We will not all sleep, but we will all be changed—in a flash, in the twinkling of an eye, at the last trumpet. For the trumpet will sound, the dead [the False Self] will be raised imperishable, and we will be changed. For the perishable must clothe itself with the imperishable [the True Self], and the mortal with immortality. When the perishable has been clothed with the imperishable, and the mortal with immortality, then the saying that is written will come true: "Death has been swallowed up in victory."*

> *"Where, O death, is your victory?*

> *Where, O death, is your sting?"*

> *The sting of death is sin, and the power of sin is the law. But thanks be to God! He gives us the victory through our Lord Jesus Christ.*

Therefore, my dear brothers and sisters, stand firm. Let nothing move you. Always give yourselves fully to the work of the Lord, because you know that your labor in the Lord is not in vain.

— **1 Corinthians 15:50–58** (NIV)

When you grasp the vitality of your True Self and experience the eternity available to you here and now, you will understand that who you truly are never dies. What is actually real never passes away. As Paul says, "we will all be changed." The eyes which observe the coming and going of all forms, including yours, see that there is no sting in death, because death is merely a change in form. The waves of life rising and crashing on the surface of the ocean do not diminish the power of the ocean. They are a part of the One. So it goes with your life. The entire ocean is contained in the wave, which is you. You rise, reaching up from the ocean. You are carried by the current moving underneath you. You fall back into the ocean from which you came.

Can you feel yourself rising? Can you feel the ocean supporting your being? Can you ride the wave while you're in it? Can you let it return you to your home? The False Self is like a wave searching for the ocean. We realize the Alpha and Omega by venturing out from our home, searching for it, returning to it, and discovering it anew, like it was the first time.

I pray that, in looking out, you don't overlook God inside.
I pray you have the courage to look into the dark.
To slay your dragons and capture their power.
I pray you breathe the fire of Love.
And feel the ecstasy of your existence.
I pray you invite your demons into heaven.
Be kind to the devil.
Show him the light.
I pray your heart rises to guide you.
I pray you walk your path.

And come to know that you are the treasure that you seek.
Amen.

Thank you for coming along on the journey of Returning to Eden with me.
Your review will help other readers discover this book.
Please consider writing an honest review of the book on the site where you
purchased it. I appreciate your help.

— **Heather Hamilton**, 2023

END NOTES

CHAPTER 1

1 Rahner, Karl. "The Spirituality of the Church and the Future," *Theological Investigations XX* (London/New York: Darton, Longman and Todd/Crossroad, 1961/1992), 149.

2 Fr. Karl Rahner (1904–1984) was an influential Jesuit priest and theologian from Germany.

3 Wintz, OFM, Jack. "7 Key Moments in the Life of St. Francis." *Franciscan Spirit Blog.* [online] Available at: <https://www.franciscanmedia.org/franciscan-spirit-blog/7-key-moments-in-the-life-of-st-francis> [Accessed 21 May 2022].

4 Keating, Thomas. "What Matters," *The Secret Embrace* (Temple Rock Company: 2018), poem VIII.

CHAPTER 2

1 Brian Zahnd is the pastor at Word of Life Church in St. Joseph, Missouri. Used with permission.

2 Bell, Rob. *What is the Bible? How an Ancient Library of Poems, Letters, and Stories Can Transform the Way You Think and Feel About Everything* (New York: HarperCollins, 2017), 110.

CHAPTER 3

1 Nicoll, Maurice. "Letter to Mr. Bush; March 27, 1941." *Psychological Commentaries on the Teaching of Gurdjieff and Ouspensky, Volume 1* (York Beach: Red Wheel/Weiser, LLC, 1996), 1–7.

2 Julian of Norwich. *Revelations of Divine Love*. Edited by Grace Warrack (London: Methuen & Company, 1901), 56.

3 Julian of Norwich is considered to be one of the greatest English mystics and the first known female writer in English.

4 Rohr, Richard. *The Universal Christ: How a Forgotten Reality Can Change Everything We See, Hope for, and Believe* (New York: Convergent, 2019), 65.

CHAPTER 4

1 Campbell, Joseph. *Thou Art That: Transforming Religious Metaphor* (Novato: New World Library, 2001), 2. From Joseph Campbell's *Thou Art That, Copyright* © Joseph Campbell Foundation (jcf.org) 2001. Used with permission.

2 Campbell, Joseph. "Cultures Linked By Man's Ideas," Houston Chronicle, 11-10-86.

3 *Joseph Campbell and The Power of Myth with Bill Moyers*. Copyright © 1988 by Apostrophe S Productions and Alfred van der Editions (New York: Doubleday oversize edition, 1988); (New York: Anchor Books Random House edition, 1991), 5.

4 Campbell, Joseph. "The Interpretation of Symbolic Forms," *The Mythic Dimension* (Joseph Campbell Foundation, 1993), 198.

5 Jung, C.G. *Modern Man in Search of a Soul* (New York: Harcourt, Brace & World, 1933), 112.

6 "Ruby Falls." *Wikipedia*, Wikimedia Foundation. [online] Available at: <https://en.wikipedia.org/wiki/Ruby_Falls> [Accessed 19 April 2022].

CHAPTER 5

1 Genesis 3:6.

2 Genesis 2:21–22.

3 Genesis 3:6.

CHAPTER 7

1 Jung, C.G. *The Development of Personality* (East Sussex and New York: Taylor and Francis, 2014), 198.

2 Jung, C.G. *Aion: The Collected Works of C.G. Jung, Vol. 9ii*. Edited and translated by Gerhard Adler

and R. F. C. Hull (Princeton: Princeton University Press, 1951/1969), para 28f.

3 Jung, C.G. *Aion: The Collected Works of C.G. Jung, Vol. 9ii*. Edited and translated by Gerhard Adler and R. F. C. Hull (Princeton: Princeton University Press, 1951/1969), para 28f.

4 Valantasis, Richard. *The Gospel of Thomas* (London and New York: Routledge, 1997), 95.

CHAPTER 8

1 Joseph Campbell and The Power of Myth with Bill Moyers Copyright © 1988 by Apostrophe S Productions and Alfred van der Editions (New York: Doubleday oversize edition, 1988), 146; (New York: Anchor Books Random House edition, 1991), 180.

2 Jonah 4:1–11.

CHAPTER 9

1 Boechler, Ethan, Campbell, Allison, et. al. *Law of Conservation of Energy* (University of Calgary, 2021). [online] Available at: <https://energyeducation.ca/encyclopedia/Law_of_conservation_of_e nergy> [Accessed 28 May 2022].

CHAPTER 11

1 von Franz, Marie-Louise, and Boa, Fraser. *The Way of the Dream* (Toronto: Windrose Films, 1988), 88.

2 Marie-Louise von Franz was a Swiss Jungian psychologist and scholar who worked for and collaborated with Carl Jung.

3 Rohr, Richard. *The Universal Christ: How a Forgotten Reality Can Change Everything We See, Hope for, and Believe* (New York: Convergent, 2019), 31.

4 Rohr, Richard. *The Universal Christ: How a Forgotten Reality Can Change Everything We See, Hope for, and Believe* (New York: Convergent, 2019), 16.

CHAPTER 12

1 Genesis 8:9.

2 Brown, Brené. *Rising Strong: How the Ability to Reset Transforms the Way We Live, Love, Parent, and*

Lead (New York: Random House, 2015).

3 Brown, Brené. "Jesus Wept." *Work of the People*. [online] Available at: <https://www.theworkoft hepeople.com/jesus-wept> [Accessed 22 May 2022].

4 Rohr, Richard. *Things Hidden: Scripture as Spirituality* (Franciscan Media: 2008), 36–37.

5 Williamson, Marianne. *A Return to Love: Reflections on the Principles of a Course in Miracles* (New York: HarperCollins, 1992), 175–176.

6 St. John Climacus was a 6th–7th century Christian monk at the monastery of Mount Sinai.

7 Coniaris, Anthony M. *Philokalia: The Bible of Orthodox Spirituality* (Minneapolis: Light & Life Publishing, 1998), 158–159.

CHAPTER 13

1 Jung, C.G. *Man and His Symbols* (London: Aldus Books, 1964), 76.

2 John 20:27.

3 Colossians 3:11b.

CHAPTER 14

1 Lewis, C.S. *The Problem of Pain* (New York: HarperOne, 1940/1996), 130.

2 Lewis, C.S. *The Great Divorce* (New York: HarperOne, 1946/1973).

3 "Divine Comedy." *Wikipedia*, Wikimedia Foundation. [online] Available at: <https://en.wikipedia.org/wiki/Divine_Comedy> [Accessed 23 May 2022].

4 Sweeney, Jon M. *Inventing Hell: Dante, the Bible, and Eternal Punishment,* 2nd ed. (Chicago: Acta, 2017), 111–112.

5 "Hell, No!: God is Good." *Center for Action and Contemplation*. [online] Available at: <https://cac.org/daily-meditations/god-is-good-2021-09-12/> [Accessed 21 May 2022].

6 Kampeas, Ron. "Gehenna Wasn't So Hellish, Archaeologist Says." *AP News*. [online] Available at: <https://apnews.com/article/af31717fc3000068267c79681f8ebe01> [Accessed 21 May 2022].

7 See Jersak, Brad. *Her Gates Will Never Be Shut: Hope, Hell, and the New Jerusalem* (Eugene: Wipf and Stock, 2009), 82–87; and Stephen John Spencer, *The Genesis Pursuit: The Lost History of Jesus Christ* (Xulon, 2007), 185–212.

8 Rohr, Richard. *The Universal Christ: How a Forgotten Reality Can Change Everything We See, Hope for, and Believe* (New York: Convergent, 2019), 100, 170.

CHAPTER 15

1 Marcus Dods was a Scottish minister and theologian.

2 Matthew 16:23.

3 Houselander, Caryll. *A Rocking-Horse Catholic* (London: Sheed and Ward, 1955), 137–140.

4 2 Corinthians 5:19.

CHAPTER 16

1 Townend, Stuart. "How Deep the Father's Love For Us." *Spotify*. <https://open.spotify.com/track/3kGPTOG6wMI7DYjCFnbvBu?si=dab09fd3c61a4aa1>.

2 Martin, Jonathan and Lowry, Mark. "God Didn't Hold the Hammer with Mark Lowry | Episode 28." *YouTube*, uploaded by The Zeitcast with Jonathan Martin, 13 September, 2019. <https://www.youtube.com/watch?v=sx0xocQ0xbA>.

3 Jersak, Brad. "Gospel in Chairs: A Beautiful Gospel 2015 Brad Jersak." *YouTube*, uploaded by Brad Jersak, 21 July, 2015. <https://www.youtube.com/watch?v=9VwP7df9BuY&t=1480s>. Originally developed by Fr. Anthony Carbo of Holy Theophany Orthodox Church in Colorado Springs, Colorado.

4 Houselander, Caryll. *A Rocking-Horse Catholic* (London: Sheed and Ward, 1955), 137–140.

5 Luke 19:1–9.

6 St. John of Kronstadt was a Russian Orthodox archpriest and saint of the Eastern Orthodox Church.

CHAPTER 17

1 Matthew 16:21–28.

2 *Moana*. Directed by John Musker and Ron Clements, performances by Auli'i Cravalho, Dwayne Johnson, Rachel House, Temuera Morrison, Jemaine Clement, Nicole Scherzinger, Alan Tudyk, et al., produced by Osnat Shurer, Walt Disney Pictures, Walt Disney Animation Studios, distributed by Walt Disney Studios Motion Pictures, 2016.

3 Campbell, Joseph. Foreword by Jean Erdman Campbell, Selected and Edited by John M. Maher and Dennie Briggs, *An Open Life: Joseph Campbell in Conversation with Michael Toms* (New York: New

Dimensions Foundation, 1989), 28.

4 See Joseph Campbell's lecture: Campbell, Joseph: "Psyche & Symbol - Apollonian vs. Dionysian Dichotomy." *YouTube*, uploaded by The Joseph Campbell Foundation, 3 December 2018. <https://www.youtube.com/watch?v=ArsS6sPhwn0>.

5 Florence + The Machine. "Shake It Out." *Spotify*. <https://open.spotify.com/track/4lY95OMGb 9WxP6IYut64ir?si=c4eebc45082d429c>.

CHAPTER 18

1 *Speculum de mysteriis ecclesiae,* Migne, P.L., vol. 172, col. 921.

2 *Harriet*. Directed by Kasi Lemmons, performances by Cynthia Erivo, Leslie Odom Jr., Joe Alwyn, Janelle Monáe, et al., produced by Perfect World Pictures, New Balloon, and Stay Gold Features, distributed by Focus Features, 2019.

3 Jung, C.G. *Mysterium Coniunctionis: The Collected Works of C.G. Jung, Vol. 14*. Edited and translated by Gerhard Adler and R. F. C. Hull (Princeton: Princeton University Press, 1954/1963/1970), para 257.

4 Matthew 3:13–17; Matthew 4:1–11.

5 Jung, C.G. *Mysterium Coniunctionis: The Collected Works of C.G. Jung, Vol. 14*. Edited and translated by Gerhard Adler and R. F. C. Hull (Princeton: Princeton University Press, 1954/1963/1970), para 258.

6 ARAS, *The Book of Symbols: Reflections on Archetypal Images* (Cologne: Taschen, 2010) 640; Edward F. Edinger, *The Mysterium Lectures* (Toronto: Inner City Books, 1995), 296.

7 Edward F. Edinger was an American psychiatrist, Jungian analyst, and writer.

CHAPTER 19

1 Campbell, Joseph. *The Hero With a Thousand Faces* (Novalto: New World Library, 2008), 77. From Joseph Campbell's *The Hero with a Thousand Faces, Copyright* © Joseph Campbell Foundation (jcf.org) 2008. Used with permission.

2 Genesis 3:24.

3 Matthew 22:13.

CHAPTER 20

1 *The Wisdom of Trauma featuring Dr. Gabor Maté.* Directed by Zaya Benazzo and Maurizio Benazzo, featuring Dr. Gabor Maté, Science and Nonduality (SAND), 2021.

2 St. Gregory Palamas was a Byzantine Greek theologian and Eastern Orthodox cleric. He is a saint in the Eastern Orthodox Church.

3 St. John of the Cross was a Spanish Catholic priest and mystic. In 1926 he was declared a Doctor of the Church by Pope Pius XI, and is commonly known as the "Mystical Doctor."

CHAPTER 21

1 Howard Thurman was an American author, philosopher, theologian, educator, civil rights leader, and prominent religious figure. He taught radical nonviolence and was a key mentor to Dr. Martin Luther King Jr.

2 Thurman, Howard. "The Sound of the Genuine" (Baccalaureate ceremony) (Spelman College), 1980 May 4, Howard Thurman audiovisual collection, MSS 394, Box 2, Folder 394–059, Archives and Manuscript Dept., Pitts Theology Library, Emory University.

3 Colossians 1:27

4 Angelou, Maya. *Wouldn't Take Nothing for My Journey Now* (New York: Bantam, 1994), 73.

5 Maya Angelou was a 20th century American author, poet, and civil rights activist.

6 Thurman, Howard. "The Sound of the Genuine" (Baccalaureate ceremony) (Spelman College), 1980 May 4, Howard Thurman audiovisual collection, MSS 394, Box 2, Folder 394–059, Archives and Manuscript Dept., Pitts Theology Library, Emory University.

CHAPTER 23

1 Spira, Rupert. *Being Myself* (Oxford: Sahaja Publications and New Harbinger Publications, 2021), Chapter 12.

2 St. Augustine's writings influenced the development of Western philosophy and Western Christianity. He is viewed as one of the most important Church Fathers of the Latin Church.

3 Augustine, *De nuptiis et concupiscentia,* 1.17.15.

4 Augustine, *Sermones,* 9.11.18.

5 *The Lion King*. Directed by Roger Allers and Rob Minkoff, performances by Jonathan Taylor Thomas, Matthew Broderick, James Earl Jones, et al., produced by Don Hahn, Walt Disney Pictures, Walt Disney Feature Animation, distributed by Buena Vista Pictures, 1994.

CHAPTER 24

1 Matthew 5:3.

CHAPTER 25

1 Guite, Malcolm. *Sounding the Seasons: Seventy Sonnets for the Christian Year* (Norfolk: Canterbury Press Norwich, 2012), 41. Used with permission.

CHAPTER 27

1 Bourgeault, Cynthia. *Love is Stronger Than Death: The Mystical Union of Two Souls* (Rhinebeck: Monkfish Book Publishing, 2014), 168.

CHAPTER 28

1 Julian of Norwich, *Revelations of Divine Love* (London: Methuen & Company, 1901), 101. This quote is a paraphrase of the original which states: "For grace worketh our dreadful failing into plenteous, endless solace; and grace worketh our shameful falling into high, worshipful rising; and grace worketh our sorrowful dying into holy, blissful life. For I saw full surely that ever as our contrariness worketh to us here in earth pain, shame, and sorrow, right so, on the contrary wise, grace worketh to us in heaven solace, worship, and bliss; and overpassing. And so far forth, that when we come up and receive the sweet reward which grace hath wrought for us, then we shall thank and bless our Lord, endlessly rejoicing that ever we suffered woe."

CHAPTER 30

1 Gungor, Michael [@michaelgungor]. "Tweet Message." *Twitter*, 4 May 2020. <https://twitter.com/michaelgungor/status/1257478191607713792>. Michael Gungor is an American singer-songwriter who led the band Gungor.

CHAPTER 31

1 Luke 8:40–47.

2 Siegel, Ethan. "Ask Ethan: How Many Atoms Do You Share With King Tut?" *Forbes*. [online] Available at: <https://www.forbes.com/sites/startswithabang/2016/05/14/ask-ethan-how-many-atoms-do-you-share-with-king-tut/?sh=27f3c6fc71a5> [Accessed 6 December 2021].

3 See F. Edinger, Edward. *Ego and Archetype* (New York: Putnam, 1972). Reprinted by Shambhala Publications (Boulder: 2017), 237.

4 Robertson Smith, William. *Lectures on the Religion of the Semites* (New York: D. Appleton and Company, 1889), 295–296.

5 William Robertson Smith was a Scottish Old Testament scholar, professor of divinity, and minister. He was an editor of the Encyclopedia Britannica. His book, *Religion of the Semites*, is highly regarded in the field of the comparative study of religion.

6 See Edinger, Edward F. *Ego and Archetype* (New York: Putnam, 1972). Reprinted by Shambhala Publications (Boulder: 2017), 247. Edinger says, "The idea that Christ sacrificed himself in order to extract or make manifest his spiritual essence is expressed in scriptural passages referring to the coming of the Paraclete." See John 16:7, John 14:16–17; John 14:25–26 RSV.

7 Acts 1:8.

8 Rohr, Richard. *The Universal Christ: How a Forgotten Reality Can Change Everything We See, Hope for, and Believe* (New York: Convergent, 2019), 33.

CHAPTER 32

1 Julian of Norwich, *Revelations of Divine Love* (London: Methuen & Company, 1901), 147.

2 Tomlin, Chris. "Good Good Father." *Spotify*. <https://open.spotify.com/track/1mWdyqs6Zvg8b1lKjDc8yB?si=b12dc79c7fef4554>.

CHAPTER 33

1 The Gospel of Mary was a part of the Papyrus Berolinensis 8502 which is a Coptic manuscript from the 5th century A.D. It was unearthed in Egypt and is a Coptic translation of an earlier Greek original. James M. Robinson, ed., "The Gospel of Mary", *The Nag Hammadi Library, second edition* (Leiden: Brill, 1984), 471–474.

2 Bourgeault, Cynthia. *The Meaning of Mary Magdalene: Discovering the Woman at the Heart of Christianity* (Boston: Shambhala Publications, 2010), 54.

3 Valantasis, Richard. *The Gospel of Thomas* (London and New York: Routledge, 1997), 95.

4 Ludwig Heinrich Heydenreich and The Editors of Encyclopedia Britannica. "Leonardo di Vinci - Anatomical Studies and Drawings." Encyclopedia Britannica, 2019. [online] Available at: <https://www.britannica.com/biography/Leonardo-da-Vinci/Anatomical-studies-and-drawings> [Accessed 21 May 2022].

5 Boehme, Jacob. *The Confessions of Jacob Boehme* (Kila, MT: Kessinger, n.d.), 41.

6 Jacob Boehme was a German philosopher, Christian mystic, Lutheran theologian, and author.

7 Nietzsche, Friedrich. *The Antichrist §34 (edited excerpt)* (New York: Alfred A. Knopf, 1923), 105.

8 Friedrich Nietzsche was a 19th century German philosopher and writer.

CHAPTER 34

1 *Acts of Peter* dates to the late 2nd century A.D. It records that the apostle Peter was crucified head down. At the end of the 4th century, Jerome wrote in his *De Viris Illustribus* ("On Illustrious Men") that the reason for this request was that Peter felt he was unworthy to die in the same manner as Jesus. However, in the Acts of Peter, the author writes that Peter's request to be crucified upside-down was to make a point: that the values of those crucifying him were inverted themselves, emphasizing the need to look beyond these values and adopt those of Jesus. *See* Pick, Bernard. *The Apocryphal Acts of Paul, Peter, John, Andrew and Thomas*, (Chicago: The Open Court Publishing Co., 1909), 118–119.

2 *The Enneagram Institute*, "The Nine Enneagram Type Descriptions." [online] Available at: <https://www.enneagraminstitute.com/type-descriptions> [Accessed 22 May 2022].

3 *Enneagrammer*, "The Nine Types." [online] Available at: https://www.enneagrammer.com/types. [Accessed 27 August 2022].

CHAPTER 35

1 Adapted from Chapter 9 and the Glossary of *Hold On to Your Kids: Why Parents Need to Matter More Than Peers*. Gordon Neufeld, Ph.D., and Gabor Maté, M.D., *Hold On to Your Kids: Why Parents Need to Matter More Than Peers* (New York: Ballantine Books, 2014), 123, 135. Also see Glossary term *tears of futility*.

2 Neufeld, Ph.D., Gordon and Maté, M.D., Gabor. *Hold On to Your Kids: Why Parents Need to Matter More Than Peers* (New York: Ballantine Books, 2014), 123.

3 Tutu, Desmond and Tutu, Mpho. *The Book of Forgiving: The Fourfold Path for Healing Ourselves and the World* (New York: HarperCollins, 2014).

4 Lucius Annaeus Seneca. *De Ira (On Anger)*, Book 2, Section 10.

CHAPTER 36

1 Campbell, Joseph. *The Hero With a Thousand Faces* (Princeton: Princeton University Press, 1968), 275.

2 St. Bernard of Clairvaux was a Burgundian abbot and helped revitalize Benedictine monasticism. He was declared a doctor or the church by Pope Pius VIII.

CHAPTER 37

1 Mother Teresa. *In the Heart of the World: Thoughts, Stories & Prayers* (Novato: New World Library, 2010).

2 Mother Teresa, Petrie, Ann, et. al. *Mother Teresa* (Petrie Productions, Inc., Distributed by Red Rose Gallerie, 433 Airport Blvd., Suite 425, Burlingame, CA. 94010, 1986), videotape.

CHAPTER 38

1 Lawrence Kushner, *The Book of Words: Talking Spiritual Life, Living Spiritual Talk* (Woodstock: Jewish Lights Publishing, 1993), 27–28.

2 Meister Eckhart was a fourteenth century Dominican friar, theologian, and mystic.

CHAPTER 39

1 Isaacson, Walter. *Einstein: His Life and Universe* (New York: Simon & Schuster, 2007), 462.

2 di Bondone, Giotto. *St. Francis of Assisi Receiving the Stigmata*, c. 1300. Located in the Louvre in Paris, France.

3 Underhill, Evelyn. *Practical Mysticism: A Little Book for Normal People* (New York: E.P. Dutton & Company, 1915), 96.

4 Evelyn Underhill was an English Anglo-Catholic writer, pacifist, and mystic.

CHAPTER 40

1 Julian of Norwich, *Revelations of Divine Love* (London: Methuen & Company, 1901), 153.

CHAPTER 41

1 Zahnd, Brian. "Monster God or Monster Man Debate 2/7." *YouTube*, uploaded by Third Way, 15 October, 2015.

<https://www.youtube.com/watch?v=aGYFjKa5n0Y>.

2 The pattern of the spiritual journey through order, disorder, and reorder is laid out in *The Wisdom Pattern* by Richard Rohr. Rohr, Richard. *The Wisdom Pattern: Order, Disorder, Reorder* (Cincinnati: Franciscan Media, 2020).

CHAPTER 42

1 Tolkien, J.R.R. *The Lord of the Rings: The Return of the King* (New York: Ballantine Books, 2012), 193.

CHAPTER 43

1 Campbell, Joseph. *Thou Art That: Transforming Religious Metaphor* (Novato: New World Library, 2001), 107. From Joseph Campbell's *Thou Art That, Copyright* © Joseph Campbell Foundation (jcf.org) 2001. Used with permission.

EPILOGUE

1 Stan Mitchell was the founding pastor at GracePointe Church in Franklin, Tennessee. Used with permission.

2 Archibald Macleish was an American writer and poet. He served as the Librarian of Congress.

3 Luke 22:62.

BIBLIOGRAPHY

Almaas, A.H. *Facets of Unity*. Boston and London: Shambhala, 2012.

———. *Keys to the Enneagram: How to Unlock the Highest Potential of Every Personality Type*. Boulder: Shambhala Publications, 2021.

Angelou, Maya. *Wouldn't Take Nothing for My Journey Now*. New York: Bantam, 1994.

ARAS. *The Book of Symbols: Reflections on Archetypal Images*. Cologne: Taschen, 2010.

Augustine. *De nuptiis et concupiscentia,* 1.17.15.

———. *Sermones*, 9.11.18.

Bell, Rob. *What is the Bible? How an Ancient Library of Poems, Letters, and Stories Can Transform the Way You Think and Feel About Everything*. New York: HarperCollins, 2017.

Boechler, Ethan; Campbell, Allison; Donev, Jason; Hanania, Jordan; Jenden, James. *Law of Conservation of Energy*. University of Calgary, 2021. https://energyeducation.ca/encyclopedia/Law_of_conservation_of_energy.

Boehme, Jacob. *The Confessions of Jacob Boehme*. Kila, MT: Kessinger, n.d.

Bourgeault, Cynthia. *Love is Stronger Than Death: The Mystical Union of Two Souls*. Rhinebeck: Monkfish Book Publishing, 2014.

———. *The Meaning of Mary Magdalene: Discovering the Woman at the Heart of Christianity*. Boston: Shambhala Publications, 2010.

Brown, Brené. "Jesus Wept." *Work of the People*. https://www.theworkofthepeople.com/jesus-wept.

———. *Rising Strong: How the Ability to Reset Transforms the Way We Live, Love, Parent, and Lead*. New York: Random House, 2015.

Campbell, Joseph. *An Open Life: Joseph Campbell in Conversation with Michael Toms*. Foreword by Jean Erdman Campbell. Selected and Edited by John M. Maher and Dennie Briggs. New York: New Dimensions Foundation, 1989.

———. "Cultures Linked By Man's Ideas," Houston Chronicle, 11-10-86.

———. *Joseph Campbell and The Power of Myth with Bill Moyers*. Copyright © 1988 by Apostrophe S Productions and Alfred van der Editions. New York: Doubleday oversize edition, 1988; New York: Anchor Books Random House edition, 1991.

———. "Psyche & Symbol - Apollonian vs. Dionysian Dichotomy."
The Joseph Campbell Foundation. *YouTube*. December 3, 2018.
https://www.youtube.com/watch?v=ArsS6sPhwn0.

———. *The Hero With a Thousand Faces*. Novalto: New World
Library, 2008.

———. *The Hero With a Thousand Faces*. Princeton: Princeton
University Press, 1968.

———. "The Interpretation of Symbolic Forms," *The Mythic Dimension*.
Joseph Campbell Foundation, 1993.

———. *Thou Art That: Transforming Religious Metaphor*. Novato:
New World Library, 2001.

Center for Action and Contemplation. "Hell, No!: God is Good."
September 12, 2021.
https://cac.org/daily-meditations/god-is-good-2021-09-12.

Coniaris, Anthony M. *Philokalia: The Bible of Orthodox Spirituality*.
Minneapolis: Light & Life Publishing, 1998.

Edinger, Edward F. *Ego and Archetype*. New York: Putnam, 1972.
Reprinted by Shambhala Publications. Boulder: 2017.

———. *The Mysterium Lectures*. Toronto: Inner City Books, 1995.

Enneagrammer. "The Nine Types." 2022.
https://www.enneagrammer.com/types.

Florence + The Machine. "Shake It Out." *Spotify*.
https://open.spotify.com/track/
4lY95OMGb9WxP6IYut64irsi=c4eebc45082d429c.

Franz, Marie-Louise von and Boa, Fraser. *The Way of the Dream*.
Toronto: Windrose Films, 1988.

Guite, Malcolm. *Sounding the Seasons: Seventy Sonnets for the Christian Year*.
Norfolk: Canterbury Press Norwich, 2012.

Gungor, Michael [@michaelgungor]. "Tweet Message." *Twitter*.
May 4, 2020.
https://twitter.com/michaelgungor/status/1257478191607713792.

Harriet. Directed by Kasi Lemmons, performances by Cynthia Erivo,
Leslie Odom Jr., Joe Alwyn, Janelle Monáe, et al., produced by
Perfect World Pictures, New Balloon, and Stay Gold Features,
distributed by Focus Features, 2019.

Heydenreich, Ludwig Heinrich and The Editors of Encyclopedia Britannica.
"Leonardo di Vinci - Anatomical Studies and Drawings."
Encyclopedia Britannica, 2019.
https://www.britannica.com/biography/Leonardo-da-Vinci/
Anatomical-studies-and-drawings.

Houselander, Caryll. *A Rocking-Horse Catholic*. London:
Sheed and Ward, 1955.

Hudson, Russ and Riso, Don Richard. *The Wisdom of the Enneagram:
The Complete Guide to Psychological and Spiritual Growth for the
Nine Personality Types*. New York: Bantam, 1999.

Isaacson, Walter. *Einstein: His Life and Universe.* New York: Simon & Schuster, 2007.

Jersak, Brad. "Gospel in Chairs: A Beautiful Gospel 2015 Brad Jersak." *YouTube.* July 21, 2015. https://www.youtube.com/watch?v=9VwP7df9BuY&t=1480s.

———. *Her Gates Will Never Be Shut: Hope, Hell, and the New Jerusalem.* Eugene: Wipf and Stock, 2009.

Julian of Norwich. *Revelations of Divine Love.* Edited by Grace Warrack. London: Methuen & Company, 1901.

Jung, C.G. *Aion: The Collected Works of C.G. Jung, Vol. 9ii.* Edited and translated by Gerhard Adler and R. F. C. Hull. Princeton: Princeton University Press, 1951/1969.

———. *Man and His Symbols.* London: Aldus Books, 1964.

———. *Modern Man in Search of a Soul.* New York: Harcourt, Brace & World, 1933.

———. *Mysterium Coniunctionis: The Collected Works of C.G. Jung, Vol. 14.* Edited and translated by Gerhard Adler and R. F. C. Hull. Princeton: Princeton University Press, 1954/1963/1970.

———. *The Development of Personality.* East Sussex and New York: Taylor and Francis, 2014.

Kampeas, Ron. "Gehenna Wasn't So Hellish, Archaeologist Says." *AP News.* March 15, 1993. https://apnews.com/article/af31717fc3000068267c79681f8ebe01.

Keating, Thomas. "What Matters," *The Secret Embrace*. Temple Rock Company: 2018.

Kushner, Lawrence. *The Book of Words: Talking Spiritual Life, Living Spiritual Talk*. Woodstock: Jewish Lights Publishing, 1993.

Lewis, C.S. *The Great Divorce*. New York: HarperOne, 1946/1973.

———. *The Problem of Pain*. New York: HarperOne, 1940/1996.

Luckovich, John. *The Instinctual Drives and the Enneagram*. New York: Enneagrammer Imprints, 2021.

Maítrí, Sandra. *The Spiritual Dimension of the Enneagram: Nine Faces of the Soul*. New York: Jeremy P. Tarcher/Putnam, 2001.

Martin, Jonathan and Lowry, Mark. "God Didn't Hold the Hammer with Mark Lowry | Episode 28." The Zeitcast with Jonathan Martin. *YouTube*. September 13, 2019. https://www.youtube.com/watch?v=sx0xocQ0xbA.

Moana. Directed by John Musker and Ron Clements, performances by Auli'i Cravalho, Dwayne Johnson, Rachel House, Temuera Morrison, Jemaine Clement, Nicole Scherzinger, Alan Tudyk, et al., produced by Osnat Shurer, Walt Disney Pictures, Walt Disney Animation Studios, distributed by Walt Disney Studios Motion Pictures, 2016.

Mother Teresa. *In the Heart of the World: Thoughts, Stories & Prayers*. Novato: New World Library, 2010.

Mother Teresa; Petrie, Ann; Petrie, Jeanette; Attenborough, Richard. *Mother Teresa*. Petrie Productions, Inc., Distributed by

Red Rose Gallerie, 433 Airport Blvd., Suite 425,
Burlingame, CA. 94010, 1986. Videotape.

Neufeld, Gordon Ph.D., and Maté, Gabor M.D., *Hold On to Your Kids:
Why Parents Need to Matter More Than Peers*. New York:
Ballantine Books, 2014.

Nicoll, Maurice. "Letter to Mr. Bush; March 27, 1941." *Psychological
Commentaries on the Teaching of Gurdjieff and Ouspensky,
Volume 1*. York Beach: Red Wheel/Weiser, LLC, 1996.

Nietzsche, Friedrich. *The Antichrist §34*. New York: Alfred A. Knopf, 1923.

Pick, Bernhard. *The Apocryphal Acts of Paul, Peter, John, Andrew
and Thomas*. Chicago: The Open Court Publishing Co., 1909.

Rahner, Karl. "The Spirituality of the Church and the Future," *Theological
Investigations XX*. London/New York: Darton, Longman and
Todd/Crossroad, 1961/1992.

Robinson, James M., editor. "The Gospel of Mary." *The Nag Hammadi
Library, second edition*. Leiden: Brill, 1984.

Rohr, Richard. *The Universal Christ: How a Forgotten Reality
Can Change Everything We See, Hope for, and Believe*.
New York: Convergent, 2019.

————. *The Wisdom Pattern: Order, Disorder, Reorder*.
Cincinnati: Franciscan Media, 2020.

————. *Things Hidden: Scripture as Spirituality*. Franciscan Media: 2008.

Rohr, Richard and Ebert, Andreas. *The Enneagram: A Christian Perspective*. Translated by Peter Heinegg. New York: Crossroad, 2016.

Seneca, Lucius Annaeus. *De Ira (On Anger)*.

Siegel, Ethan. "Ask Ethan: How Many Atoms Do You Share With King Tut?" *Forbes*. May 14, 2016. https://www.forbes.com/sites/startswithabang/2016/05/14/ask-ethan-how-many-atoms-do-you-share-with-king-tut/?sh=27f3c6fc71a5.

Smith, William Robertson. *Lectures on the Religion of the Semites*. New York: D. Appleton and Company, 1889.

Speculum de mysteriis ecclesiae, Migne, P.L., vol. 172, col. 921.

Spencer, Stephen John. *The Genesis Pursuit: The Lost History of Jesus Christ*. Xulon, 2007.

Spira, Rupert. *Being Myself*. Oxford: Sahaja Publications and New Harbinger Publications, 2021.

Sweeney, Jon M. *Inventing Hell: Dante, the Bible, and Eternal Punishment,* 2nd ed. Chicago: Acta, 2017.

The Enneagram Institute. "The Nine Enneagram Type Descriptions." 2021. https://www.enneagraminstitute.com/type-descriptions.

The Lion King. Directed by Roger Allers and Rob Minkoff, performances by Jonathan Taylor Thomas, Matthew Broderick, James Earl Jones, et al., produced by Don Hahn, Walt Disney Pictures, Walt Disney Feature Animation, distributed by Buena Vista Pictures, 1994.

The Wisdom of Trauma featuring Dr. Gabor Maté. Directed by Zaya
  Benazzo and Maurizio Benazzo, featuring Dr. Gabor Maté, Science and
  Nonduality (SAND), 2021.

Thurman, Howard. "The Sound of the Genuine" (Baccalaureate ceremony)
  (Spelman College),1980 May 4, Howard Thurman audiovisual collection,
  MSS 394, Box 2, Folder 394–059, Archives and Manuscript Dept., Pitts
  Theology Library, Emory University.

Tolkien, J.R.R. *The Lord of the Rings: The Fellowship of the Rings.*
  New York: Ballantine Books, 2012.

Tomlin, Chris. "Good Good Father." *Spotify.*
  https://open.spotify.com/track/1mWdyqs6Zvg8b1lKjDc8yB?si=
  b12dc79c7fef4554.

Townend, Stuart. "How Deep the Father's Love For Us." *Spotify.*
  https://open.spotify.com/track/3kGPTOG6wMI7DYjCFnbvBu?si=
  dab09fd3c61a4aa1.

Tutu, Desmond and Tutu, Mpho. *The Book of Forgiving:*
  The Fourfold Path for Healing Ourselves and the
  World. New York: HarperCollins, 2014.

Underhill, Evelyn. *Practical Mysticism: A Little Book for Normal*
  People. New York: E.P. Dutton & Company, 1915.

Valantasis, Richard. *The Gospel of Thomas.* London and New York:
  Routledge, 1997.

Wikipedia. 2022. "Divine Comedy." Last Modified August 9, 2022.
  https://en.wikipedia.org/wiki/Divine_Comedy.

———. 2022. "Ruby Falls." Last Modified April 19, 2022. https://en.wikipedia.org/wiki/Ruby_Falls.

Williamson, Marianne. *A Return to Love: Reflections on the Principles of a Course in Miracles*. New York: HarperCollins, 1992.

Wintz, Jack OFM. "7 Key Moments in the Life of St. Francis." *Franciscan Spirit Blog*. May 9, 2020. https://www.franciscanmedia.org/ franciscan-spirit-blog/7-key-moments-in-the-life-of-st-francis.

Zahnd, Brian. "Monster God or Monster Man Debate 2/7." *YouTube*. October 15 2015. https://www.youtube.com/watch?v=aGYFjKa5n0Y.

ABOUT THE AUTHOR

Heather Hamilton lives near Atlanta, Georgia, with her husband and three children. She received her B.A. in Journalism from Georgia State University and spent many years doing video production before discovering her love of writing. After filming and editing stories with people from all over the world—celebrities, orphans, religious leaders, royal family members, political figures, and everyday people—Heather realized the common threads and themes intertwining all humans across religions, cultures, classes, and demographics. She is passionate about fostering human connection through storytelling, writing, art, and exchanging ideas.

To keep in touch with Heather, you can sign up for her newsletter at:

https://www.ReturningtoEden.com

You can also follow her on social media at:

https://www.instagram.com/heatherhamilton1
https://www.facebook.com/heatherhamiltonauthor

For more information about Heather Hamilton,
or to contact her for speaking engagements, please visit
www.ReturningToEden.com.

Many Voices. One Message.

For more information, please visit
www.quoir.com

CPSIA information can be obtained
at www.ICGtesting.com
Printed in the USA
LVHW031255020223
738347LV00004B/18